Recipe Hall of Fame
Quick & Easy
Cookbook

★

*Winning Recipes
from Hometown America*

Gwen McKee and Barbara Moseley have worn out three vans traveling the highways and byways of our beautiful country in search of the best cookbooks and the best recipes in America.

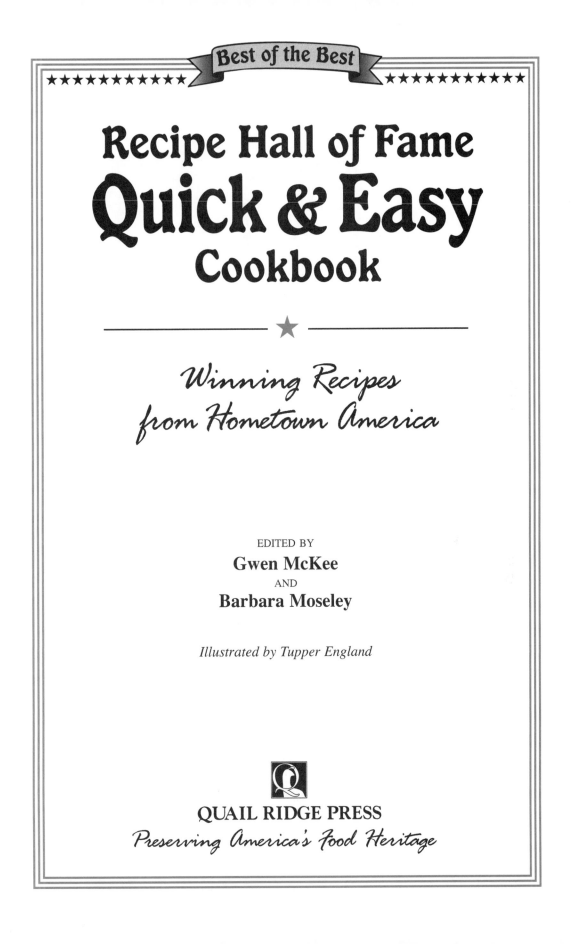

Best of the Best

★★★★★★★★★★★★ ★★★★★★★★★★★★

Recipe Hall of Fame
Quick & Easy
Cookbook

─────── ★ ───────

Winning Recipes
from Hometown America

EDITED BY
Gwen McKee
AND
Barbara Moseley

Illustrated by Tupper England

QUAIL RIDGE PRESS
Preserving America's Food Heritage

★★★★★★★★★★★★★★★★★★★★★★★★

Library of Congress Cataloging-in-Publication Data

Recipe hall of fame quick & easy cookbook: winning recipes from hometown
    America / edited by Gwen McKee and Barbara Moseley;
    illustrated by Tupper England.
        p. cm. — (Best of the best)
    Includes index.
    ISBN 1-893062-26-0
    1. Quick and easy cookery. 2. Cookery, American I. Title: Quick &
easy cookbook. II. McKee, Gwen. III. Moseley, Barbara. IV. Quail
Ridge Press cookbook series.
TX833.5 .R43 2001
641.5'55—dc21   2001019080

Paperbound edition (ISBN 1-893062-26-0)
First printing: 93,000 copies, April 2001
Second printing: 47,000 copies, June 2001
Third printing: 5,000 copies, June 2005
Fourth printing: 32,000 copies, July 2006

Ringbound edition (ISBN 1-893062-56-1)
First printing: 12,000 copies, May 2004
Second printing, 14,000 copies, January 2005

Printed in Canada
Book design by Cynthia Clark
Cover photos by Greg Campbell

QUAIL RIDGE PRESS
P. O. Box 123 • Brandon, MS 39043 • e-mail: info@quailridge.com
www.recipehalloffame.com • www.quailridge.com

Contents

Cincinnati is a great place to walk—up hills, across bridges, and through its lovely parks. After checking out the Serpentine Wall and some of the pig statues around Sawyer Point, we take a break before deciding not to tackle the "Big Mac" Bridge.

★★★★★★★★★★★ ★★★★★★★★★★★

"Quick and Easy" are words that get immediate attention, particularly in the area of food preparation. "Wow, if I can cook it fast and it tastes good, give me the recipe!" is a phrase we hear more and more often. With this in mind, we have put together the *Recipe Hall of Fame Quick & Easy Cookbook,* a time-saving collection of 546 recipes that will put delicious meals on your table in the least amount of time.

As with its predecessors, *The Recipe Hall of Fame Cookbook* and the *Recipe Hall of Fame Dessert Cookbook*, all of the recipes in this book have been collected from the database of the BEST OF THE BEST STATE COOKBOOK SERIES (over 12,000 recipes). This highly acclaimed series of individual state cookbooks contains recipes that have already been judged superior. The RECIPE HALL OF FAME SERIES is literally the *Best* of the Best of the Best. The three-part criteria for selection is the same for all Recipe Hall of Fame books in that the recipes must deliver: 1) Taste, 2) Taste, and 3) **Taste!**

A quick and easy recipe in our estimation 1) *should* require a small amount of work; 2) it *should not* require you to read the directions a half dozen times to figure out what you should be doing; 3) it *should not* require a long list of ingredients; and further, 4) these ingredients *should* be the type you will likely have on hand. And though most are start-to-finish quick, we have also included dishes we call "fix and forget"—the kind that are great to take out of the oven, or to come home to, smelling wonderful and ready to serve! All of these recipes will prove to be the ones you will delight in cooking and serving over and over again.

We have frequently added "Editor's Extras" to some of the recipes. These offer suggestions for enhancement, including variations, substitutions, helpful hints, or whatever we found would make preparing a particular recipe more versatile. And further, we have added "Even Easier" comments that will help you prepare the dish even more efficiently.

In today's busy world, Americans seem to be spending less time cooking, yet they realize the value of sharing meals with family and friends, and lament this loss of quality time together. Eating out used to be a sometimes treat—now it has become, for many, a way of life. But from all the feedback we get from people all over America, they really want to eat more at home. Their fondest memories are of times spent around a table of home-cooked food . . . Thanksgiving dinner is talked about in tones of reverence. This cookbook will get you back into the

★★★

kitchen, and back around the table with your family, with less effort than ever for a good homemade meal.

This cookbook will also be of particular value to the young or inexperienced cook, those who are usually asked to bring the chips or napkins to the party. Wouldn't it be a kick instead to contribute a delicious hors d'oeuvre or a sinfully scrumptious dessert that you made yourself? Older children who help with family meals will love the choices and dishes they can make on their own. These simple and easy recipes will result in cooking successes that will instill confidence, and likely lead to more and more enjoyment in the kitchen and at the dinner table.

In our years of research, we have traveled throughout America learning about its people and what they most enjoy cooking and eating. We invite you to travel around the country with us, by way of the chapter opening photographs, to some of the places we have visited. It has been quite an experience, even frustrating at times—making a wrong turn or getting there only minutes after the store closed. It was sometimes a little scary wandering into unknown territory in the dark, but it was mostly exciting and rewarding and fun, and always informative. Everywhere we went, we met interesting and helpful people, some of whom have become dear friends.

We wish to thank all of the incredibly good and creative cooks who contributed a choice recipe to a cookbook that made it to our BEST OF THE BEST STATE COOKBOOK SERIES, and then further made it to the RECIPE HALL OF FAME SERIES. They have all contributed to our goal of *Preserving America's Food Heritage*.

We wish to thank all the in-house people who have contributed to the development of this book. These include Tupper for her illustrations, Greg for his cover photos, all the recipe testers (and tasters), and particularly our "we-can-do-it" staff.

We hope the *Recipe Hall of Fame Quick & Easy Cookbook* will help you solve that dilemma of modern-day life, "How can I get delicious food on the table in the least amount of time?" With this cookbook, the solution is *easy*.

Gwen McKee and Barbara Moseley

Beverages & Appetizers

★★★★ ★★★★

Behind the Breakers, the Vanderbilts' summer home in Newport, Rhode Island, we take an early morning stroll on the Cliff Walk. It is so pretty seeing these huge mansions, one after another, so beautifully landscaped, while feeling the sea breeze and hearing the lapping waves.

9

★★★★★★★★★★★★ ★★★★★★★★★★★★

Hot Chocolate Mix

1 (8-quart) box powdered milk
1 (2-pound) box Quik (powdered chocolate mix)

½–1 cup powdered sugar
1 (8 to 10-ounce) jar coffee creamer

Combine all ingredients in very large bowl. Store in 5-quart ice cream bucket or other sealed container. To use, add ¼ cup mix for each mug of boiling water.

Feeding the Flock (Minnesota)

Hot Peppermint Chocolate

Refreshing and warm on a cold winter night.

3 cups hot milk, divided
8 chocolate peppermint patties (the small ones)

⅛ teaspoon salt
1 cup cream

Combine ½ cup hot milk with chocolate peppermint patties. Add salt and 2½ cups hot milk; heat to simmering. Add cream.

Touches of the Hands & Heart (Ohio)

Wassail

When the weather outside is frightful . . .

2 quarts apple cider
2 cinnamon sticks
½ cup lemon juice

1 cup light corn syrup
1 (12-ounce) can pineapple juice
½ teaspoon nutmeg

Boil and simmer cider and cinnamon sticks for 5 minutes. Add rest of ingredients and serve hot.

Caring is Sharing (Illinois)

Hot Buttered Rum

This is supposed to have been the Pilgrims' brew, and when made in quantity, it was kept hot by dipping a hot iron in the bowl—the iron was called a loggerhead. Hot buttered rum was a remedy for everything from chills to snakebite and is still a help when the thermometer drops below zero.

1 teaspoon confectioners' sugar
¼ cup rum

1 tablespoon butter
¼ cup boiling water

Heat the glass you will serve in or use a hot mug. Put the sugar in, and add the remaining ingredients. Fill the glass or mug with boiling water and serve at once. You may sprinkle the top with nutmeg—I use cinnamon. Serves 1.

My Own Cook Book (New England)

Witches' Brew

Drink with halloween spirit.

1 gallon apple cider
12 ounces frozen orange juice
  concentrate, thawed

1 gallon cranberry juice
1 pound dry ice

Mix juices in large container; add dry ice broken in big pieces for steam effect.

Anoka County 4H Cook Book (Minnesota)

Dry ice is frozen carbon dioxide, a gas that we exhale, that plants use in photosynthesis, and the same gas that is added to water to make soda water. It is so cold (-109.3 degrees F.), that it's "hot," and so you must wear gloves or use a towel when handling it. Though great for ice chests since there is no messy melting into liquid, it should not be stored in your freezer, as it is so cold it may make the thermostat turn off. Of course if your freezer were broken, dry ice would save all your frozen foods.

Coffee Liqueur

This homemade Kahlua has to age two weeks, but is so easy to make, so nice to have on hand, so delightful to serve.

⅓ cup instant coffee
3½ cups sugar
2 cups water

1 fifth vodka
3 tablespoons plus 1 teaspoon
   vanilla

Combine coffee, sugar and water. Heat until dissolved; cool. Add vodka and vanilla. Pour into half-gallon glass container. Age 2 weeks. Use as is for Kahlua or serve mixed with milk.

A Taste of the Holidays (Georgia)

★ **Editor's Extra:** My sweet little mother made batches of this and put it in sterilized brown bottles (she had friends save bottles from other kinds of liquors—the bottles had to be dark glass), dated them and then gave them as treasured gifts—the older ones were the best!

Sunday Punch

So easy and so very good.

1 (46-ounce) can pineapple juice
2 (46-ounce) cans apple juice

3 quarts ginger ale

Chill juices and ginger ale. Make ice ring of apple juice with cherries and orange slices. Can do ahead. Serves 40.

Mountain Elegance (North Carolina)

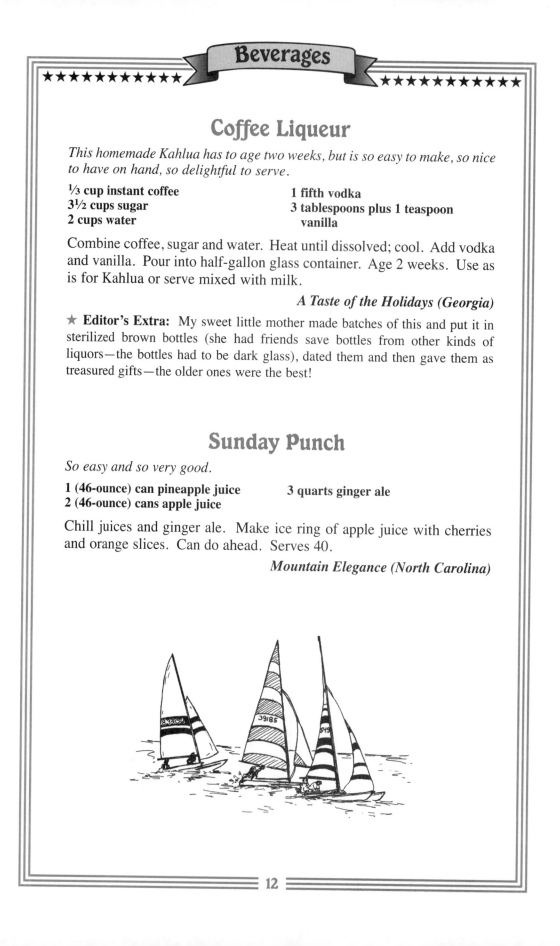

Strawberry Lemonade Punch

½ cup instant tea (not lemon
  flavored)
5 cups water
1 (12-ounce) can frozen lemonade
  concentrate

½ cup sugar
1 package frozen sliced
  strawberries
Vodka or champagne (optional)

Mix tea, water, lemonade, and sugar together, then add strawberries. Vodka or champagne may be added to taste. Easy. Do ahead (except strawberries). Serves 8–10.

With Hands & Heart Cookbook (Missouri)

★ **Editor's Extra:** I make ½ recipe at a time and whirl it in a blender. Great summertime refresher.

Hurricane Punch

1 large can Hawaiian Punch
1 (12-ounce) can frozen orange
  juice
1 (6-ounce) can frozen lemonade

¾ cup sugar
Rum
Cherries
Orange slices

In large bowl mix punch, orange juice, lemonade and sugar. Fill (16-ounce) glasses with crushed ice and add 4 ounces rum per glass. Fill glasses with punch. Garnish with cherries and orange slices. Makes 4–6 hurricanes.

Nibbles Cooks Cajun (Arkansas)

Pina Coolada

1 cup pineapple juice
½ teaspoon coconut extract

1 cup skim milk
1 cup crushed ice (optional)

Blend and serve cold. Makes 2½ cups.

Breakfasts Ozark Style (Missouri)

Angel Frost

1 (6-ounce) can frozen pink
  lemonade, thawed
1 cup milk
1 (10-ounce) package frozen
  strawberries in syrup, partially
  thawed

1 pint vanilla ice cream
Fresh strawberries (optional)

In a blender, place first 4 ingredients in the order given; blend until smooth. Pour into glasses. Garnish with fresh strawberries, if desired. Yields approximately 4–6 servings.

Sharing God's Bounty (Great Plains)

Amaretto Freeze

Delicious as an after dinner drink or as a frozen dessert.

⅓ cup amaretto liqueur
1 tablespoon dark brown sugar
1 quart vanilla ice cream

Whipped cream
Maraschino cherries

Mix amaretto and brown sugar together and stir until the sugar is dissolved. Combine the Amaretto mixture and the ice cream in container of blender and process until smooth.

   You may serve immediately in brandy snifters or pour mixture into parfait glasses. Fill ¾ full and freeze. When ready to serve, top with a spoon of whipped cream and a cherry. Serves 6 as an after dinner drink. Double recipe to serve 6 for a parfait. (Pictured on cover.)

Pineapple Gold (Mississippi)

★ **Editor's Extra:** I make this with non-fat vanilla yogurt so I can justify refills. Better plan on making several batches.

★★★★★★★★★★★★   ★★★★★★★★★★★★

Smoothie

1 cup ice
1 cup skim milk
1 (3-ounce) scoop low-fat vanilla
   frozen yogurt

½ cup frozen strawberries
½ banana

Combine all ingredients in blender for approximately 30 seconds. Serves 6.

Amount per serving: Cal: 268; Grams of fat: 1.9; Chol: trace; Sod: 44mg; % of Fat: 6%

Eat To Your Heart's Content! (Arkansas)

Orange Julius

1 (6-ounce) can frozen orange juice
   concentrate
1 cup milk
1 cup water

½ cup sugar
1 teaspoon vanilla
5–6 ice cubes

Blend in blender 30 seconds. Makes 6 cups.

The Country Gourmet (Mississippi)

Orange Blush

1 (6-ounce) can frozen orange juice
   concentrate, thawed
1 cup cranberry juice

4 tablespoons sugar
16 ounces club soda
Mint for garnish

Combine orange juice concentrate, cranberry juice, and sugar. Chill. Just before serving, stir in club soda. Pour over crushed ice in goblets. Yields 6 servings.

Bear in Mind: Add sprigs of fresh mint or lemon balm to each goblet. For extra zip, add vodka.

Unbearably Good! (Georgia)

Cheese Ring

1 bunch finely chopped green onions
Red and black pepper, to taste
1 pound grated Cheddar cheese
1 cup mayonnaise
1 cup finely chopped nuts
1 jar red plum preserves

Combine ingredients, except preserves. Pour into greased (Pam) round bowl to form cheese ring. Place on serving dish and top with red plum preserves.

Kooking with the Krewe (Louisiana II)

Baked Brie with Caramelized Apple Topping

A perfect pairing of flavors and textures.

1 large Granny Smith apple, peeled,
  cored and coarsely chopped
  (about 2 cups)
½ cup pecan pieces
⅓ cup (packed) brown sugar
2 tablespoons Kahlua
1 (about 2-pound) wheel brie, rind
  left on

Mix apple with pecans, brown sugar, and Kahlua. Set aside. Place brie in shallow, oven-proof dish; top with apple mixture. Bake at 325° 10–15 minutes, or until topping is bubbly and cheese is softened. Serve with lavosh or water crackers. Makes 16–20 servings.

Palates (Colorado)

Boursin Cheese

This will keep for a couple of weeks in refrigerator.

8 ounces sweet butter, room
  temperature
2 (8-ounce) bars cream cheese,
  room temperature

1 clove garlic, chopped
½ teaspoon each: basil, chives,
  dill, marjoram, thyme and black
  pepper

Mix sweet butter and cream cheese together. Add remaining ingredients, mixing well. It's best to use fresh herbs. Serve with crackers and fruit.

Cookin' in the Spa (Arkansas)

★ **Editor's Extra:** This will make you want to start an herb garden! But don't hesitate to use the dried variety. Sooo good to have on hand. Good gift, too!

Home-Style Boursin

2 (8-ounce) packages cream
  cheese, softened
¼ cup mayonnaise
2 teaspoons Dijon mustard

2 tablespoons chopped chives
2 tablespoons dill weed
1 clove garlic, minced

In a bowl, mix all ingredients together.

For party spread, simply spread on favorite little party breads. For party ball, shape into a ball and roll in ½ cup crushed pecans. Wrap in clear wrap and refrigerate for 3 days. Serve on cheese board with favorite breads or crackers.

Tony Chachere's Second Helping (Louisana II)

★ **Editor's Extra:** Mine looked more like a flying saucer at first, but after I folded the clear wrap over it, it was easier to shape. It would probably have been fantastic in 3 days, but it was eaten long before then!

Wisconsin is the No. 1 cheese-producing state in the country, with nearly ⅓ of the total annual U.S. cheese production. Wisconsin is the nation's only producer of Limburger cheese. Colby cheese was invented in Colby, Wisconsin. Brick cheese was invented in Wisconsin, and is named for its shape—and because cheesemakers originally used bricks to press moisture from the cheese.

Chocolate Chip Cheese Ball

A sweet surprise!

3 (8-ounce) packages cream cheese
2 teaspoons vanilla
1–2 teaspoons cinnamon
1 cup powdered sugar

1 (12-ounce) bag mini-chocolate
  chips
½–1 cup chopped pecans

Soften cream cheese and mix with vanilla, cinnamon, sugar, and chips. Form into 1 very large or 2 medium-size cheese balls. Roll in pecans. Refrigerate overnight. Serve with ginger snaps and/or vanilla wafers.

Hopewell's Hoosier Harvest II (Indiana)

Pumpkin Cheese Ball

1 (8-ounce) package cream cheese,
  softened
1 (16-ounce) package shredded
  Cheddar cheese

½ cup pumpkin
1 (4-ounce) package thin-sliced beef,
cut up
Chopped nuts

Mix first 4 ingredients together. Shape into ball. Roll in nuts to cover. Keep refrigerated. Serve with crackers.

Franklin County Homemakers Extension Cookbook (Illinois)

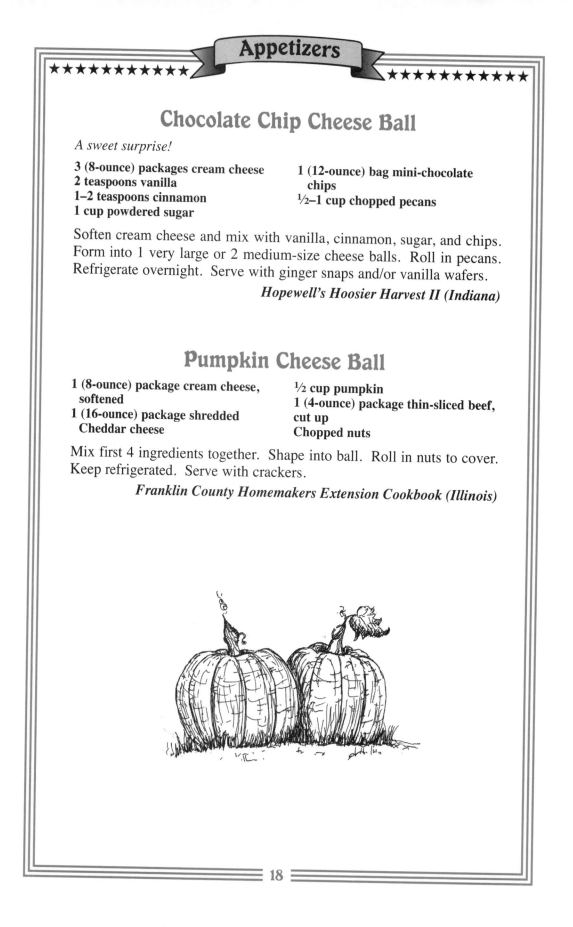

Mustard Dip

This is addictive!

8 ounces sour cream
8 ounces mayonnaise
8 ounces yellow mustard
¼ cup dry chopped onion

1 package original Hidden Valley
  Dressing Mix
½ cup sugar
3 teaspoons horseradish

Mix all together. Serve with pretzels.

Sharing Our Best (Iowa)

★ **Editor's Extra:** Try this with veggies, pita chips, Tostitos, or even as a sandwich spread. Keeps well in the fridge.

Dill Dip

Serve with fresh vegetable strips.

½ pint Hellmann's Mayonnaise
1 tablespoon grated onion
½ pint sour cream

1½ teaspoons chopped parsley
1½ teaspoons dill weed
1 teaspoon cumin

Mix and serve with fresh asparagus spears, sliced zucchini, green onions, cherry tomatoes, celery, carrot sticks, cauliflower or radishes.

Square House Museum Cookbook (Texas)

★ **Editor's Extra:** This is also good with crackers, chips, crusty bread . . . truly a delicious dip.

In 1756, while Duc de Richelieu was defeating the British at Port Mahon, his French chef was creating a victory feast that included a sauce made of cream and eggs. When the chef realized that there was no cream in the kitchen, he improvised by substituting olive oil for cream. A new culinary masterpiece was born, and the chef named it "Mahonnaise" in honor of the Duc's victory at Port Mahon. In 1903, German immigrant Richard Hellmann opened a delicatessen in New York City. His wife's recipe for mayonnaise was featured in salads and it became so popular that he began selling it in "wooden boats" that were used for weighing butter.

Cream Cheese and Chutney Canapé

This is a quick recipe and may be made the day before using.

1 (8-ounce) package cream cheese
¼ cup chutney
¼ teaspoon dry mustard

1 teaspoon curry powder
Pineapple half (optional)
Toasted almonds, for topping

Blend first 4 ingredients well. Chill for at least 4 hours. Scoop out a pineapple half and fill with mixture. Top with toasted almonds. Serve with crackers. Yields 12 servings.

Cooking with Tradition (Georgia)

★ **Editor's Extra:** This is great to stuff in celery or dates.

Jane's Broccoli Dip

1 cup chopped onion
1 stick margarine
2 packages frozen, chopped broccoli
1 (4-ounce) can sliced mushrooms
1½ (9-ounce) rolls garlic cheese

1 cup slivered almonds
2 (10½-ounce) cans mushroom soup
Tabasco sauce and Worcestershire
 sauce to taste

Sauté onion and margarine in large pot. Add broccoli and simmer, covered, until tender. Add remaining ingredients, heat till smooth, and serve hot with corn chips. Makes 4 cups.

Bell's Best (Mississippi)

★ **Editor's Extra:** This is a very popular party dip. Serve it in a crock pot to keep it warm. Good with Melba rounds.

Corbin's Bean Dip

1 (8-ounce) package cream cheese
1 (16-ounce) can refried beans
1 (8-ounce) carton sour cream

1 (10-ounce) jar salsa
Shredded Cheddar cheese

Mix first 4 ingredients together; place in casserole dish and cover with cheese. Bake at 350° until hot and cheese is melted. Serve with corn chips or tortilla chips.

MDA Favorite Recipes (Ohio)

★★★★★★★★★★★ ★★★★★★★★★★★

Mexican Confetti Dip

This is a great source of protein. Great for lunch.

1 (12-ounce) can whole kernel corn,
    drained
1 (15.5-ounce) can black beans,
    drained

⅓ cup fat-free Italian Salad
    Dressing
1 (16-ounce) jar of your favorite
    salsa

Mix all together. Chill. Presto! You're done! Serve with Baked Tostito
Chips. Yields 6 servings (approximately 8 ounces each serving).

Per serving: Cal 78; Fat .75g

Variations: Warm a flour tortilla in microwave. Fill center with ¼ cup
of dip. Fold up as you would a burrito. Or toss ½ cup with 1½ cups of
your favorite lettuces for a tasty twist to your salad!

Down Home Cookin' Without the Down Home Fat (Ohio)

Traveling Taco Dip

1 (16-ounce) can refried beans
2 cups sour cream
8 ounces frozen guacamole, thawed
1 (7-ounce) can diced green chiles

1 (7-ounce) can chopped black
    olives, drained
2 plum tomatoes, diced
4 ounces shredded Cheddar cheese

Spread the refried beans over the bottom of a 10-inch pie plate. Top with
layers of sour cream, guacamole, green chiles, black olives, tomatoes,
and cheese. Refrigerate, covered, until chilled. Serve with tortilla chips.
Serves 8–10. (Pictured on cover.)

Tucson Treasures (Arizona)

Hot Mushroom Dip

4 tablespoons butter
1 clove garlic, minced
1 pound mushrooms, sliced
2 tablespoons chopped parsley

½ teaspoon salt
¼ teaspoon pepper
1 cup sour cream

Melt butter in saucepan. Add garlic, mushrooms, parsley, salt, pepper. Cook until mushrooms are tender. Fold in sour cream. Serve in chafing dish with Melba toast.

Best of Bayou Cuisine (Mississippi)

Tuna Dip

Lightning fast!

1 (6-ounce) can spring water tuna
1 (8-ounce) carton sour cream

1 package Good Seasons Italian
    Dressing

Drain tuna and mash. Add sour cream and dressing mix. Mix well. Chill. Make a day ahead.

Shared Treasures (Louisiana II)

★ **Editor's Extra:** Good with canned shrimp, too. This may be better made a day ahead, but we usually can't wait long enough to find out.

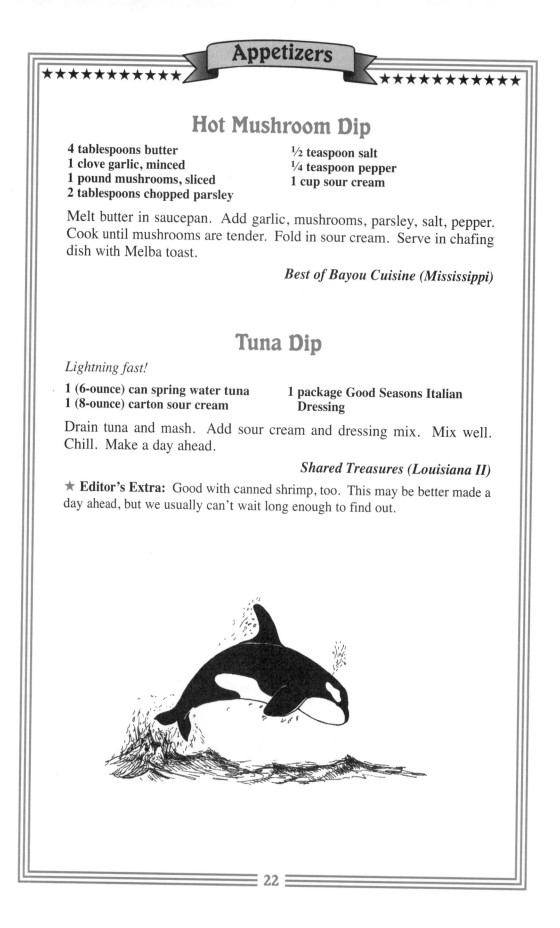

Sooie Cheese Dip

½ pound pork sausage
½ pound ground round beef
1 can Cheddar cheese soup
1 (8-ounce) jar taco sauce

1 (4-ounce) jar mushroom stems
  and pieces
1 pound process American cheese,
  cubed

Brown sausage and beef. Drain well. Add remaining ingredients, stirring often. Heat until cheese melts.
     Serve hot with your choice of chips or French bread cubes. Serves 12.

Cookin' in the Spa (Arkansas)

Nacho Cheese Dip

2 pounds ground beef, browned and
  drained
2 pounds Velveeta cheese, melted

1 can cream of mushroom soup
1 (8-ounce) jar picante sauce

Combine ingredients and serve hot with tortilla chips. Crockpot works well.

The Joy of Sharing (Great Plains)

★ **Even Easier:** Cut cheese in cubes—melts faster!

7 Layer Dip

2 small cans diced jalapeño peppers
2 cans chopped black olives
1 package taco mix
1 pint sour cream
1 (15-ounce) can chili with beans

1 (8-ounce) container guacamole
8 ounces grated sharp cheese
8 ounces grated Monterey cheese
2 or 3 medium-size tomatoes, diced

Put peppers and olives on bottom of a 9x13-inch baking dish, then taco mix. Make layers of sour cream, chili, guacamole and cheeses. Then, on the top, put tomatoes and more olives, if desired. Dip with tortilla chips.

Diversity is Delta's Main Dish (California)

★★★★★★★★★★★★   ★★★★★★★★★★★★

Amaretto Cheese Spread

1 (8-ounce) package cream cheese
¼ cup amaretto liqueur

1 (2½-ounce) package slivered
almonds, sautéed in butter

Soften cream cheese and blend in amaretto. Form a ball and chill until firm. Before serving, cover with almonds and allow to reach room temperature. Serve with thinly sliced apples and pears.

  This also may be served as after-dinner fruit and cheese.

Putting on the Grits (South Carolina)

Asparagus Ham Rolls

16 asparagus stalks, cooked
4 thin slices of boiled ham
½ cup grated sharp Cheddar
cheese

1 cup medium white sauce
(2 tablespoons butter,
2 tablespoons flour, 1 cup
milk, salt and pepper)

Put 4 asparagus stalks on each ham slice. Roll up and fasten with a toothpick. Broil for 5 minutes on each side. Add cheese to heated sauce. Stir till melted and pour over ham rolls. Broil to golden brown. Garnish with toast points.

Dan River Family Cookbook (Virginia)

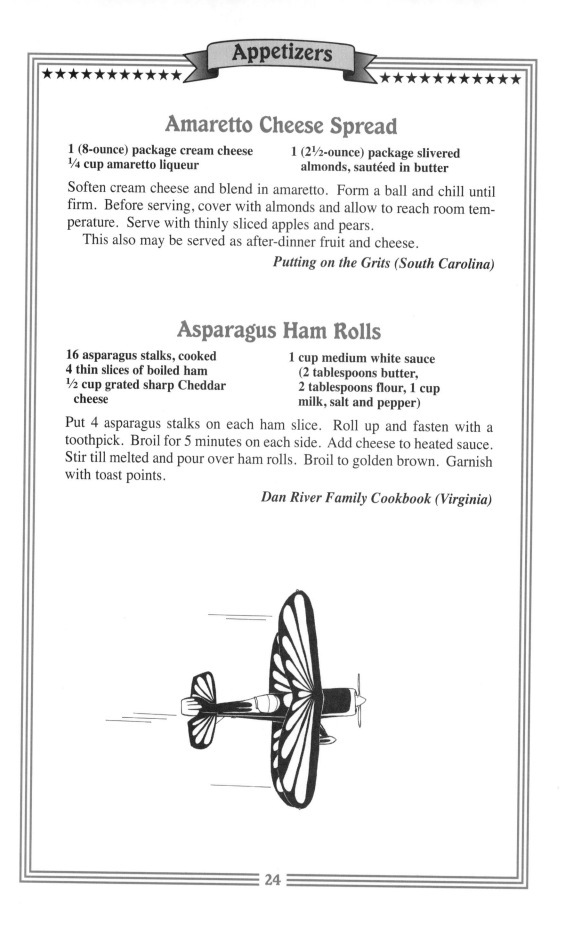

★★★★★★★★★★★   ★★★★★★★★★★★

Kate's Last-Minute Artichoke Spread

A house classic, this recipe is in constant demand by our guests who try to guess the secret flavorings. There aren't any. It's fast, simple, and just plain wonderful.

1 (14-ounce) can artichoke hearts, water packed
1 clove garlic, peeled and mashed

3 tablespoons good mayonnaise
Hungarian paprika

Drain the artichokes and squeeze out the water from each one. Chop finely and transfer them to a small saucepan. Add the garlic and mayonnaise. Blend well.

To blend and enhance the flavors, warm over low heat, stirring constantly. Do not let it boil. Turn spread into a serving bowl, sprinkle with paprika, and offer with your favorite crackers. Serves 10–12.

Recipes from a New England Inn (New England)

Hot Artichoke Cheese

1 (8½-ounce) can artichokes, drained, and cut in small bite-size pieces

1 cup grated Parmesan cheese
1 cup Hellmann's Mayonnaise

Mix together and bake in flat baking dish 20 minutes at 350° until brown on top.

Serve hot on crackers. Triple for large casserole. Hellmann's is a must. (This brand does not make the casserole greasy.)

Carolina Cuisine Encore! (South Carolina)

Curry Mayonnaise

1 cup mayonnaise
1 tablespoon curry powder

2 tablespoons brown sugar
½ cup dried cranberries

Mix first 3 ingredients well. Add dried cranberries. Use as spread for turkey or ham sandwiches.

Stirling City Hotel Afternoon Tea (California)

Shrimp Stuffed Celery

Good quickie hors d'oeuvre.

1 (4½-ounce) can broken shrimp
  washed and drained
1 teaspoon dried chives
3 tablespoons finely chopped onion
5 black olives, pitted, finely chopped

2 tablespoons slivered almonds
Dash of lemon juice
Enough mayonnaise for consistency
Celery stalks, cut in 3-inch pieces

Mix first 7 ingredients thoroughly. Stuff celery and arrange on platter.

Ship to Shore I (North Carolina)

Shrimp Butter

1 (8-ounce) package cream cheese
1 stick real butter, softened
2 tablespoons lemon juice
1 small can shrimp, drained

4 chopped green onions
1 tablespoon sugar
¼ teaspoon seasoned salt

Soften cream cheese and butter. Place all ingredients into a bowl and mix with a mixer until smooth. Serve cold with crackers or at room temperature for sandwich spread.

Fiftieth Anniversary Cookbook (Louisiana II)

Shrimply Devine

The #1 hors d'oeuvre at the party!

1 (8-ounce) package cream cheese
1 cup sour cream
1 (⅝-ounce) package Italian Salad
  Dressing Mix

2 tablespoons finely chopped green
  pepper
½ cup finely chopped shrimp
1 teaspoon lemon juice

Blend cheese with remainder of ingredients. Chill at least 1 hour before serving. Makes 1⅔ cups. Serve with crackers, tortilla chips, Melba toast, etc. (Pictured on cover.)

A Collection of Recipes from St. Matthew Lutheran Church (Illinois)

Easy Party Dip

Sure to be one of your favorite dips. You will be surprised.

1 cup Hellmann's Mayonnaise
1 cup chopped onion
8 ounces Swiss cheese, shredded

2 artificial lobster tails or 3 sea
legs or 12 cooked shrimp

Simply mix first 3 ingredients in a small casserole dish. For color and added taste, shred one or a combination of seafood mentioned above. Mix well. Cover casserole dish. Bake at 350° until cheese is melted, approximately 15–20 minutes. Serve warm on a Ritz cracker.

Indiana's Finest Recipes (Indiana)

Crab Meat Dip

1 (8-ounce) package cream cheese
½ cup mayonnaise
1 (12-ounce) package imitation
  crab meat

½ teaspoon dill weed
Dash of garlic salt
Dash of Worcestershire sauce
1 cup sour cream

Mix cream cheese and mayonnaise well; add (cut up) crab and seasonings; fold in sour cream. May be made the day before serving. Serve in round bread, on crackers or buns.

Visitation Parish Cookbook (Iowa)

★ **Editor's Extra:** A 5-minute quickie, this is good spread on any kind of crackers, and great for stuffing celery. Imitation crab meat is actually fish that tastes something like crab—without the shells! You can find packages in the seafood department.

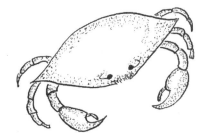

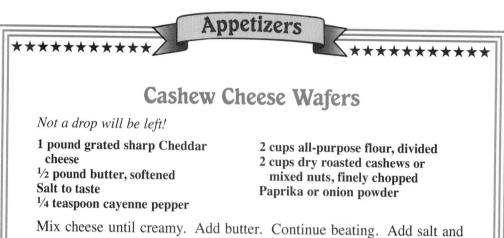

★★★★★★★★★★★★ ★★★★★★★★★★★★

Cashew Cheese Wafers

Not a drop will be left!

1 pound grated sharp Cheddar cheese	**2 cups all-purpose flour, divided**
½ pound butter, softened	**2 cups dry roasted cashews or mixed nuts, finely chopped**
Salt to taste	**Paprika or onion powder**
¼ teaspoon cayenne pepper	

Mix cheese until creamy. Add butter. Continue beating. Add salt and pepper; add 3 tablespoons flour. Blend well. Continue adding flour until mixture becomes soft dough and can be rolled into balls without sticking. Add finely chopped nuts. Dust hands and fork with flour. Form small balls. Flatten with fork on cookie sheet. Bake at 325° about 20 or 25 minutes. Sprinkle with paprika while hot, after you remove from oven, or sprinkle with onion powder. Better after the first day. Keep in tin. Yields approximately 100.

Huntsville Entertains (Alabama)

★ **Editor's Extra:** Mix in food processor or in mixer bowl with dough hook. Cut recipe in half to make it quicker. These are great for tailgate parties and take-alongs.

Hot Sausage Puffs

1 pound raw, hot seasoned sausage
3 cups Bisquick Baking Mix
¼ cup water

12 ounces sharp Cheddar cheese, shredded

Mix all together. Form into balls and bake at 375° for 15 minutes. Serve piping hot. Can be frozen. If frozen, place in 300° oven for 10 minutes, then bake.

Susie's Cook Book (Pennsylvania)

★ **Editor's Extra:** Forming the balls may take a *little* time; get somebody to help you—these are delicious!

Pepperoni Puffs

Very easy and freezes beautifully!

1 cup all-purpose flour
1 teaspoon baking powder
1 cup milk
1 egg

¼ cup grated Cheddar cheese
1 (3½-ounce) package diced pepperoni (1 cup)

Combine first 5 ingredients and mix thoroughly. Add pepperoni and mix until evenly distributed throughout the mixture. Allow batter to stand for 15 minutes. Grease mini-muffin pans or spray with nonstick vegetable spray. Fill each cup ¾ full. Bake at 350° for 25–35 minutes or until browned. Yields 60 puffs.

Connecticut Cooks III (New England)

Tortilla Roll-Ups

1 (4-ounce) can chopped green chiles
3 green onions, chopped
1 (8-ounce) package cream cheese, room temperature

½ teaspoon garlic salt
3 large flour tortillas
Salsa or picante sauce

Mix chiles, onions, cream cheese, and garlic salt together. Spread this on the tortillas, roll up, and refrigerate until chilled. Cut into bite-size pieces. Serve salsa on the side.

Hopewell's Hoosier Harvest II (Indiana)

Shaved Ham Oven Sandwiches

Good make-ahead for parties, picnics, tailgates. Freezes and pleases.

½ cup butter, room temperature
2 tablespoons Dijon mustard
1½ tablespoons poppy seeds
1¼ teaspoons Worcestershire sauce

½ medium onion, finely grated
8 cracked pepper sandwich rolls
1 pound shaved boiled ham
8 slices Swiss cheese

Preheat oven to 400°. Mix together butter, mustard, poppy seeds, Worcestershire sauce, and onion. Split rolls and spread mixture thinly on both sides. Divide the ham between the rolls, top with 1 slice of Swiss cheese, and replace sandwich tops.

Wrap sandwiches in aluminum foil and warm at 400° for 10 minutes, or until cheese melts. Serves 8.

Settings (Pennsylvania)

★ **Editor's Extra:** Be creative and try different kinds of buns. We like trays of 24 party rolls—you can slice them in half all at once.

Chocolate Fondue and Fresh Fruit

A perfect dessert and coffee event.

Fruit chunks or angel food cake
1 (12-ounce) bag Hershey Real
  Chocolate Chips

1 cup sour cream
¼ cup Grand Marnier or Crème
  de Cacao

Arrange fruit (fresh apples, bananas, grapes, peaches, pears, pineapple) or cake attractively on a platter. Cover and place in refrigerator. Melt chocolate chips in saucepan or microwave, taking care not to scorch. Add sour cream to chocolate. Whisk cream and chocolate quickly with a wire whisk. Add liqueur and whisk until blended well. Place warm fondue in attractive bowl. Use fondue forks to dip cool fruit or cake into chocolate.

There Once Was a Cook... (Pennsylvania)

★ **Editor's Extra:** Chocolate melts well in a heavy glass bowl in the microwave, 2 minutes on HIGH, then stir.

★★★★★★★★★★★   ★★★★★★★★★★★

Heavenly Fruit Dip

½ cup sugar
2 tablespoons flour
1 cup pineapple juice

1 egg, beaten
1 tablespoon butter or margarine
1 cup whipping cream, whipped

Combine sugar, flour, juice, egg, and butter in heavy saucepan. Cook over medium heat, stirring constantly until smooth and thick. Let cool completely. Fold in whipped cream. Serve with fresh fruit—especially good with sliced apples.

Note: Use ½ cup orange juice and ½ cup pineapple juice instead of all pineapple juice. Also use 2 cups nondairy whipped topping instead of 1 cup whipped cream.

More Goodies and Guess-Whats (Colorado)

Caramel Apple Dip

1 (8-ounce) package cream cheese
1 cup brown sugar, packed
1 teaspoon vanilla

½ cup chopped dry roasted
  peanuts (optional)

Cream all together. Serve with crisp apple slices. (Granny Smiths do especially well.)

Cooking with Grace (Wisconsin)

★ **Editor's Extra:** Trying to get your kids to eat more fruit? Offer sliced apples with this delicious dip and watch them go for it!

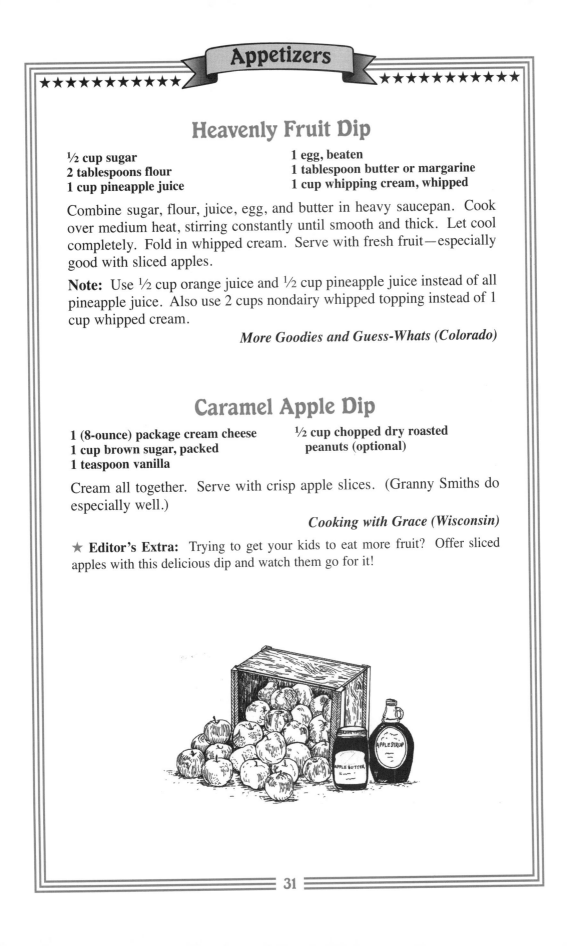

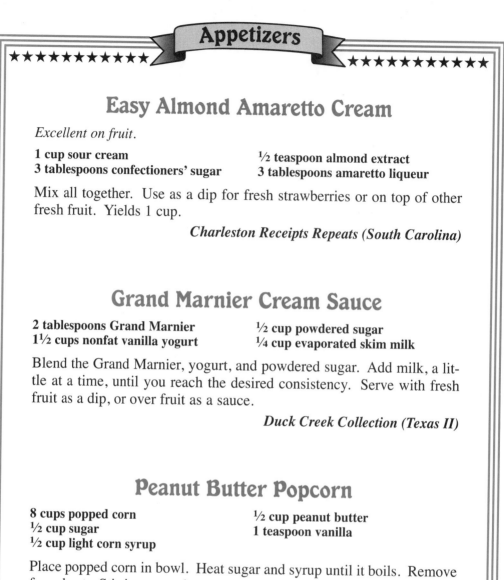

Easy Almond Amaretto Cream

Excellent on fruit.

1 cup sour cream
3 tablespoons confectioners' sugar

½ teaspoon almond extract
3 tablespoons amaretto liqueur

Mix all together. Use as a dip for fresh strawberries or on top of other fresh fruit. Yields 1 cup.

Charleston Receipts Repeats (South Carolina)

Grand Marnier Cream Sauce

2 tablespoons Grand Marnier
1½ cups nonfat vanilla yogurt

½ cup powdered sugar
¼ cup evaporated skim milk

Blend the Grand Marnier, yogurt, and powdered sugar. Add milk, a little at a time, until you reach the desired consistency. Serve with fresh fruit as a dip, or over fruit as a sauce.

Duck Creek Collection (Texas II)

Peanut Butter Popcorn

8 cups popped corn
½ cup sugar
½ cup light corn syrup

½ cup peanut butter
1 teaspoon vanilla

Place popped corn in bowl. Heat sugar and syrup until it boils. Remove from heat. Stir in peanut butter and vanilla; mix well. Pour over corn, and coat. Can make into popcorn balls.

New Beginnings Cookbook (Iowa)

Because more popcorn is consumed there per capita than anywhere else—an average of four pounds per person per year—Minneapolis-St. Paul is the Popcorn-Eating Capital of the World.

★★★★★★★★★★★ ★★★★★★★★★★★

Spicy Red Pecans

¼ cup butter or margarine
2 teaspoons ground red chile

¾–1 teaspoon garlic salt
3 cups pecan halves

In large skillet, melt butter over medium heat. Stir in red chile, garlic salt, and pecans. Cook and stir pecans 4–5 minutes until browned and well coated with chile.

Recipes from Arizona with Love (Arizona)

Shrimp Cheesies

1 (4-ounce) jar Old English
pasteurized processed cheese
spread
½ cup butter, softened

1 tablespoon mayonnaise
½ teaspoon garlic powder
1 (4-ounce) can shrimp, diced
6 English muffins

Combine first 5 ingredients in mixing bowl or blender container. Mix until well blended and fairly smooth. Cut each muffin half into 4 pieces. Spread each ¼ muffin with 1 teaspoon of cheese mixture and place on baking sheet. Broil for 3–5 minutes or until golden brown.

These can be frozen by placing on a baking sheet and allowing to freeze. They can then be placed in a freezer bag and stored until needed. Broil while still frozen. Serves 16–18.

Philadelphia Homestyle Cookbook (Pennsylvania)

Chiles and Cheese Bake

Serve hot and bubbly—hold on a warming tray.

1 (4-ounce) can chopped green chiles
2 cups (8 ounces) shredded
Longhorn or sharp Cheddar cheese

1 egg
1 tablespoon water
Corn chips

Heat oven to 350°. Spread undrained chiles evenly in a 9-inch pie pan. Sprinkle grated cheese over chiles. Beat egg with water until blended, then spread over cheese. Bake 15–20 minutes until cheese is hot, bubbly, and lightly browned. Serve with corn chips. Hold on warming tray so cheese stays soft. Serves 8–10.

Lasting Impressions (Georgia)

Jalapeño Cheese Squares

4 eggs
2 cups shredded sharp Cheddar
  cheese
1 (4-ounce) jar sliced pimentos,
  drained

1 (4-ounce) jar sliced jalapeños,
  drained (or diced green chiles)

Preheat oven to 400°. Coat an 8x8-inch baking pan with cooking spray or oil. Set aside. Beat eggs with fork in medium bowl. Add remaining ingredients and blend thoroughly, mixing by hand. Pour into prepared pan and bake approximately 20 minutes or until set. Let cool slightly and cut into squares. Serve hot or cold. Makes 8 servings.

Vistoso Vittles II (Arizona)

★ **Editor's Extra:** My friend made half a recipe in a small Corningware dish and it worked perfectly. This can be served as a side dish, or try doubling the recipe for a great breakfast entrée.

Shrimp Pizza

Serve this pizza cold.

2 (8-ounce) packages cream cheese
  (softened)
1 (8-ounce) jar cocktail sauce

1 pound shrimp (cooked and cut up)
½ cup chopped green onion
1 cup shredded mozzarella cheese

Spread cream cheese on pizza pan. Spread cocktail sauce on top of cream cheese. Arrange shrimp on top of cocktail sauce. Sprinkle on onion and cheese. Serve with crackers or taco chips.

The Fishlady's Cookbook (Illinois)

★ **Editor's Extra:** This is as pretty as it is popular.

Approximately three billion pizzas are sold in the U.S. each year. Each man, woman, and child in America eats an average of 46 slices (23 pounds) of pizza per year. Pepperoni is America's favorite topping—anchovies is least favorite.

Vegetable Pizza

1 can crescent rolls
4 ounces cream cheese
½ cup mayonnaise

½ package Hidden Valley Original
   Recipe Dressing
Diced fresh vegetables

Spread rolls flat and press together on pizza pan; bake according to directions on package.

Mix cream cheese, mayonnaise and Hidden Valley dressing well. Spread on cooled crescent roll crust.

Dice choice of fresh vegetables to spread on top of mixture. (You can use diced cauliflower, green onions, broccoli flowerets, mushrooms, radishes, green pepper, celery, tomatoes, whatever you wish. Do not use cucumbers.)

Old Fashioned Cooking (Illinois)

Mini Party Pizzas

½ pound sausage or hamburger
1 teaspoon oregano
1 clove garlic, minced
1 tube refrigerator biscuits

1 small can tomato paste
1 cup shredded cheese
¼ cup grated Parmesan cheese

Brown and drain meats. Add oregano and garlic. On greased baking sheet, flatten 10 refrigerator biscuits to 4-inch circles with a rim. Fill with tomato paste and meat. Sprinkle with cheeses. Bake at 450° for 10 minutes.

New Beginnings Cookbook (Iowa)

★ **Even Easier:** To save a step, mix the tomato paste with the drained meat.

Easy Appetizer

1 package bologna   **Horseradish, to taste**
1 package cream cheese, whipped

Spread each piece of bologna with cream cheese that has been mixed with a little horseradish, if desired. Layer the bologna until all pieces are used. Wrap stack of layered bologna and place in refrigerator. When ready to serve, cut into bite-size triangular wedges.

Crystal Clear Cooking (Michigan)

★ **Editor's Extra:** This is an extremely quick hors d'oeuvre that will surprise your guests. You can substitute most any kind of sliced deli meat for the bologna. Fun to stack in smaller layers and cut in different shapes, or roll each spreaded slice, and cut in half or thirds, then pierce with decorative toothpicks.

Crockpot Hors D'Oeuvres

1 (10-ounce) jar chili sauce
1 (10-ounce) jar grape jelly

1 package small sausage links (can be cut in half)

Melt chili sauce and jelly in saucepan. Brown sausage links. Put everything in crockpot on low for full flavor. Use toothpicks to spear.

Home Cooking II (Indiana)

Teriyaki Tidbits

1 (10-ounce) jar apricot preserves
½ cup barbecue sauce
1–2 tablespoons teriyaki sauce
1 pound wieners, cut in 1-inch pieces (or cocktail franks)

1 (15¼-ounce) can pineapple chunks, drained
1 large green pepper, cut into ¾-inch squares

In large saucepan over medium heat, combine preserves, barbecue sauce, and teriyaki sauce. Stir in wieners, pineapple, and green pepper. Heat thoroughly. Transfer mixture to chafing dish, keeping warm over low heat. Serve with toothpicks. Stick pretzels can be used instead.

We Love Country Cookin' (Great Plains)

★ **Editor's Extra:** When a friend, Annette, made this, she said the dipping never stopped till it was gone. A sure-fire winner.

Jezebel Sauce

An old recipe that's always enjoyed.

1 (18-ounce) jar pineapple preserves
1 (18-ounce) jar apple jelly
1 (5-ounce) jar horseradish

1 (1⅛-ounce) can dry mustard
1 tablespoon cracked black pepper (optional)

Blend in mixer, or by hand. Serve with ham, cheese slices and crackers, or over a bar of cream cheese.

This keeps in refrigerator for several weeks. Makes a nice Christmas or other occasion remembrance packaged in small attractive jars and wrapped in colored cellophane.

Turnip Greens in the Bathtub (Louisiana)

★★★★★★★★★★★ ★★★★★★★★★★★

Harlequin Dip

Bring on the tortilla chips!

2 (4-ounce) cans chopped green chiles
2 (4½-ounce) cans chopped black
olives
3 tomatoes, chopped

4 green onions, chopped
2 tablespoons wine vinegar
1 tablespoon oil
Salt and pepper to taste

Combine all ingredients and mix well. Makes 8–10 servings.

Simply Simpatico (New Mexico)

Delicious Mexican Salsa

1 (28-ounce) can crushed or
chopped tomatoes
1 (8-ounce) can tomato sauce
1 teaspoon salt
¼ teaspoon pepper

¼ teaspoon garlic salt
1 teaspoon crushed red pepper
3 small green onions, chopped
Cilantro to taste

Mix ingredients in order. Refrigerate for ½ hour before serving.

Cooking with Cops (Arizona)

Refresh stale potato chips, crackers or other such snacks by putting a plateful in the microwave oven for about 30-45 seconds. Let stand for one minute to crisp. Cereals can also be crisped this way.

Bread & Breakfast

You can't go through Hurricane Mills without checking out the local cuisine. We discovered that "them vittles" were decidedly, deliciously Tennessee.

★★★★★★★★★★★ ★★★★★★★★★★★

Spinach Corn Bread Puff

10½ ounces frozen chopped spinach
1 (7-ounce) box cornbread mix
4 eggs, beaten
6 tablespoons butter, melted

1 medium onion, chopped
1 (8-ounce) carton cottage cheese
½ teaspoon salt

Thaw spinach and squeeze out all the water. Combine spinach and all remaining ingredients. Stir just until moistened. Pour into greased 9-inch pie plate. Bake at 400° for 25 minutes or until lightly browned. Serves 6.

Uptown Down South (South Carolina)

★ **Editor's Extra:** Older recipes show larger sizes; you'll likely find a 10-ounce box of spinach and a 6-ounce package of cornbread mix . . . works deliciously.

Herb Bread

1 teaspoon oregano
1 teaspoon garlic salt
3 tablespoons Parmesan cheese

2 teaspoons parsley flakes
½ pound soft butter
1 loaf French bread

Mix first 5 ingredients well. Slice bread. Butter generously on both sides. Wrap in foil and bake at 350° for 15–20 minutes. (Any extra butter is great on popcorn.)

The Guild Cookbook II (Indiana)

Speidini

1 long loaf French bread
1 pound grated mozzarella cheese

½ pound bacon, fried and crumbled
1 stick butter, melted

Slice bread on diagonal into about 20 slices, but do not slice through the bottom crust. Place on long sheet of heavy foil and stuff the cheese and bacon into the slices. Pour the melted butter slowly over the bread. Wrap the foil to enclose the loaf and bake at 350° about 25 minutes. Serves 8–10. Delicious with soup and a green salad.

Plantation Country (Louisiana)

Popovers Patrick Henry

No popovers we have tasted equal these in flavor and simplicity. A special treat any time.

3 eggs
1 cup milk

1 cup flour
¾ teaspoon salt

Have eggs and milk at room temperature. Mix all ingredients in bowl together and beat hard for 2 minutes. Grease 11–12 cups of muffin tin with vegetable shortening or lard. Pour batter from pitcher, filling each cup ½–¾ full. Place in cold oven and set temperature for 450°. Bake for 25 minutes. Expect them to fall when removed, for that is the nature of popovers. Butter heavily (with the real dairy product) and serve.

More Delectable Cookery of Alexandria (Virginia)

Cheezy Hot French Bread

Practically a meal in itself!

1 long loaf French bread
½ cup margarine, softened
1 tablespoon prepared mustard
¼ cup minced onion

2 tablespoons poppy seeds
1 (8-ounce) package sliced Swiss
   cheese, cut in thirds
2 slices bacon, cooked and crumbled

Slice loaf horizontally into 2 large pieces. Combine margarine, mustard, onion, and poppy seeds. Spread on bread and top with cheese. Place slices in a foil "boat" and sprinkle bacon on top. Bake 15 minutes in 375° oven; cut in serving pieces. Serves 8–12.

Home at the Range IV (Great Plains)

★ **Even Easier**: This can be made even faster and easier by using bottled bacon bits. There are real bacon bits and artificial bacon bits—read the labels. Approximately 2 tablespoons equal 2 slices of bacon.

Cream Cheese Biscuits

1 (3-ounce) package cream cheese
1 stick butter

1 cup all-purpose flour
½ teaspoon salt

Soften cream cheese and butter. Mix all ingredients and roll out to ¼-inch or less thickness. Cut with small cookie cutter. Place on ungreased baking sheet and bake at 350° for 20 minutes or 400° for 10 minutes. Makes about 40 small biscuits.

Flavored with Tradition (South Carolina)

★ **Editor's Extra:** These are thin biscuits, almost like cookies—bring on the jam!

Quick (and I Mean Quick) Herb Rolls

These may be prepared ahead of time.

½ cup butter
1½ teaspoons parsley flakes
½ teaspoon dill weed
1 tablespoon onion flakes

2 tablespoons Parmesan cheese
1 (12-ounce) can Hungry Jack
  biscuits

Melt butter in 9-inch pan. Mix herbs and cheese together and stir into butter. Let stand (15–30 minutes). Cut biscuits into halves and swish around in herb butter to coat all sides. Bake at 425° for 12–15 minutes. (Pictured on cover.)

Family Secrets (Mississippi)

★ **Editor's Extra:** These are buttery-good! Sometimes I use a 9x13-inch pan—it allows the rolls to spread more and have crispier crusts. Delicious both ways.

★★★★★★★★★★★★ ★★★★★★★★★★★★

Hot Pull-Apart Biscuits

These are "olé" spicy!

1 (10-biscuit) package refrigerated biscuits
3 tablespoons margarine, melted
½ teaspoon chili powder

½ cup shredded Cheddar cheese
¼ cup chopped jalapeño peppers

Cut biscuits into quarters. Combine margarine and chili powder in a 9-inch pie plate. Place biscuit pieces in pie plate and toss to coat each piece with margarine mixture. Sprinkle cheese and peppers on top. Bake at 350° for 15 minutes or until brown.

Shattuck Community Cookbook (Oklahoma)

★ **Editor's Extra:** Fun to watch tasters exclaim: "These are *hot!*"—then go back for another one.

Farmers Hall Tea Room's Sour Cream Biscuits

Delicious! Perfect biscuits!

2 cups self-rising flour
4 tablespoons shortening

⅔ cup sour cream
½–¾ cup milk

Mix flour, shortening and sour cream together. Add milk until mixture is thick enough to cling to a spoon. Drop by tablespoonfuls onto a greased pan. Bake in 450° oven for 8–10 minutes. Serve immediately. Yields 2 dozen.

South Carolina's Historic Restaurants (South Carolina)

★ **Editor's Extra:** Leftover biscuits are great split and toasted. Try spreading softened butter on sliced leftover rolls and breads, then wrap in foil and freeze. Next morning pop them right in the oven in the wrapping . . . so good you'll make extra just to have leftovers.

Bruschetta

The original garlic bread.

2 garlic cloves (1 minced, 1 cut)
3 Roma tomatoes, diced
Extra virgin olive oil (about ¾ cup)

10 fresh basil leaves, finely chopped
Salt and pepper
4 slices Tuscan country bread

Mix together minced garlic, tomatoes, olive oil, basil, salt and pepper. Set aside. Grill both sides of the bread. Rub one side of the bread with a garlic clove. Then add tomato mixture. Grill again for 30 seconds. Garnish with basil leaf. *Buon Appetito!!!*

International Garlic Festival Cookbook (California)

Super-Easy Ham and Cheese Muffins

Great for breakfast, lunch or supper, and with a bowl of soup.

2 cups self-rising flour
½ teaspoon baking soda
1 cup milk

½ cup mayonnaise
½ chopped cooked ham
½ cup shredded Cheddar cheese

In a large bowl, combine flour and baking soda. Combine remaining ingredients; stir into dry ingredients just until moistened. Fill paper-lined muffins cups ⅔ full. Bake at 425° for 16–18 minutes, or until golden brown on top. Makes 18.

Woodbine Public Library (Iowa)

Yogurt Muffins

2 cups flour
¼ cup sugar
1 tablespoon baking powder
½ teaspoon baking soda
½ teaspoon salt

¼ cup melted butter
1 (8-ounce) container plain yogurt
¼ cup milk
1 egg
½ teaspoon vanilla

Combine dry ingredients; combine liquid ingredients. Mix the 2 together until moistened. Bake at 425° for 25 minutes.

Home Cookin': First Congregational United Church of Christ (Michigan)

Mexican Muffins

2 English muffins
Butter
Guacamole
4 eggs, scrambled

Monterey Jack cheese, grated
Cheddar cheese, grated
Salsa

Toast the English muffin halves and butter lightly. Keep warm. On each half, put a scoop of guacamole and approximately one scrambled egg. Top with grated cheeses; broil. Serve with fresh salsa. Serves 4.

Steamboat Entertains (Colorado)

Gloria's Corn Bread Muffins

Oooo . . . these are good!

1 cup self-rising cornmeal
1 (8-ounce) carton sour cream
1 (8½-ounce) can cream-style corn

½ cup vegetable oil
2 eggs, beaten

Mix all ingredients together and bake in greased muffin tins at 400° for 20 minutes. Makes 12.

Tasting Tea Treasures (Mississippi)

★ **Even Easier:** Smaller muffins (24) only take 12 minutes to bake.

When our country was young, cornmeal was the pioneers' "flour," as corn was easier than other grains to make into meal. It could be milled by hand in a mortar and pestle made of wood or stone.

Applesauce Puffs

Best when served warm with coffee.

2 cups packaged biscuit mix
¼ cup sugar
1 teaspoon cinnamon
½ cup applesauce

¼ cup milk
1 egg, slightly beaten
2 tablespoons salad oil

TOPPING:
2 tablespoons melted margarine
½ cup sugar

1 teaspoon cinnamon

Combine biscuit mix, ¼ cup sugar, and 1 teaspoon cinnamon. Add applesauce, milk, egg and oil. Beat vigorously for 30 seconds. Grease 2 small muffin tins and fill ⅔ full (yields 24) or 1 regular muffin tin (yields 12). Bake in 400° oven for 12–16 minutes. Dip tops in melted butter and then into sugar mixed with cinnamon. Can be frozen.

Bravo (North Carolina)

Alegra's Six Week Muffins

These are the best bran muffins I have ever tasted.

1 (15-ounce) box Raisin Bran
3 cups sugar
5 cups flour
5 teaspoons baking soda

2 teaspoons salt
4 eggs, beaten
1 cup oil
1 quart buttermilk

In a very large bowl, mix Raisin Bran, sugar, flour, soda, and salt. Add eggs, oil and buttermilk. This batter will keep up to six weeks in the refrigerator. As you are ready to use it, fill muffin tins ⅔ full and bake at 400° for 15–20 minutes, depending on tin size. Yields 4–5 dozen.

The Lazy Gourmet (California)

★ **Editor's Extra:** I make these all the time! I like it just as well with ⅓ less sugar.

You have to be eighteen to vote, but you can be younger to have a law passed. . . . Many elementary school classes around the nation have petitioned their legislature to declare an official "state food," and many have been passed into law. As a result, New York now claims the apple muffin as their official food; Massachusetts, the corn muffin; and Minnesota, the blueberry muffin. Not all states chose a type of muffin, though . . . North Carolinians chose a vegetable, the sweet potato as their state food.

Lemon Poppy Seed Bread

1 package lemon cake mix
1 (3-ounce) package instant vanilla
  pudding
½ cup (scant) salad oil
1 cup water
4 eggs
¼ cup (1 ounce) poppy seeds

Mix the above ingredients with an electric mixer. Pour into 2 greased and floured 9x5-inch bread pans. Bake at 350° for 40 minutes, or until toothpick comes out clean. (Or you may make 4 small loaves, and bake them for 30–35 minutes.) Drizzle with icing while bread is still warm.

ICING:
1 cup powdered sugar
2 tablespoons lemon juice

Mix together.

Centennial Cookbook (Minnesota)

★ **Editor's Extra:** You won't believe how good this is! Fun to wrap mini-loaves for take-along gifts.

Strawberry Bread

3 cups flour, sifted
1 teaspoon baking soda
1 teaspoon salt
2 teaspoons cinnamon
2 cups sugar
4 eggs, beaten
1½ cups vegetable oil
1 cup chopped pecans
1½ pints fresh strawberries, sliced

Preheat oven to 350°. In a bowl combine flour, soda, salt, cinnamon, and sugar, and mix well.

Mix eggs and oil and add to dry ingredients. Stir in pecans. Fold in strawberries until moistened.

Pour into 2 greased 9x5-inch loaf pans and bake for 50–60 minutes or until toothpick inserted in center comes out clean. Yields 2 loaves.

One Magnificent Cookbook (Illinois)

★ **Editor's Extra:** My granddaughter asked me to leave out the pecans, so of course, I did . . . superb!

Monkey Toes

Takes five minutes to prepare and is ready by the time the coffee is made!

2 cans cheap biscuits
½ cup sugar
1 teaspoon cinnamon
½ cup chopped nuts (optional)

½ stick butter or margarine
½ cup brown sugar
1 tablespoon vanilla

Preheat oven to 350°. Cut each biscuit into 4 pieces. Combine the white sugar and cinnamon in a plastic bag. Shake the cut-up biscuits (a few at a time) in this mixture. Put biscuit pieces in a well-greased pan (loaf, Bundt or angel). Evenly add nuts, if desired. In a saucepan melt butter and brown sugar. When smooth and hot, add vanilla. Stir thoroughly and pour or spoon over the biscuit pieces. Bake 20–25 minutes or until done. Makes 5 servings.

Grade A Recipes (Colorado)

★ **Editor's Extra:** You don't have to use the least expensive biscuits—this is delicious with any kind of canned biscuits.

No-Peek Rolls

18 frozen dinner rolls
½ cup melted margarine
¾ cup packed brown sugar

1 (3-ounce) package butterscotch pudding and pie filling mix (not instant)
¼ cup chopped pecans

Place rolls in greased 9x13-inch baking pan. Blend margarine and brown sugar in bowl. Spoon over rolls. Sprinkle pudding mix over rolls. Sprinkle with pecans. Place cold in oven before going to bed. The next morning bake at 350° for 20 minutes. Invert onto waxed paper. Yields 18 rolls.

Approximately Per Roll; Cal 269; Prot 5.3g; T Fat 8.2g; Chol 1.7mg; Carbo 44.2g; Sod 381.2mg; Potas 108.4mg.

Laurels to the Cook (Pennsylvania)

★ **Editor's Extra:** I like to bake these in a Bundt pan, up to 24 rolls. Let them sit in the pan about 10 minutes before inverting, so that good syrup has time to firm up and stick to the rolls. Everybody loves these.

Rum Rolls

Fun for overnight guests and holiday company.

½ cup sugar
¼ cup butter

¼ cup light rum
1 tray Pepperidge Farm Party Rolls

Boil first 3 ingredients for 1 minute. Pour over tray of Pepperidge Farm party rolls. Follow directions on rolls to heat.

For Crying Out Loud...Let's Eat (Indiana)

Mock Beignets

2 cans refrigerated biscuits (plain)
Sifted powdered sugar

Hot grease (shortening or oil)

Cut biscuits in half and roll flat with a rolling pin. Drop in hot grease, a few at a time. Turn once. Watch carefully as they brown quickly. Drain on absorbent paper. Sprinkle with powdered sugar. Yields 40 doughnuts. (Pictured on cover.)

Recipes and Reminiscences of New Orleans I (Louisiana)

★ **Editor's Extra:** Serve these with café au lait and you'll be magically transported to the French Quarter in New Orleans.

Sandwich Surprise

Terrific!

2 cups crumbled, crisp bacon
1 cup finely chopped or shaved
  pecans

¼ cup finely chopped or shaved
  bell pepper
Mayonnaise

Mix first 3 ingredients together. Add enough mayonnaise to bind the mixture and to make it spreadable on bread. Terrific! Proportions can vary according to individual taste. Yields 10–12 sandwiches.

Talk About Good II (Louisiana)

★ **Editor's Extra:** This is also great to stuff into hollowed-out cherry tomatoes or celery.

Meatless Summer Sandwiches

Yummy!

3 cups shredded Swiss cheese
⅔ cup chopped tomato (best when
  homegrown)

½ cup chopped green onion
⅔ cup mayonnaise
1 loaf pumpernickel or rye bread

Mix cheese, tomato, green onion, and mayonnaise. Spread on bread, making sandwiches. Wrap individually in foil. Bake at 350° for 25 minutes. Serve hot. Yields 6–8 sandwiches.

Duluth Woman's Club 70th Anniversary Cookbook (Minnesota)

Heath Brunch Coffeecake

2 cups flour
¼ pound softened butter
1 cup brown sugar
½ cup white sugar
1 cup buttermilk (or regular milk
  with 1 teaspoon vinegar)

1 teaspoon baking soda
1 egg
1 teaspoon vanilla
½ package Heath miniatures,
  approximately 16 bars
¼ cup chopped pecans or almonds

Blend flour, butter, and sugars. Remove ½ cup mixture. To rest, add buttermilk, baking soda, egg, and vanilla. Blend well. Pour into greased and floured 9x13-inch pan. Crush the Heath bars finely; mix with nuts and ½ cup of mixture. Sprinkle over top of batter; bake at 350° for 30 minutes.

Note: It's easier to crush the Heath bars if they are refrigerated first.

The Centennnial Society Cookbook (Minnesota)

★ **Even Easier:** Heath Bars come in regular and miniatures, and also "Bites," all found in the candy section. Toffee baking chips (Heath Bits) can be found in the baking section. Since many recipes were conceived before all these choices were available, we had to do our own hammering to make pieces . . . now it's your choice.

Peach Coffee Cake

Delicious served warm or cold—offer whipped topping.

1 (18-ounce) package yellow cake mix
1 (21-ounce) can peach pie filling
3 eggs

3 tablespoons sugar
1 teaspoon cinnamon

Mix together by hand the cake mix, pie filling, and eggs. Spread in a 9x13-inch pan that has been sprayed with vegetable oil. Stir together sugar and cinnamon. Sprinkle over cake batter. Bake, uncovered, at 350° for 30 minutes. Test with a toothpick. Yields 8 servings.

Variation: For Apple Coffee Cake, substitute spice cake mix and apple pie filling. (You may want to cut up the apples a bit.)

The Give Mom a Rest (She's on Vacation) Cookbook (Great Plains)

★ **Even Easier:** I keep a mixture of cinnamon and sugar (⅔ cup sugar mixed with 1 tablespoon cinnamon) in a large spice container—not only is it convenient for all sorts of recipes, but kids love it on hot buttered toast.

Almond Crusted Oven Pancakes

Oven pancakes make a spectacular breakfast, and for all their puffed glory, they are amazingly easy to prepare. Its concave center can be filled with fresh fruits or simply sprinkled with sugar and lemon juice. The pancake in its various forms will bring exclamations of admiration for your prowess in the kitchen.

3 large eggs	1 teaspoon sugar
½ cup milk	Pinch of nutmeg (optional)
½ cup all-purpose flour	2 tablespoons butter
½ teaspoon salt	½ cup blanched slivered almonds

Preheat oven to 425°. Select a round skillet or a quiche pan. Combine eggs, milk, flour, salt, and sugar, and whirl in a blender or beat with a wire whip. If using a blender, scrape down its sides to be certain all the flour is in the batter, and whirl again until creamy. If you are baking the pancake in a skillet, place it over a burner, add butter and almonds, and sauté the almonds for 2 minutes. If a quiche pan is used, place in the oven with the butter until melted, add the almonds and let cook about 2–3 minutes. Carefully pour in the batter and bake 20 minutes. The pancake will rise with the sides encrusted with almonds. Serve filled with fresh fruit, if desired, or with cooked apples on the side. Serves 4 amply.

Quick Breads, Soups & Stews (Oklahoma)

Blender Apple Pancakes

1 egg	1 medium apple, peeled and sliced
1 tablespoon sugar	1 cup evaporated milk
1 tablespoon soft butter	1 cup pancake mix

Place egg, sugar, butter, apple, and milk in blender. Blend. Add pancake mix and blend. Fry as for ordinary pancakes.

Three Rivers Cookbook I (Pennsylvania)

★ **Editor's Extra:** Biscuit mix can sub for the pancake mix.

Popover Pancake

It's fun to watch it pop and it's mighty good, too!

½ cup all-purpose flour
½ cup milk
2 eggs, slightly beaten

¼ cup butter
2 tablespoons confectioners' sugar
Juice of ½ lemon

Preheat oven to 425°. In mixing bowl combine flour, milk, and eggs. Beat lightly. The batter will be slightly lumpy. Put butter into a 12-inch round frying pan with heatproof handle. Place in oven until very hot. Pour in the batter, return to oven, and bake 20 minutes or until pancake is puffed all around sides of the pan and golden brown. Remove from oven and sprinkle with confectioners' sugar and lemon juice. Serve immediately. Serves 2–3. (Pictured on cover.)

Cook and Deal (Florida)

★ **Editor's Extra:** We baked half of this in a small iron skillet for the cover photo shoot. It "popped" before we could get its picture made. But it surely was delicious!

Cottage Pancakes

These pancakes are very light.

3 eggs, separated
1 whole egg
1 cup cottage cheese, small curd
  (or ricotta cheese)

¼ cup flour
¼ teaspoon salt
1 apple, grated
Margarine or butter for frying

Beat 3 egg whites until stiff; set aside. Place whole egg and egg yolks in bowl with cottage cheese, flour, salt, and apple. Blend well. Fold in beaten egg whites. Heat butter or margarine in skillet. Drop batter by tablespoonfuls into skillet and fry until golden brown. Turn only once.

Apples Etc. Cookbook (California)

There is an International Pancake Race held annually in Liberal, Kansas. On Shrove Tuesday (the day before Lent begins), women contestants run 415 yards through the main streets of town flipping pancakes in skillets.

Jell-O Flavored Syrups

Easy, delicious, and a great gift in a bottle, carafe or jar.

½ small box cherry or raspberry
  or strawberry or your favorite
  flavor Jell-O

½ cup boiling water
1 pint white Karo

Dissolve Jell-O in boiling water. Stir into white Karo. Use over pancakes, waffles, fried mush or fritters.

Seems Like I Done It This A-Way II (Oklahoma)

Oven Baked French Toast

¼ cup butter, melted
2 tablespoons sugar
½ teaspoon cinnamon
3 eggs

¾ cup orange juice
8 slices sourdough bread, ¾-inch
  thick and cut on an angle, or
  Texas toast

Pour melted butter into large pan, large enough for all 8 slices. Swirl the butter to coat the pan. Mix sugar and cinnamon together, sprinkle over butter. Beat eggs with orange juice and dip each slice of bread for 15 seconds on each side. Lay in pan. Bake at 425° for 10–15 minutes.

Par Excellence (Arizona)

Bob's French Toast

3 eggs
4 tablespoons milk
¼ teaspoon vanilla

2 tablespoons sugar
Sliced bread (8 slices)
Butter and powdered sugar

Mix first 4 ingredients thoroughly in shallow bowl. Dip each side of bread in batter (do not soak). Fry in ¼-inch hot shortening (450° in electric skillet) on both sides until brown crust forms. Butter and sprinkle with powdered sugar. Serves 4.

A Cook's Tour of Shreveport (Louisiana II)

Everyday Waffles

1¾ cups all-purpose flour
½ teaspoon salt
3 teaspoons baking powder
2 eggs yolks (beaten)

1¼ cups milk
½ cup melted shortening or
　salad oil
2 stiffly beaten egg whites

Sift dry ingredients. Combine egg yolks, milk, and shortening; stir into dry ingredients. Fold in egg whites. Bake in hot waffle iron. When steam no longer appears, waffle is done. Don't raise cover during baking. Makes 8 waffles.

Dinner Bell (Pennsylvania)

★ **Even Easier:** To make this speedier, use self-rising flour in place of first 3 ingredients.

Cranberry Breakfast Pie

2 cups fresh cranberries
½ cup chopped walnuts
½ cup brown sugar
1 stick melted butter or margarine

1 cup white sugar
1 teaspoon almond extract
1 cup flour
2 beaten eggs

Grease large pie pan or 9x9-inch cake pan. Put washed cranberries in pan and sprinkle with walnuts and brown sugar. Combine butter, white sugar, almond extract, flour, and eggs, and pour over contents in pan. Bake at 350° for 40–45 minutes, till lightly brown. Can be served with vanilla yogurt as a topping. Makes 8 servings.

Inn-describably Delicious (Illinois)

★ **Editor's Extra:** Buy fresh cranberries in season. They freeze well and can usually be put into recipes right out of the freezer.

Cream Cheese Brunch Bars

2 tubes crescent rolls
2 (8-ounce) packages cream cheese, softened

1½ cups sugar, divided
1 egg, separated
1–2 teaspoons cinnamon

Spread one tube of crescent rolls in 9x13x2-inch pan, patting edges together to form crust. Meanwhile, whip softened cream cheese, one cup sugar, and egg yolk together. Spread on layer of rolls. Top with other tube of rolls. Glaze with beaten egg white. Mix together ½ cup sugar and cinnamon. Sprinkle over egg white. Bake at 350° for 20 minutes. Makes 24 bars.

Recipe from Candlelight Bed and Breakfast, Belle Fourche
South Dakota Sunrise (Great Plains)

★ **Editor's Extra:** I make half of this in an 8x8-inch pan, and my husband and I eat the whole thing! I bought a can of French bread by mistake (it was right next to the crescent rolls), and though it made a more firm coffee cake, it was a delicious mistake.

Creamed Eggs on Toast

¼ cup margarine
¼ cup flour
2 cups milk

½ teaspoon salt
4 eggs, hard boiled
6 slices bacon, fried

Melt margarine and blend in flour. Add milk (gradually) and salt, stirring continuously. Slice eggs and crumble in bacon. Add to cream sauce. Serve with or over toast.

Amish Country Cookbook II (Indiana)

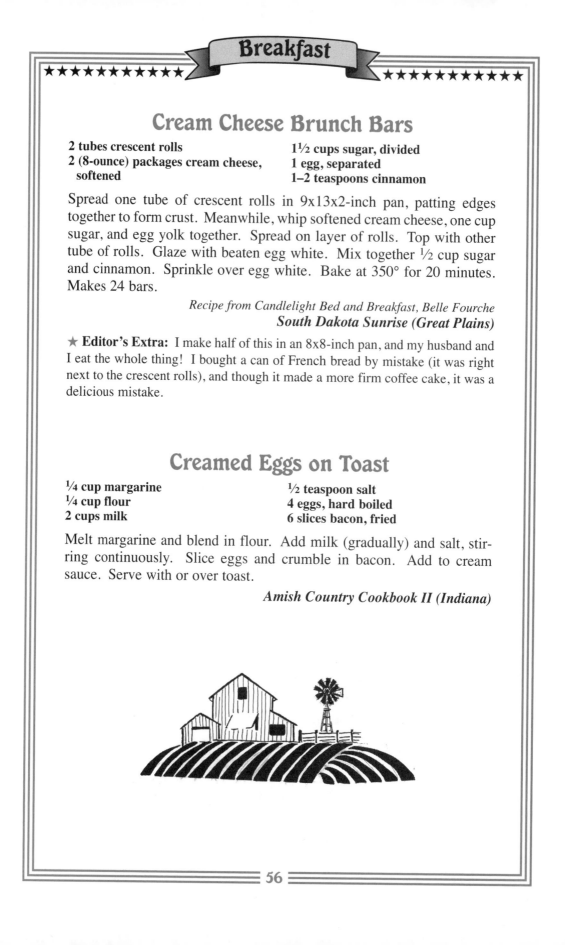

★★★★★★★★★★★ ★★★★★★★★★★★

Oeufs Crevettes

FOR EACH SERVING:

1 teaspoon butter
3 or 4 shrimp, cooked and peeled
1 egg

Salt and pepper
1 tablespoon cream
1 tablespoon Swiss cheese, grated

Melt butter in ramekin or custard cup. Add shrimp. Break egg over shrimp. Season. Pour on cream and top with cheese. Bake at 400° for 8–10 minutes.

The Twelve Days of Christmas Cookbook (Mississippi)

★ **Editor's Extra:** "Oeufs" is French for eggs, and "crevettes" are shrimp— an interesting combination, merci beaucoup.

Impossible Bacon Quiche

12 slices bacon, cooked and crumbled
1 cup shredded natural Swiss cheese
⅓ cup chopped onion
2 cups milk

1 cup Bisquick Baking Mix
4 eggs
¼ teaspoon salt
⅛ teaspoon pepper

Preheat oven to 400°. Lightly grease a 10-inch deep-dish pie plate. Sprinkle bacon, cheese, and onion in the pie plate. Beat milk, Bisquick, eggs, salt and pepper in a medium-size bowl with electric mixer until smooth, about 1 minute. Pour into pie plate.

Bake in hot oven for 35 minutes or until top is golden brown and knife inserted halfway between center and edge comes out clean. Let stand 5 minutes before cutting. Garnish with tomato slices and cooked bacon strips, if you wish. Refrigerate any leftovers.

Covered Bridge Neighbors Cookbook (Missouri)

A 5,000-egg omelet? Absolutely. Abbeville, Louisiana has a festival around the occasion.

Incredibly Easy Chile Rellenos

Great supper dish.

1 large (27-ounce) can green chile
  strips
1 pound sharp Cheddar cheese, cut
  in strips

12 eggs
½ teaspoon salt
1½ cups milk

Wash chiles and remove seeds. Wrap chile strips around cheese strips. Place side by side in a shallow, 9x13-inch greased baking dish. Beat eggs with salt, then add milk and mix well. Pour over stuffed chiles. Bake 50–60 minutes in a 350° oven. Do not overbake, since it toughens the protein in both eggs and cheese. Serves 6–8.

Arizona Highways Heritage Cookbook (Arizona)

★ **Even Easier:** Okay to use 3–5 (4-ounce) cans of whole mild green chiles, and already grated cheese. This is awesome!

Breakfast Burritos

Breakfast Burritos are popular at the Albuquerque Balloon Fiesta in October, where everyone gets up before dawn to watch 500 to 600 hot-air balloons ascend.

2 strips bacon, fried
1 scrambled egg
Shredded Monterey Jack cheese
  (2 tablespoons)

1 flour tortilla
Red or green salsa to taste

Roll bacon, egg, and cheese in flour tortilla. Serve with salsa.

Variations: Cooked crumbled or sliced chorizo may be substituted for bacon for a spicier burrito. Fried, grated or cubed potatoes can be added.

License to Cook New Mexico Style (New Mexico)

Potato Scramble

Great for brunch or a quick supper.

¼ cup butter
½ large package frozen grated
  potatoes
1 small onion, grated
8 eggs, beaten

3 tablespoons cream
1 cup chopped bacon or ham
Salt and pepper to taste
1 cup grated Cheddar cheese

Melt butter in sauté pan and add potatoes and onion. Cook over medium heat until lightly browned. Combine next 4 ingredients. Pour over potatoes and cook as for scrambled eggs. Add cheese. Heat until melted. To serve, cut in pie wedges.

Bravo (North Carolina)

Sausage Casserole

3 slices bread, toasted and cubed
1 pound sausage, browned and
  drained
1 cup grated cheese

6 eggs
2 cups milk
1 teaspoon salt
1 teaspoon dry mustard

Spray dish with Pam. Place bread cubes in casserole dish. Sprinkle sausage over bread cubes. Sprinkle cheese over sausage. Mix together eggs, milk, salt, and dry mustard. Pour over sausage and cheese. Bake 1 hour at 350°.

Cooking with Class (Virginia)

★ **Editor's Extra:** This can be refrigerated overnight and baked in the morning.

Winter Morning Peaches

2 (16-ounce) cans sliced peaches
2 tablespoons margarine or butter
⅓ cup brown sugar

½ teaspoon cinnamon
2 tablespoons cornstarch
¼ cup cold water

In saucepan over medium heat, heat peaches, margarine, brown sugar, and cinnamon. Stir cornstarch into cold water and add to peaches. Cook and stir until thickened. Cool slightly and spoon into individual dishes. Serve warm. Makes 6–8 servings.

Inn-describably Delicious (Illinois)

★★★★★★★★★★★★ ★★★★★★★★★★★★

Pan Fried Apples, 1919

These make a great camp meal anywhere, even at the backyard barbecue.

3 or 4 large, tart apples, cored and
  sliced
2 tablespoons bacon drippings or
  butter

⅓ cup wild honey or brown sugar
Salt and cinnamon

Heat apple slices in hot bacon drippings in skillet until they soften, stirring to turn over. Add honey or brown sugar and a little salt and cinnamon, if desired. The honey or sugar will glaze the slices if allowed to remain on the fire, covered, 5–10 minutes, depending on heat.

Arizona Highways Heritage Cookbook (Arizona)

Tomato Gravy

¼ cup Crisco (or bacon drippings)
6 level tablespoons flour
1 cup milk

1 cup water
1½ cups stewed (canned) tomatoes
1 teaspoon salt

In large skillet, melt Crisco on high heat. Add flour and stir constantly until it is slightly brown. Remove from heat. Let cool. Mix together the milk and water. Add to Crisco-flour mixture and stir until well blended. Add tomatoes. Put back on heat and stir until thickened. Add salt.

Variation: To make Old-Fashioned White Gravy, use the same recipe, but omit the tomatoes. Black pepper is also good in this gravy. This was always an old standby when food was scarce during depression days. Some of those "necessities" turned out to be favorite foods.

Kum' Ona' Granny's Table (Alabama)

Soups

The drive into Princeton, New Jersey, in the snow is almost indescribable, sort of like you're inside a Courier and Ives painting. After a recommended local lunch, good research, and an invigorating walk around the beautiful campus, we left feeling much smarter.

★ ★ ★ ★ ★ ★ ★ ★ ★ ★ ★   ★ ★ ★ ★ ★ ★ ★ ★ ★ ★ ★

Pumpkin Bisque

This has replaced the pumpkin pie on our Thanksgiving menu. I serve it in cups in the living room with hot cheese crisps or mushroom rolls.

1 large onion, sliced	2 cups cream
¼ cup butter	1½ teaspoons salt
½ teaspoon curry powder	2½ cups chicken stock
2 cups canned pumpkin	

Sauté onion in butter until wilted. Sprinkle with curry powder and cook a minute or two longer. Combine in a blender or food processor with pumpkin, and process until mixed. Stir in cream and salt and continue to process. Pour into a large saucepan and add chicken stock. Heat slowly, until very hot. Serves 6–8.

The New Gourmets & Groundhogs (Pennsylvania)

★ **Editor's Extra:** Lots of soup recipes get their flavor from chicken broth or stock. Easy to buy it in a can. But you can make it yourself by putting chicken (even frozen) in a crockpot with 4–5 cups of water and seasoning, and let it cook all night or all day. Now you have cooked chicken you can enjoy in all sorts of recipes (see poultry chapter), and you have that wonderful broth. Freeze it in small enough containers so you can put it directly into the soup pot. Once you do this, you'll never want to be without it.

Onion Soup in the Microwave

1 cup thinly sliced onions	½ cup shredded Swiss cheese
2 tablespoon margarine	2 tablespoons grated Parmesan
1 can condensed beef broth	cheese
1 slice toasted French bread	

In 1-quart glass dish, combine onions and margarine. Cook 2–3 minutes until onions are soft. Stir. Add beef broth and cook on HIGH for 2–3 minutes. Stir. Pour into large soup bowl. Cover mixture with bread slice and sprinkle with cheeses. Cook, uncovered, for 45 seconds on HIGH until cheese is melted. Serves 1.

Thank Heaven for Home Made Cooks (Wisconsin)

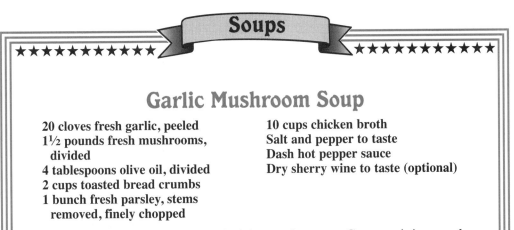

Garlic Mushroom Soup

20 cloves fresh garlic, peeled
1½ pounds fresh mushrooms,
  divided
4 tablespoons olive oil, divided
2 cups toasted bread crumbs
1 bunch fresh parsley, stems
  removed, finely chopped

10 cups chicken broth
Salt and pepper to taste
Dash hot pepper sauce
Dry sherry wine to taste (optional)

Finely chop garlic and 1 pound of the mushrooms. Cut remaining mushrooms into thin slices. In a 4-quart saucepan, heat 2 tablespoons of the olive oil and sauté garlic and mushrooms for 3 minutes. Remove from pan and set aside. Sauté bread crumbs in remaining oil. Add garlic and mushroom mixture to crumbs, stir in parsley and sauté for 5 minutes. Add broth and simmer, stirring frequently for 15 minutes. Season to taste with salt, pepper, hot pepper sauce, and dry sherry, if desired. Yields 8–10 servings.

Note: If a thicker soup is desired, stir in a few teaspoons of cornstarch dissolved in a little cold water and simmer for a few minutes until soup clears and thickens.

Celebrating California (California)

Elegant Mushroom Soup

This soup is elegant enough to serve to dinner guests. Top the servings with a dollop of Créme Fraîche or sour cream and chopped parsley or green onion tops.

1 pound mushrooms, coarsely
  chopped
4 green onions with tops, coarsely
  chopped
½ cup butter
⅓ cup flour
¼ teaspoon dry mustard

2 teaspoons salt
Cayenne pepper to taste
¼ teaspoon black pepper
2 cups chicken broth
2 cups whipping cream or
  half-and-half
⅓ cup sherry (optional)

Sauté the mushrooms and green onions in the butter in a saucepan for 5 minutes. Stir in the flour, dry mustard, salt, cayenne pepper, and black pepper. Stir in the chicken broth and cream gradually. Simmer until thickened and smooth, stirring constantly. Add the sherry. Serves 4.

Generations (Illinois)

Ham and Potato Chowder

¼ cup butter
1 medium onion, minced
¾ cup diced ham
½ cup chopped celery
1½ cups finely diced raw potatoes

¼ cup flour
1½ teaspoons salt
¼ teaspoon pepper
4 cups milk

In large saucepan, melt butter and sauté onion, ham, and celery. Add potatoes and cook 10 minutes longer. Remove from heat and add flour, salt, and pepper. Mix well. Add milk and return to heat. Warm slowly—do not let boil. If not served immediately and soup thickens, add warm water to thin to desired consistency. Serves 4–6.

Silver Dollar City's Recipes (Missouri)

Artichoke Soup

3 (14-ounce) cans artichoke hearts, drained
3 (10¾-ounce) cans cream of mushroom soup

1 pint whipping cream
2 cups chicken broth
½ cup dry white wine
6 drops hot pepper sauce

Place about ⅓ cup of the artichokes in the bottom of a blender or food processor. In a large bowl, combine the soup, whipping cream, broth, white wine, and hot pepper sauce. Add part of this liquid mixture to the artichokes and blend until puréed. Repeat with remaining artichokes and liquid until all has been puréed. Pour puréed soup into a large saucepan and heat over a low heat. Serve hot. Yields 6–8 servings.

Note: People will think you spent hours in the kitchen preparing this soup.

From A Louisiana Kitchen (Louisiana)

★**Editor's Extra:** Make ⅓ recipe for an elegant candlelight dinner in a hurry! And this is even good without the wine!

All artichokes grown commercially in the U.S. are grown in California. Artichokes are rich in iodine, a nutrient not found in most foods. In fact, they rank 7th among fruits and vegetables in vitamin and mineral content, and are a good source of vitamins A, B, and C, as well as potassium. At the same time, artichokes are low in fat and sodium.

Dilled Potato Soup

Preparation time: 10 minutes!

1 (10¾-ounce) can cream of potato
  soup
1 soup can milk
Dash white pepper

⅛ teaspoon salt
1 teaspoon dried dill
⅔ cup sour cream

Mix soup, milk, pepper, salt, and dill in soup pan. Heat until hot, stir-ring constantly with wire whisk. Stir in sour cream. Pour into bowls and sprinkle with paprika for color. Serves 2 heartily, 3 well, 4 in small bowls.

Rush Hour Superchef! (Missouri)

Cream of Zucchini Soup

4 cups zucchini, thickly sliced
  (seeded, if large)
1 medium onion, quartered
1 can chicken broth
1 teaspoon salt

¼ teaspoon pepper
½ teaspoon dried basil
1½ cups milk
½ cup cream

Combine zucchini, onion, chicken broth, salt, pepper, and basil in pan. Cover and simmer about 20 minutes or until tender. Cool slightly and pour into blender. Cover and purée at high speed. (May be frozen at this point.) When ready to serve, add milk and cream and heat. Serves 6.

Favorites for All Seasons (Arizona)

Quick Broccoli Soup

1 (10-ounce) package frozen
  chopped broccoli
1 can cream of mushroom soup
  (undiluted)

1½ cups milk
2 tablespoons butter or margarine
⅛ teaspoon pepper
4 ounces shredded cheese

Cook broccoli in large saucepan, (do not salt); drain well. Stir in remaining ingredients. Cook over medium heat, stirring constantly until thoroughly heated. Serves 6.

Our Favorite Recipes (Illinois)

Broccoli Chowder

1 pound fresh broccoli
1 (13¾-ounce) can chicken broth,
  divided
1½ cups skim milk
1 cup evaporated skim milk

½ cup lean cubed ham
Salt to taste (optional)
¼ teaspoon pepper
1 cup shredded lite Swiss cheese

Combine broccoli stalks and ½ can chicken broth in casserole dish. Cover and cook 5 minutes on HIGH in microwave. Remove broccoli and cool, cutting into small pieces. Add remaining broth to dish with milk, ham, salt, and pepper. Microwave 5 minutes or until mixture boils. Stir in broccoli and cheese and microwave 3 minutes. Yields 4 servings.

Cal 244; Chol 38mg; Sat Fat 4g; Fat 8g; Sod 374mg; Pro 24g; Cho 19g; Exchanges 2 meats, 2 milks, 1 vegetable

Just For Kids (Louisiana II)

★ **Editor's Extra:** Try this with beef broth, too. The hardest part is chopping the broccoli!

The bagged salads and wrapped pre-cut vegetables now on the market can be nutrient savers as well as time savers. According to research at the University of Kentucky, the special plastic wrap and bags used for most of these products help keep them fresh longer and reduce the loss of vitamin C and beta carotene by regulating the amount of water, oxygen, and carbon dioxide inside.

Instant Borscht

Easy, fun soup—gorgeous color.

1 medium onion
1 cup canned sliced beets, save juices
Thin peel from ½ lemon
¾ teaspoon salt
Pepper to taste

2 tablespoons sugar
1 cup condensed beef broth
3 tablespoons sour cream
2½ tablespoons lemon juice

With metal blade in place, use food processor to chop onion; add beets, lemon peel, salt, pepper, and sugar. Turn on and add all other liquid ingredients including saved beet juice. Blend until smooth. Serve chilled with a dollop of sour cream on top. Can also be done in a blender. Very easy. Do ahead. Serves 4.

Culinary Classics (Georgia)

Hot Tomato Bouillon

1 can condensed tomato soup
1 can beef broth
⅓ teaspoon prepared horseradish
  (wet)
1 dash Tabasco sauce

1 cup water
1 tablespoon sherry (optional)
Sour cream or unsweetened
  whipped cream

Simmer all but sherry and cream 5 minutes. Add sherry. Add cream just before serving to float on top of cup. Serves 6.

Atlanta Natives' Favorite Recipes (Georgia)

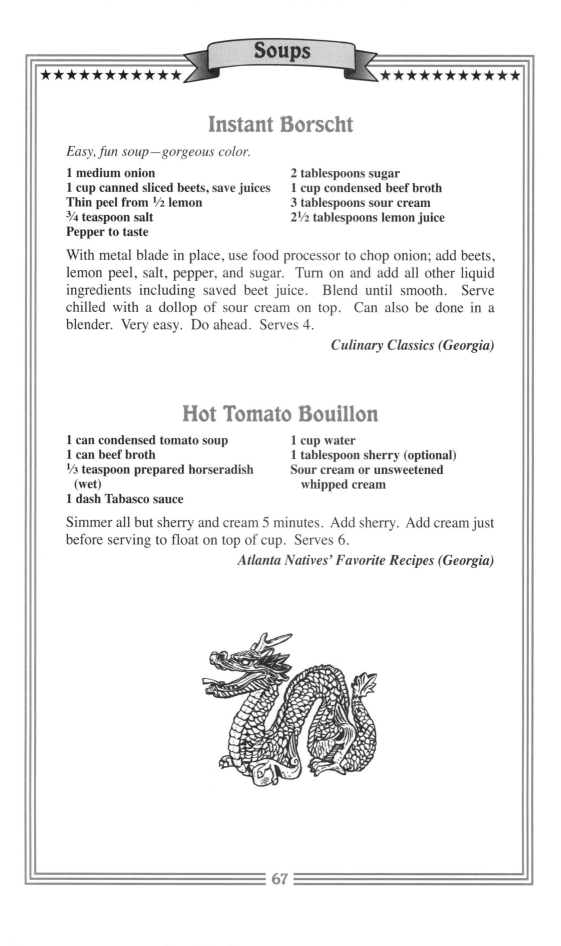

Wedding Soup

Don't wait for a wedding to try this one.

2 eggs
¼ cup bread crumbs
¼ cup grated Romano cheese
Lemon rind to taste

Pinch of nutmeg
3 cups chicken broth
Parsley

Mix first 5 ingredients. Let stand a few minutes. Drop by teaspoonfuls into boiling chicken broth and simmer until done. Garnish with parsley. This recipe makes 2 servings; just multiply as needed.

Variation: Make a portion of your own favorite meatballs recipe. Form into balls about the size of marbles. When egg drop is done, add meatballs to broth and cook a few minutes. Makes 2 servings.

Our Favorite Recipes (Minnesota)

Cream of Corn Soup

A Tea Room recipe from the Woman's Exchange.

1 can cream-style corn
1 cup milk
1 cup light cream
2 chicken bouillon cubes or 2
  teaspoons chicken stock base

Salt and white pepper to taste
½ stick butter
Chopped parsley

Blend corn in blender. Combine with milk, cream and bouillon cubes. Add salt and pepper. Pour into saucepan, bring to boil, stirring constantly. Add butter. Garnish with chopped parsley. Serves 4–6.

Woman's Exchange Cookbook II (Tennessee)

Corn is grown in more countries than any other crop. The U.S. grows more corn than any other country in the world, producing 41% of the planet's corn.

Corn Chowder in a Flash

Serve with a good green salad and/or a fried cheese sandwich. Makes for a good supper or lunch.

1 medium onion, chopped
3 tablespoons of butter or margarine
1 (10½-ounce) can potato soup

¾ soup can of milk or light cream
1 can cream-style corn
Salt and pepper to taste

Sauté onion in butter. Add remaining ingredients and heat until hot; do not boil. Serves 2.

Collectibles II (Texas)

Camping Chowder

A can of this, a can of that. Just too easy to be so good.

Polish sausage, thinly sliced, or
  1 can minced clams
2 medium onions, minced (or dried
  onion flakes)
3 cups water
1 (16-ounce) can cream-style corn
1 (13-ounce) can evaporated milk

1 (14-ounce) can cream of potato
  soup (or canned potatoes)
1 teaspoon salt
⅛ teaspoon pepper
4 tablespoons butter (optional)
2 cloves garlic, minced (optional)

Brown sausage and drain on paper towels. If you use fresh onions, brown with sausage. Dump remaining ingredients in a pot with sausage and onions and heat slowly. Serves 5–6.

On the Road Again Cookbook (California)

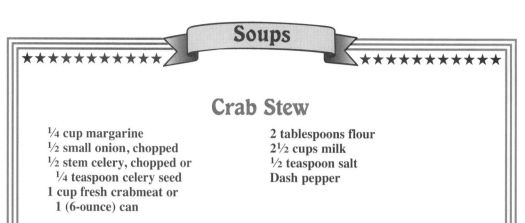

Crab Stew

¼ cup margarine
½ small onion, chopped
½ stem celery, chopped or
  ¼ teaspoon celery seed
1 cup fresh crabmeat or
  1 (6-ounce) can

2 tablespoons flour
2½ cups milk
½ teaspoon salt
Dash pepper

Melt margarine in heavy saucepan. Add chopped onion and celery and sauté until tender, but not brown. Add crabmeat and stir for a minute or two. Sprinkle flour over crabmeat and stir well. Add milk and stir constantly until thickened. Season. Serve in bowls with crisp crackers. Serves 4.

Strictly For Boys (South Carolina)

★ **Editor's Extra:** This also works with chicken or shrimp—a great first course, or a meal with a hearty salad.

Creole Crab Gumbo

Quick to fix, fabulous to eat.

½ cup sliced onion
4 tablespoons butter
4 tablespoons flour
1 pound crabmeat
1 pound okra, cut up
5 cups canned tomatoes

1 cup diced green pepper
2 garlic cloves, crushed
1 teaspoon ground nutmeg
2 teaspoons salt
Freshly ground black pepper
2 cups water

Sauté onion in butter 10 minutes. Stir in flour and brown. Add crabmeat and other ingredients. Bring to a boil, reduce heat, cover, simmer for 1 hour. Serves 6.

Louisiana's Original Creole Seafood Recipes (Louisiana)

★ **Editor's Extra:** Gumbo is not a "quick" recipe, but this is the quickest, tastiest you can make! Use frozen vegetables (okra, onion, green pepper) for speedier preparation. The flavor intensifies overnight, so plan to make ahead—freezes beautifully.

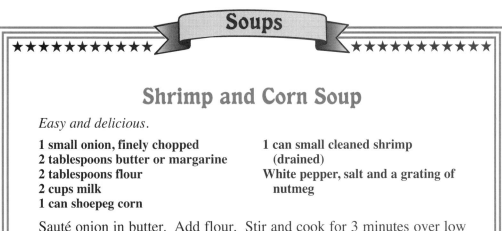

Shrimp and Corn Soup

Easy and delicious.

1 small onion, finely chopped
2 tablespoons butter or margarine
2 tablespoons flour
2 cups milk
1 can shoepeg corn

1 can small cleaned shrimp
  (drained)
White pepper, salt and a grating of
  nutmeg

Sauté onion in butter. Add flour. Stir and cook for 3 minutes over low heat. Slowly add milk and blend (a wire whisk is handy for this). Add corn and cook for 3–5 minutes over low heat stirring constantly. Lastly add drained shrimp. Season to taste with pepper, salt, and a pinch of nutmeg. Serves 4.

The Pilgrimage Garden Club Antiques Forum Cookbook (Mississippi)

★ **Editor's Extra:** Fresh boiled shrimp or crab makes this even better.

Shrimp Bisque

1 pound shrimp, boiled and peeled
4 tablespoons butter
4–5 tablespoons flour
1 quart milk
2 teaspoons salt

3 teaspoons lemon juice
1/2 teaspoon Tabasco
Dash white pepper
Sherry
Lemon slices

Grind shrimp in blender or food processor. Combine butter and flour in saucepan. Add milk and salt and stir until thickened. Add lemon juice, Tabasco, and pepper. Add shrimp and sherry (approximately 2 tablespoons per serving). Serve hot with lemon slice floating on top. Serves 6–8.

Savannah Style (Georgia)

★ **Editor's Extra:** The secret to tender shrimp is to cook them quickly in order to preserve their sweet, delicate flavors. Most shrimp cook in as little as 3 minutes—when they're pink, they're done. And don't let them sit in the cooking liquid, as they will continue to cook and get tough. Plunge them into cold water to stop the cooking process. One pound of raw shrimp in their shells equals about 1/2 pound peeled and cooked shrimp.

Shrimp are in season from May to October, and 95% of the shrimp caught come from the warm waters of the South Atlantic and Gulf states.

Oyster Stew

1 pint oysters with liquid
¼ cup butter
1 cup milk
½ cup cream

½ teaspoon salt
¼ teaspoon pepper
⅛ teaspoon paprika

Pour oysters and liquid into a saucepan. Bring to a brisk boil until edges of oysters begin to shrivel and curl. Add butter and stir until melted. Reduce to medium heat. Add milk and cream (curdling will occur only if milk is beginning to sour). Season with salt and pepper. Increase heat and bring to light boil. Sprinkle with paprika and serve hot. Serves 4.

Note: When using fresh oysters (right out of the shell), one cup water may be used for liquid.

Big Mama's Old Black Pot (Louisiana II)

Easy Clam Chowder

This tastes pretty authentic!

3 slices bacon, minced
1 small onion, minced
1 can cream of potato soup
1½ soup cans milk

1 can minced clams, undrained
1 tablespoon butter or margarine
Salt and pepper

Fry bacon in a large saucepan until crisp. Remove bacon and set aside. Discard all but 1 tablespoon fat. Sauté onion in fat until transparent. Add potato soup, milk, clams and clam broth. Add reserved bacon. Heat, but do not boil. Season with butter, salt, and pepper. Serves 4.

Berkshire Seasonings (New England)

Clams have been around for 400 million years—more or less. New Englanders use the Native American word "quahog" for the hardshell clams used in their delicious chowders.

Ham and Cannellini Soup

So easy, so fast, so good!

2 (15.8-ounce) cans cannellini (white
  beans), drained
1½ cups chicken broth, divided
½ cup chopped celery

2 ounces (½ cup) fully cooked
  smoked ham, chopped
Black pepper, to taste
¼ cup chopped red onion

In food processor or blender, purée 1 can of beans with ¾ cup chicken
broth. Scrape into a medium-sized saucepan. Stir in remaining beans
and broth, celery, and ham. Bring to a boil over medium heat. Cover
and simmer 15 minutes. Season with pepper. Ladle into bowls. Sprinkle
with chopped onion. Makes 5 cups or 4 servings.

A Heritage of Good Tastes (Arkansas)

★ **Editor's Extra:** Cannellini (Italian) are large white kidney beans. We used
the easy-to-find Great Northern whites.

Chili Soup

This is good!!

1 pound hamburger
1 onion, chopped
2 tablespoons flour
¼ cup brown sugar

1 can kidney beans
1 (11½-ounce) can tomato juice
Chili powder

Brown hamburger and onion. Drain grease. Add 2 tablespoons flour and
brown sugar; stir. Add kidney beans and tomato juice. Add chili powder to taste. Simmer for 15 minutes. Serves 4–6.

Salem Mennonite Cookbook (Ohio)

★ **Editor's Extra:** Good with V-8 instead of tomato juice. Try serving this
over rice or noodles to stretch it—also good on Texas toast or hamburger buns
for a super lunch treat.

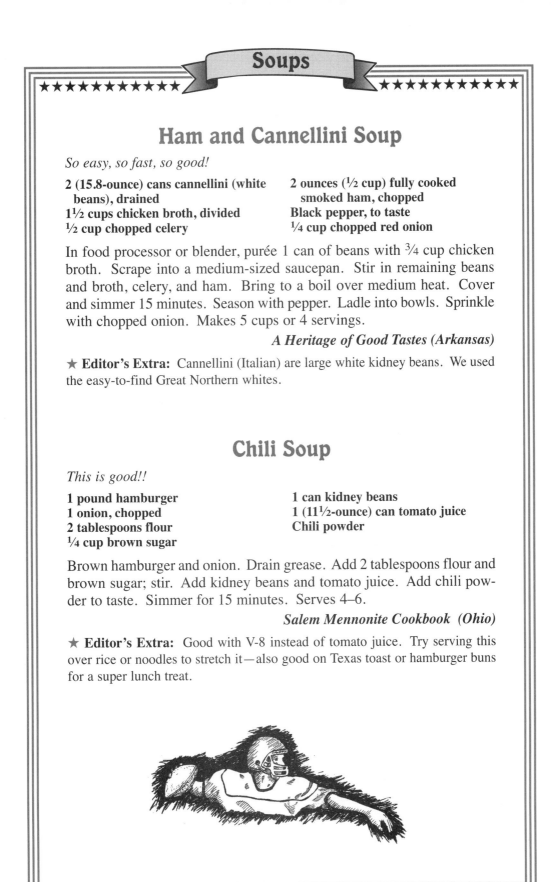

Taco Soup

2 pounds ground meat
1 onion, chopped
1 can chopped green chiles
1 can hominy or corn or both
2 cans pinto beans

3 cans tomatoes
1 package dry taco mix
1 package dry Hidden Valley Salad
   Dressing Mix
2½ cups water

Brown the ground meat and onion together. Add the remaining ingredients. Mix all together and simmer 30 minutes. Serves 12–15.

Our Best Home Cooking (New Mexico)

Chicken Tortilla Soup

1 can cream of chicken soup
1 can fiesta nacho cheese soup
2 soup cans milk
1 can green chile enchilada sauce

1 can chicken meat
Tortilla chips
Sour cream (optional)

In a saucepan, mix soups and milk. Heat till hot and add enchilada sauce and chicken. Heat and serve. Put crushed tortilla chips on top. Can garnish with sour cream, if you like. Serves 4–5.

Cookin' with Farmers Union Friends (Great Plains)

Salads

★★★★ ★★★★

*Sometimes the lap of the ocean waves is irresistible, and we just
have to let the waves wash the grit of the road off our feet.
And for golfers like us, a fun place like Myrtle Beach, South Carolina,
offers lots of other diversions, too.*

★★★★★★★★★★★ ★★★★★★★★★★★

Mary's Salad

1 medium head Boston or bibb
  lettuce, torn into pieces
½ avocado, peeled and thinly sliced
1 (11-ounce) can mandarin
  oranges, chilled and drained
½ cup chopped pecans, toasted
2 green onions, thinly sliced
Pepper to taste
⅓ cup Italian dressing

Combine all ingredients except dressing in salad bowl. Just before serving, add dressing and toss gently. Yields 6 servings.

Deep in the Heart (Texas II)

Mushroom Salad

A must-try for mushroom lovers.

1 large package fresh mushrooms,
  sliced
2 bunches green onions (tops, too),
  chopped
1 (8-ounce) package mild Cheddar
  cheese, cubed

DRESSING:
½ cup salad oil
¼ cup wine vinegar
1 tablespoon sugar
3 heaping teaspoons Cavender's
  Greek Seasoning

Place mushrooms, onions, and cheese in bowl. Mix all dressing ingredients together. Pour over salad just before serving. Yields 4 servings or more.

Shattuck Community Cookbook (Oklahoma)

★ **Editor's Extra:** Colby Jack cheese is my favorite in this tasty salad.

Wilted Lettuce Salad

SALAD:
1 bunch leaf lettuce, torn
4–6 green onions, thinly sliced
6–8 radishes, thinly sliced

Toss lettuce, onions, and radishes in a large salad bowl; set aside.

DRESSING:
4–5 bacon strips
1 tablespoon lemon juice
2 tablespoons red wine vinegar
1 teaspoon sugar
½ teaspoon pepper

In a skillet, cook bacon until crisp. Remove to paper towels to drain. To the hot drippings, add lemon juice, vinegar, sugar, and pepper; stir well. Immediately pour dressing over salad; toss gently. Crumble the bacon and sprinkle on top. Yields 6–8 servings.

Mrs. Noah's Survival Guide (New Mexico)

★ **Editor's Extra:** Because heads of lettuce, broccoli, cauliflower, onions, and all fresh vegetables differ so much in size, use serving sizes only as a rule of thumb.

Crunchy Broccoli Salad

4 cups chopped broccoli
1½ cups seedless red grapes, halved
1 cup mayonnaise
⅓ cup sugar
2 tablespoons cider vinegar
12 slices bacon, cooked and
   crumbled
¼ cup shelled sunflower nuts

Combine broccoli and grapes. Mix mayonnaise, sugar, and vinegar. Add to broccoli and toss. Chill. Before serving, add bacon and sunflower nuts. Toss well. Makes 6 servings.

Note: May substitute chopped pecans for sunflower nuts, or raisins for grapes.

Honest to Goodness (Illinois)

Apple cider was a highly popular early American beverage. Cider is made by pressing the juice from fruit (usually apples). Referred to as "sweet" cider, it can be drunk straight or diluted with water. If allowed to ferment, it becomes "hard" cider, and can range widely in alcohol content. Apple cider is also used to make vinegar and brandy.

Broccoli and Cauliflower Salad

Easy to make. Tastes great.

1 head broccoli, broken up
1 head cauliflower, broken up
1 small onion, chopped

1 pint jar Miracle Whip
½ cup Bac-Os
½ cup Parmesan cheese

Layer broccoli, cauliflower, and onion in large bowl. Then frost with layer of Miracle Whip. Sprinkle Bac-Os and layer of Parmesan cheese; chill overnight. Stir before serving. Serves 6–8.

St. Joseph's Parish Cookbook (Iowa)

Spinach-Apple-Cheese Salad

2 hard-cooked eggs, diced
1 large apple, diced
1 small onion, diced
¼ pound bleu cheese, crumbled

½ cup mayonnaise
½ cup sour cream
Salt and pepper to taste
1 pound spinach, washed

Combine all ingredients except the spinach. Break the spinach into bite-size pieces. Add the salad mixture to the spinach just before serving. Serves 4–6.

Appletizers (Ohio)

★ **Editor's Extra:** Use packaged baby spinach for quicker prep.

Strawberry Spinach Salad

2 bunches spinach

2 pints strawberries, washed and quartered

Arrange spinach and strawberries in layers in a glass bowl. Add dressing at last minute and toss. Enjoy! (Pictured on cover.)

DRESSING:

½ cup sugar
1½ teaspoons minced onion
2 tablespoons sesame seeds
1 tablespoon poppy seeds

¼ teaspoon Worcestershire sauce
¼ teaspoon paprika
½ cup vegetable oil
¼ cup cider vinegar

Put all dressing ingredients in blender. Blend on low until mixed.

Families Cooking Together (New Mexico)

★ **Editor's Extra:** This pretty 2-ingredient salad is made even prettier by the thick, tasty, seed-rich dressing you can make in advance. So delicious, you will want to use it on lots of other salads, too.

Spinach Salad & Sour Cream Dressing

1 (1-pound) bag fresh spinach
½ cup sour cream
½ cup sugar
3 tablespoons vinegar
4 teaspoons horseradish

½ teaspoon mustard
¼ teaspoon salt
1 (15-ounce) carton small curd cottage cheese
1 cup pecans, halved

Rinse, remove stems and break up spinach. Blend next 6 ingredients and pour over spinach. Add cottage cheese and pecans. Toss and serve. Serves 10.

Bringing Grand Tastes to Grand Traverse (Michigan)

Renowned comic-strip character, Popeye the Sailor Man, is perhaps the most famous native of Victoria, Texas. The Victoria *Advocate* is credited as the first newspaper in the nation to run Elzie Segar's comic strip, originally called "Thimble Theatre," which starred the spinach-eating hero. The spinach industry credited Popeye and Segar with a 33% increase in spinach consumption from 1931 to 1936.

Sunny Spinach Salad

1 pound spinach, torn into bite-size
  pieces
1 (6-ounce) package dried apricots,
  chopped

1 medium red onion, thinly sliced
⅓ cup toasted salted sunflower
  seeds

Combine ingredients. Good served with vinaigrette dressing. Serves 8–10.

More of the Four Ingredient Cookbook (Texas II)

Spinach Salad

Get prepared fresh spinach for quicker fixing.

6–8 strips of crisp bacon, crumbled
2 hard-boiled eggs, chopped
½ cup sliced mushrooms

Fresh spinach and leaf lettuce, torn
  into bite-size pieces
Small purple onion, sliced

DRESSING:
1 cup oil
¾ cup sugar
⅓ cup ketchup

¼ cup vinegar
1 teaspoon Worcestershire sauce

Mix dressing ingredients and heat to dissolve sugar. This dressing may be warm or at room temperature, but should be poured over the salad ingredients immediately before serving.

Favorite Recipes (Ohio)

★ **Editor's Extra:** You'll have to cook the bacon while the eggs boil, so this one is borderline easy—but so good, we gave it a thumbs up!

Bean Salad

This make-ahead dish goes great with whatever's on the grill.

1 cup oil
1½ cups vinegar
2 cups sugar

2 teaspoons salt
½ teaspoon pepper

Heat to boiling. Cool, then pour over the following:

1 can green beans, drained
1 can yellow beans, drained
1 can kidney beans, drained
1 can lima beans, drained

1 can English peas, drained
2 small onions, sliced
2 medium green or red peppers,
  sliced

Mix well. Can be refrigerated for several weeks. Serves 12–16. (Pictured on cover.)

500 Favorite Recipes (South Carolina)

Marinated Green Beans

¼ cup dairy sour cream
2 tablespoons Italian salad dressing
1 (8-ounce) can cut green beans,
  drained

1 tomato, peeled, cubed and
  drained
2 tablespoons finely chopped onion

Thoroughly combine sour cream and Italian dressing. Add beans, tomato, and onion; mix well. Chill 3–4 hours before serving. Serve in lettuce cups. Serves 2–4.

Quasquicentennial / St. Olaf of Bode (Iowa)

Cold Corn Salad

2 cans shoe peg corn, drained
2 green onions, chopped
1 large bell pepper, chopped
½ cup chopped celery

Black pepper
Mayonnaise
2 medium tomatoes, chopped

Drain corn well; add green onions, bell pepper, celery, lots of black pepper, and a little mayonnaise to hold salad together. Just before serving, add chopped tomatoes. Serves 4–6.

Bouquet Garni (Mississippi)

Kentucky Fried Coleslaw

2½ pounds cabbage, shredded
1 carrot, shredded

½ medium onion, chopped
1 green pepper, chopped (if desired)

Mix together cabbage, carrot, onion, and green pepper. Set aside.

DRESSING:
¼ cup oil
1 cup Miracle Whip
¼ cup tarragon vinegar

½ teaspoon salt
1 cup less 2 tablespoons sugar

Mix together oil, Miracle Whip, vinegar, salt, and sugar; stir and pour over cabbage mixture. Serves 16.

Recipes and Memories (Minnesota)

★ **Editor's Extra:** Quicker with packaged shredded cabbage.

West Special Dressing

Something different, a must-try, so good on lettuce.

2 cups mayonnaise
¼ cup milk
1 tablespoon white vinegar
1 teaspoon garlic powder
1 teaspoon onion powder

½ teaspoon salt
¼ teaspoon pepper
1 tablespoon sugar
2 teaspoons dry parsley

Mix all ingredients well and refrigerate in a covered container. This will keep for weeks.

Note: Use white pepper instead of black pepper in this, as well as other recipes. It is more finely ground, nearly invisible.

Singing in the Kitchen (Iowa)

Hudson's House Dressing

½ quart mayonnaise
2 dashes Tabasco
3 tablespoons crushed black pepper
¼ cup Parmesan cheese, grated

½ ounce lemon juice
⅛ teaspoon garlic powder
¼ cup water
2 dashes Worcestershire sauce

Mix all ingredients well and serve over a tossed green salad. Top with croutons. Yields approximately ¾ quart.

Hudson's Cookbook (South Carolina)

Honey-Mustard Salad Dressing

¼ cup cider vinegar
¼ cup puréed onion
¼ cup sugar
1 cup honey

1 (6-ounce) jar spicy brown mustard
1½ cups mayonnaise
1¼ cups buttermilk

Combine all ingredients and mix well. Refrigerate between uses.

It's About Thyme (Indiana)

City Club Salad Dressing

The favorite dressing at the Grand Rapids Women's City Club.

⅓ cup sugar
3 tablespoons honey
1 teaspoon salt
1 teaspoon dry mustard

1 teaspoon celery seed
1 teaspoon paprika
1 cup salad oil
¼ cup vinegar

Mix sugar, honey, and seasonings. Gradually add oil and vinegar alternately, beating with rotary beater or blender. Perfect topping for grapefruit sections and avocado. Yields 1⅔ cups.

The Junior League of Grand Rapids Cookbook I (Michigan)

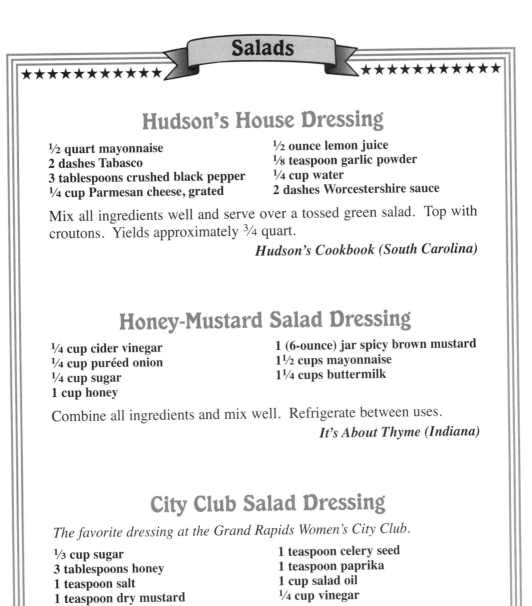

Michigan produces lots of soybeans—an ideal food helpful in lowering cholesterol and in the prevention of many cancers. Soybean oil is used in more than 80% of all cooking oils and salad dressings, and in 90% of all margarines produced. Ford, in 1940, was the first to use soybean plastics in automobiles.

Ramen Salad

1 package chicken Ramen noodles
¾ package already-grated cabbage
4 green onions, diced

2 tablespoons sunflower seeds
½ cup sliced almonds

Mix together shortly before serving.

DRESSING:

½ cup salad oil
2 tablespoons sugar
3 tablespoons vinegar

½ teaspoon pepper
Seasoning packet from noodles

Mix together and let stand a few minutes. Toss together the salad and dressing. Serve immediately.

First Christian Church Centennial Cookbook (Iowa)

Rice Salad

Good with cold turkey or ham.

1½ cups Minute Rice
1 package frozen peas in butter sauce
¾ cup mayonnaise
⅓ cup Durkee's sauce

¾ teaspoon curry powder
½ teaspoon dry mustard
1 cup diced celery
1 tablespoon grated onion

Cook Minute Rice as directed. Cook peas as directed and drain. Add all other ingredients to rice and peas while still warm. Toss lightly and chill several hours or overnight. Serves 6–8.

Atlanta's Pet Recipes (Georgia)

★ **Editor's Extra:** Durkee's sauce, popular in the South, can be found near the mayos and mustards in your grocer's condiments section.

Savage Rice Salad

4 hard-cooked eggs
3 cups cooked rice
½ cup chopped onion
½ cup pickle relish

¼ teaspoon pepper
1 cup mayonnaise
1 teaspoon dry mustard
¼ cup diced pimiento

Chop eggs finely. Combine all ingredients thoroughly. Chill and serve.

Great Grandmother's Goodies (Pennsylvania)

Ham and Rice Salad

1 boil-a-bag rice (Success)
1 (6-ounce) package boiled ham,
  diced
2 green peppers, diced

½ cup sour cream
½ cup mayonnaise
1 small can pineapple rings
Lettuce

Mix prepared rice, diced ham, and green peppers in bowl. Combine sour cream and mayonnaise and mix in. Serve on drained pineapple rings on lettuce. Serves 4.

Alone at the Range (Florida)

Quick Ham Salad

2 (6¾-ounce) cans chunk ham
4 tablespoons sweet pickle relish
2 tablespoons mayonnaise (or just
  enough to hold mixture together)

2 tablespoons vinegar
Generous dash of lemon and pepper
  seasoning

Flake ham with fork and add other ingredients; mix well. Refrigerate until ready to use.

Use this salad for sandwiches, and as an appetizer spread on crackers. It can also be served as a salad on lettuce with crackers.

Gatlinburg Recipe Collection (Tennessee)

Black Bart's Seafood Ambrosia

1–1½ cups white-meat fish, cooked
  and flaked
1 medium red onion, chopped
4 stalks celery, chopped
½ green pepper, chopped
1 large dill pickle, chopped

2 tablespoons salad oil
2 tablespoons lemon juice
1 tablespoon parsley flakes
1 teaspoon salt
1 cup mayonnaise

Mix thoroughly. Refrigerate in airtight container until ready to use. Serve on lettuce leaves with tomato garnish. Serves 6–8.

Nice to Know: This is good served as a dip with crackers or stuffed into jalapeño or banana pepper halves for a fire-breathing surprise.

Thyme Waves (Florida)

★ **Editor's Extra:** We prepared this for a TV show in Florida by cooking fresh fish in a hot pot in our hotel room. When we got to the studio, we opened the sealed container of chopped onions, and it got everybody's attention very quickly! But after we mixed and served it, they all proclaimed it a definite winner.

Shrimp-Filled Avocado Shells

1 avocado, halved and seeded
Fresh lemon or lime juice
½ cup cooked small shrimp
¼ cup minced water chestnuts
2 green onions, minced

2–3 tablespoons mayonnaise
½–1 teaspoon curry powder to
  taste
Salt and freshly ground pepper
Lettuce leaves

Sprinkle cut edges of avocado with lemon or lime juice. Combine all remaining ingredients except lettuce and toss lightly. Mound in avocado halves. Set each on lettuce-lined plate. Cover and chill until ready to serve. Serves 2.

Spindletop International Cooks (Texas)

Avocados are sold unripened; allow a few days for them to ripen before you use them. You can speed up the ripening process by putting the avocado in a brown paper bag. When puréed with a little lemon juice, they can be frozen in an airtight container for later use. Avocados have been grown in California since 1871.

Crab Salad

1 pound crabmeat, picked over well
2 hard-cooked eggs, chopped
2 stalks celery, sliced diagonally
1 sweet red pepper, julienned
⅓ cup chopped parsley

⅓ cup your favorite French or
  Italian dressing
Salt and pepper to taste
Fresh spinach leaves

Mix all ingredients except spinach leaves together. Season to taste. Serve on a bed of fresh spinach leaves. Yields 6 servings.

The Flavor of Waverly (Pennsylvania)

Basil Chicken Salad

2 celery stalks, diced
2 scallions, finely chopped
⅓ cup crushed almonds

10 leaves fresh basil, cut
1 (10-ounce) can chicken meat
2 tablespoons Miracle Whip

Chop celery, scallions, nuts, and basil. Mix with chicken and Miracle Whip. Serve on lettuce bed and garnish with basil.

Herbal Favorites (Michigan)

Bon Appétit's Celebrated Chicken Salad

At Bon Appétit, salad days never end. So it is with all who have a youthful passion for salad. Chicken salad is an all-time favorite.

3 whole boiled chicken breasts,
  chopped and deboned
1 cup Hellmann's Mayonnaise
¾ cup celery, chopped

¾ cup green grapes, diced
½ cup dried parsley or fresh
  parsley, chopped

Mix together and serve any way your heart desires. We suggest our chicken salad in sandwiches, in tomatoes, and in avocados, or on a lettuce-lined plate with fresh fruit and vegetables. Yields 4–6 servings.

Fessin' Up with Bon Appétit (Louisiana II)

★ **Editor's Extra:** Buy boneless chicken tenders—they boil or stir-fry fast.

★★★★★★★★★★★ ★★★★★★★★★★★

Quick and Easy Tomato Aspic

2 cups V-8 juice, divided
1 small box lemon gelatin
½ teaspoon onion salt

½ teaspoon Worcestershire sauce
Celery, chopped (optional)
Green pepper, chopped (optional)

Bring 1 cup V-8 juice to a boil and pour over gelatin. Stir to dissolve. Add 1 cup cold V-8, onion salt, and Worcestershire sauce. Add celery and pepper, if desired. Pour into mold. Refrigerate until firm.

The What in the World Are We Going to Have for Dinner? Cookbook (Virginia)

Easy Tomato Aspic

You may not ever make it any other way.

1 (14½-ounce) can stewed tomatoes
1 box lemon Jell-O

¼ cup chopped olives

Heat stewed tomatoes. Add Jell-O. Stir until thoroughly dissolved. Add chopped olives, pour into molds, and chill until congealed. Serves 6. (Pictured on cover.)

Florence Cook Book (Alabama)

★ **Editor's Extra:** The lemon Jell-O adds a nice sweetness. This is so attractive in fancy-shaped molds, like the pretty heart pictured on the cover. Also good using olive salad in place of the olives.

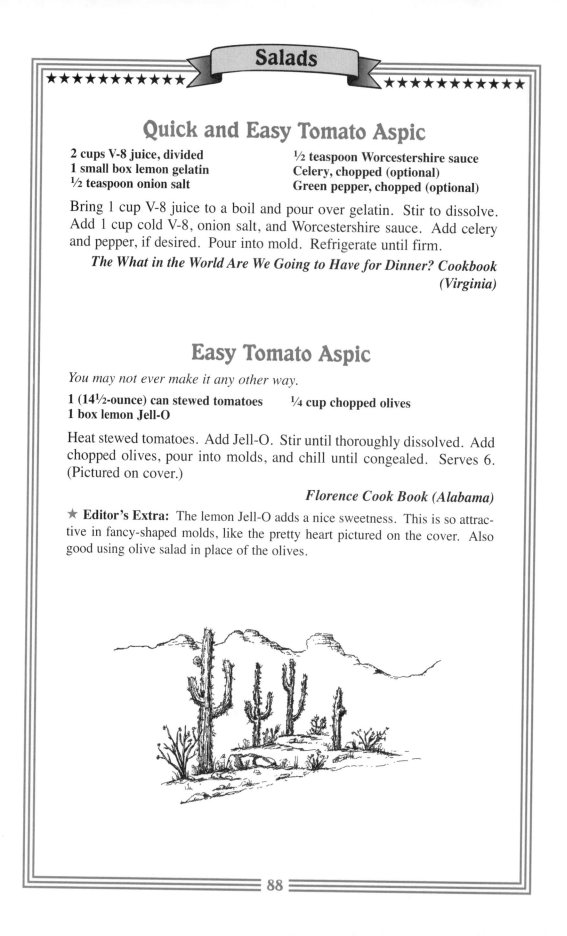

Cranberry Raspberry Salad

1 (3-ounce) package raspberry
  gelatin
¾ cup hot water
1 can whole cranberry sauce

1 (8-ounce) can crushed pineapple
1 cup seedless grapes
½ cup chopped nuts

Dissolve gelatin in hot water in casserole or Jell-O mold. Add cranberry sauce and crushed pineapple. As it begins to thicken, add grapes and nuts. Chill. Serves 6.

More Goodies and Guess-Whats (Colorado)

★ **Editor's Extra:** Pretty orange and red salads look even more colorful on leafy green lettuce, or with a sprig of mint atop.

Mom's Cranberry Salad

3 bananas, cubed
2 tablespoons lemon juice
1 can jellied cranberry sauce, cubed
1 (15-ounce) can crushed pineapple,
  drained

1 (8-ounce) carton frozen whipped
  topping, thawed
½ cup sugar
1 cup nuts, chopped
2 drops red food coloring (optional)

Stir cubed bananas in lemon juice to keep from turning dark. Fold all ingredients together gently. Freeze in 9x13-inch pan. Serves 8–10.

The Farmer's Daughters (Arkansas)

★ **Editor's Extra:** Anytime I have drained pineapple juice, I put it in my orange juice carton for next morning's breakfast drink.

Native Americans used cranberries as medicine and for poultices to draw poison from arrow wounds. The juice was a natural dye for rugs, blankets and clothing. They also mixed mashed cranberries with deer meat to make pemmican, a convenience food that kept for long periods of time. Some say the cranberry gets its name from Dutch and German settlers who called it "crane berry" because its petals resembled the head of a crane. Others say the name came from colonists who saw cranes feeding on the red berries. Legend has it cranberries were served at the first Thanksgiving in 1621. The U.S. produces some 4.84 million barrels of cranberries in a given year. End to end, that's about 1.75 million miles.

Gertie's Cranberry Salad

1 large package strawberry Jell-O
2 cups boiling water
1 small can crushed pineapple

1 can whole cranberry sauce
1 (10-ounce) package frozen
  strawberries

Dissolve Jell-O in the boiling water. Add the pineapple, cranberry sauce, and frozen strawberries. Mix well. Chill until set. Serves 8.

Recipes from the Flock (Minnesota)

Pineapple Salad

1 (6-ounce) package apricot Jell-O
1 (15½-ounce) can crushed pineapple
2 cups buttermilk

1 (8-ounce) carton Cool Whip
1 cup or less chopped pecans
  (optional)

Boil together the Jell-O and crushed pineapple. Cool, and add the buttermilk, Cool Whip, and pecans. Pour in 9x13-inch pan and chill. Serves 6–8.

Home at the Range III (Great Plains)

Delightful Orange Salad

2 small cans mandarin oranges
1 large can pineapple chunks
½ cup maraschino cherries
3 bananas, sliced
1 pint sour cream

1 (12-ounce) carton Cool Whip
1 (3-ounce) package orange Jell-O
½ cup chopped nuts
2 cups miniature marshmallows

Drain fruits well. Mix sour cream, Cool Whip and dry Jell-O until blended. Fold in fruits, nuts, and marshmallows. Chill in a 9x13-inch pan. Serves 8–10.

Heavenly Delights (Arizona)

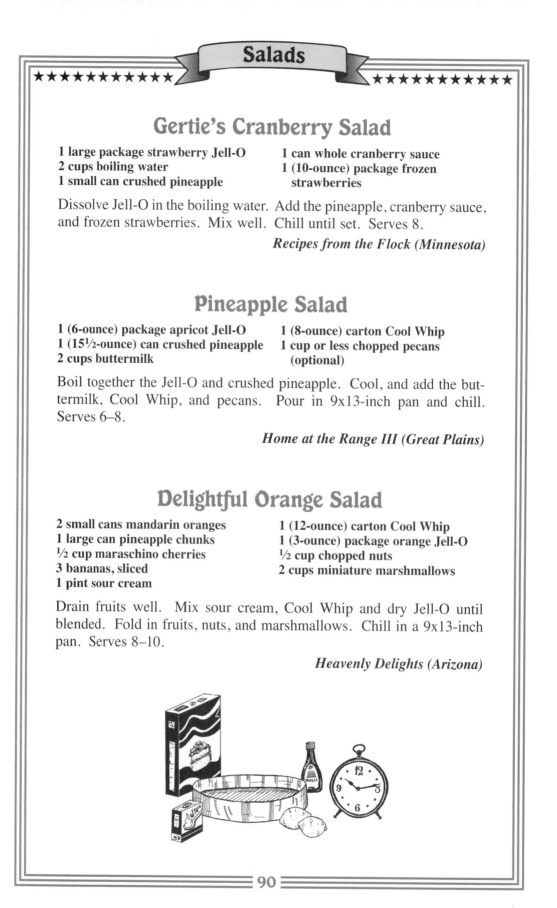

Orange Delight Quick Salad

1 (3-ounce) package orange Jell-O
1 small carton cottage cheese
1 small can mandarin oranges
1 small can crushed pineapple
1 cup Cool Whip
½ cup mini-marshmallows
Maraschino cherries for garnish

Pour dry Jell-O powder over cottage cheese in serving bowl or dish. Now drain a can of mandarin oranges, and pineapple. Mix in thoroughly with Jell-O mixture and add a cup of Cool Whip. Add mini-marshmallows. Put in refrigerator to chill. Use maraschino cherries for decoration on top.

Favorite Recipes (Iowa)

Orange Jell-O Salad

2 cups water
1 small package orange Jell-O
1 small package tapioca pudding
1 small can mandarin oranges, drained
1 carton Cool Whip (any size)

Put water, Jell-O, and tapioca pudding in saucepan. Bring to boil, stirring constantly. Put in bowl. Let cool in refrigerator about 15 minutes. Mix oranges and Cool Whip with Jell-O and pudding. Refrigerate one hour before serving. Serves 6–8.

Centerville Community Centennial Cookbook (Great Plains)

★ **Editor's Extra:** This works with other flavors of Jell-O—lemon is especially nice.

Mandarin Orange Salad

2 (3-ounce) packages orange gelatin
1½ cups boiling water
1 pint orange sherbet
1 (11-ounce) can mandarin oranges, drained
1 (20-ounce) can crushed pineapple, drained

Dissolve gelatin in boiling water. Add sherbet and stir until melted. Add fruit, stir, and pour into mold. Chill. Serves 12–15.

Country Cupboard Cookbook (Georgia)

Sunshine Salad

1 (3-ounce) package lemon Jell-O
1 cup hot water
1 cup cold water
1 tablespoon vinegar

1 cup grated carrots
1 cup crushed pineapple, drained
½ cup chopped nuts (if desired)

Dissolve Jell-O in bowl with hot water. Add cold water and vinegar. Then add the carrots, pineapple, and nuts. Refrigerate until set. Serves 8.

Spotsylvania Favorites (Virginia)

Watergate Salad

1 (8-ounce) container Cool Whip
1 small package pistachio instant
   pudding mix
⅓ cup cherries, chopped

1 large can crushed pinneapple,
   drained
½ cup pecans, chopped
½ cup miniature marshmallows

Mix Cool Whip and pudding together. Add remaining ingredients. Chill. Serves 6–8.

Southwest Cookin' (Arkansas)

Pear Mousse

1 (29-ounce) can pears
1 (6-ounce) package lemon Jell-O

1 (8-ounce) package cream cheese
1 (8-ounce) carton Cool Whip

Drain pears, reserving juice. Heat juice to boiling and add the Jell-O. Cool. Place pears and cream cheese in blender and blend till smooth. Pour in a large bowl and fold in cooled Jell-O mixture and Cool Whip till smooth. Place in serving dish and refrigerate. Garnish with fresh fruit of any kind. Serves 8.

Treasured Recipes from Treasured Friends (Minnesota)

Pears are cousins to apples. In North America, the first pear trees arrived with early colonists in the 1700s, where they thrived until blights became severe. Most pears are now commercially grown west of the Rockies where ideal growing conditions exist.

★★★★★★★★★★★★★★★★★★★★★★★★

Gelatin Cottage Cheese Salad

3 cups cottage cheese
1 (16-ounce) container frozen
  non-dairy whipped topping
1 (14-ounce) can mandarin oranges,
  drained

1 (16-ounce) can crushed pineapple,
  drained
2 (3-ounce) packages fruit-flavor
  gelatin

Mix cottage cheese and whipped topping; fold in fruit. Sprinkle gelatin over the mixture and blend well. Refrigerate until ready to serve. Serves 8–10.

Connecticut Cooks III (New England)

Apricot Salad

1 (3-ounce) package vanilla pudding
  (not instant)
1 can apricots, reserve juice

1 small can mandarin oranges
1 (8-ounce) carton Cool Whip

Cook pudding with 2 cups apricot juice (if you don't have enough juice, add water to make 2 cups). Cool. Add oranges (drained) and cut-up apricots; add Cool Whip. Mix well and chill. Serves 6.

Sharing our Best / Bergen Lutheran Church (Minnesota)

★ **Editor's Extra:** A small can of mandarin oranges is in the 11-ounce range; a large can, 14.

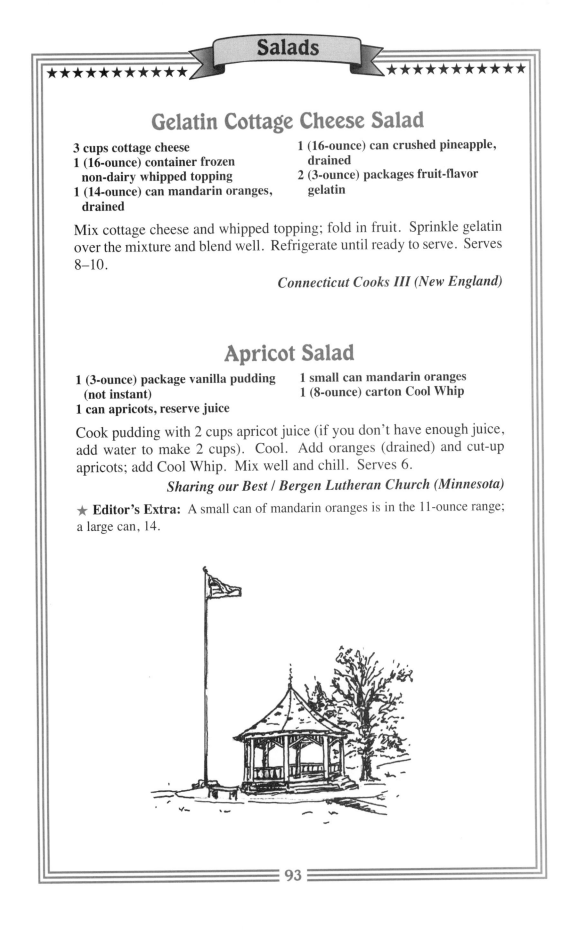

Easy Green Salad

2 (3½-ounce) boxes instant
  pistachio pudding mix
1 (16-ounce) container sour cream
½ cup chopped nuts

1 (20-ounce) can crushed pineapple,
  drained
½ cup flaked coconut

Combine ingredients in mixing bowl; mix until thoroughly blended. Pour into crystal serving dish, cover, and refrigerate until chilled. Serves 8–10.

Connecticut Cooks III (New England)

Fantastic Fruit Salad

This is a wonderful fruit salad for special holiday dinners.

2 cans mandarin oranges
2 (15-ounce) cans pineapple chunks
1 (16-ounce) package frozen
  strawberries, thawed

1 can peach pie filling
1 can apricot pie filling
2 bananas, sliced

Drain oranges, pineapple, and strawberries. In a mixing bowl, combine all ingredients; gently mix together. Place in a beautiful crystal bowl for serving. Serves 16.

I Cook—You Clean (Texas II)

Frozen Fruit Salad

Easy enough for children to make.

1 (10-ounce) package frozen
  strawberries, thawed, drained
1 (21-ounce) can apricot or peach
  pie filling

1 large can crushed pineapple,
  drained
½ cup sugar
1 cup whipping cream, whipped

Mix all ingredients together and pour into 9x9-inch pan. Freeze several hours. Cut into squares and serve each on lettuce leaf. Keeps well in freezer, covered. Serves 9.

Brunch Basket (Illinois)

Amazing Grace Salad

Delicious.

1 can sweetened condensed milk
3 tablespoons lemon juice
1 large carton Cool Whip

1 large can crushed pineapple,
  drained
1 cup chopped nuts

Mix all ingredients together for a good salad. Set in refrigerator prior to serving. Serves 6–8.

Variation: For Cherry Pineapple Salad, omit lemon juice and nuts, add 1 sliced banana and use 1 medium can pineapple and 1 medium carton Cool Whip, then add 1 can cherry pie filling. Pour into a pan and freeze.

A Taste of South Carolina (South Carolina)

Quick Salad

1 (8-ounce) package cream cheese
1 can condensed milk
1 can lemon pie filling
1 (8-ounce) carton Cool Whip

1 (15½-ounce) can crushed
  pineapple, drained
Nuts (if desired)

Mix the cream cheese and condensed milk together. Add the rest of the ingredients together and stir. Spread in a long dish and chill. Serves 8–10.

Centennial Cookbook (Oklahoma)

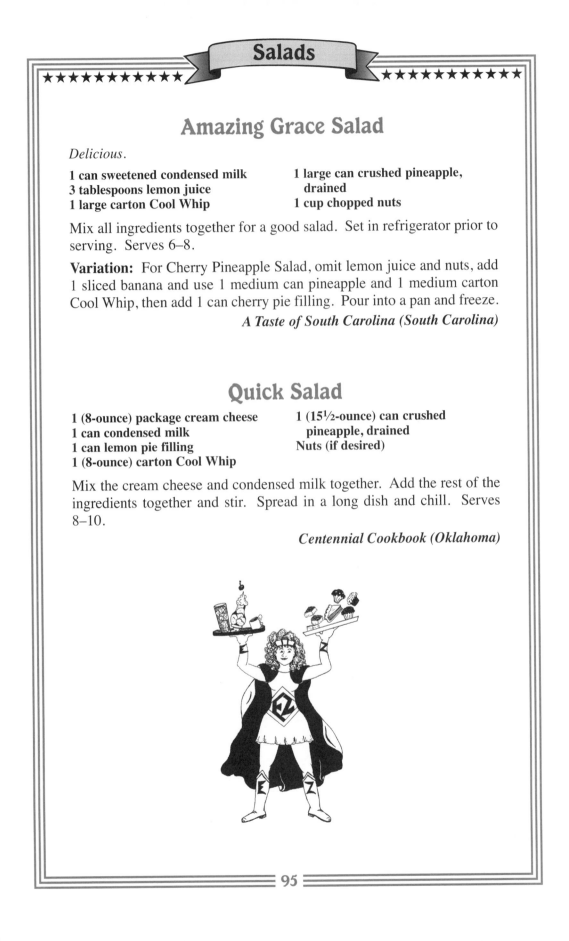

Cookies and Cream Salad

2 cups buttermilk
2 small packages instant vanilla
  pudding
16 ounces Cool Whip
1 package crushed fudge stripe
  cookies

2 small cans mandarin oranges,
  drained
1 small can crushed pineapple,
  drained

Mix together first 3 ingredients. Add remaining ingredients. Keeps well in fridge for 2–3 days. Serves 10–12.

Sharing Our "Beary" Best II (Great Plains)

Caramel Apple Salad

4–6 Snickers candy bars, frozen
4–6 Granny Smith apples, chopped
1 (8-ounce) carton Cool Whip

1 (3-ounce) package dry instant
  vanilla pudding

Smash frozen candy bars in wrappers with hammer. Mix all ingredients together. Serves 6–8.

Note: You can use other candy bars: Milky Way, KitKat, Twix, and others. These are all good, but the peanut flavor in the Snickers makes the salad.

Trinity Lutheran Church of Norden Anniversary Cookbook (Wisconsin)

Vegetables

In San Francisco, we walk up Filbert Street past Saints Peter and Paul Church, and tackle the uphill climb to Coit Tower. The view on top is well worth it. The fresh fruit and sourdough bread and seafood, especially at Fisherman's Wharf, is also well worth the trip from anywhere.

★★★★★★★★★★★★ ★★★★★★★★★★★★

Cheesy Potato Sticks

2 tablespoons butter
2 tablespoons all-purpose flour
¼ teaspoon salt
Dash pepper
1 cup milk

1 cup shredded Cheddar cheese,
  divided
1 (16-ounce) package frozen
  French fried potatoes

Melt butter over low heat. Blend in flour, salt and pepper. Add milk all at once. Cook quickly, stirring constantly until thickened and bubbling. Add half the shredded cheese. Stir until the cheese melts. Place potatoes in 10x6x1½-inch casserole dish. Pour milk mixture over top. Top with remaining cheese. Bake at 350° for 45 minutes. Serves 4.

Dishes from the Deep (Arizona)

Nacho Potato Slices

2 medium potatoes (about 12 ounces)
2 tablespoons thinly sliced green
  onion
2 tablespoons finely chopped green
  pepper

¼ cup bottled taco, barbecue, or
  spaghetti sauce
⅓ cup shredded Cheddar cheese

Scrub potatoes. Trim ends. Cut potatoes into ⅜-inch thick slices. In an 8x8x2-inch microwave-safe baking dish, arrange potato slices, putting smaller slices in the center. Sprinkle with green onion and green pepper.

Cover with vented clear plastic wrap. Cook on 100% power (HIGH) for 7–10 minutes or until tender, giving the dish a half-turn once. Drizzle sauce over slices. Sprinkle with shredded cheese. Cook uncovered, for 30–60 seconds more or until cheese is melted. Makes 4 servings.

Visions of Home Cook Book (New England)

★ **Editor's Extra:** Our friend Dawn gave us a great bell pepper tip. Buy fresh peppers, wash, halve and core, then freeze in Ziploc bags. When a recipe calls for chopped green or red pepper, hammer the pepper right through the bag! Perfect chopped peppers!

Dilled New Potatoes

Elegant, simple, and delicious!

**16 small new potatoes, washed but
  not peeled**
½ cup butter, melted

3 tablespoons fresh snipped dill weed
Salt to taste
Pepper to taste

In a large saucepan, cover potatoes with cold water. Place on high heat and boil 20 minutes or until fork tender. Drain. Place in a serving bowl, toss in butter, dill, salt and pepper. Serves 8.

Please Don't Feed the Alligators (South Carolina)

★ **Editor's Extra:** Dried dill weed works great; use half as much.

Hot Potato Salad

Like twice-baked potatoes without all the hassle.

**1 (12-ounce) package instant
  potatoes**
1 pint sour cream

6–8 green onions, chopped
1 cup crumbled fried bacon
8 ounces grated Cheddar cheese

Prepare potatoes according to directions. Put in buttered 9x13-inch dish. Spread sour cream on top of potatoes. Sprinkle with green onions. Add bacon; top with cheese. Bake at 350° for 20 minutes. Serves 12.

High Cotton Cookin' (Arkansas)

★ **Even Easier:** This makes enough to feed an army. I use a 2-ounce package of potatoes, ⅓ cup sour cream, 1 green onion (or 2 teaspoons dried), and a tablespoon of bottled real bacon bits topped with ⅓ cup cheese, and baked for 15 minutes in a small casserole dish. Serves 2–3 deliciously.

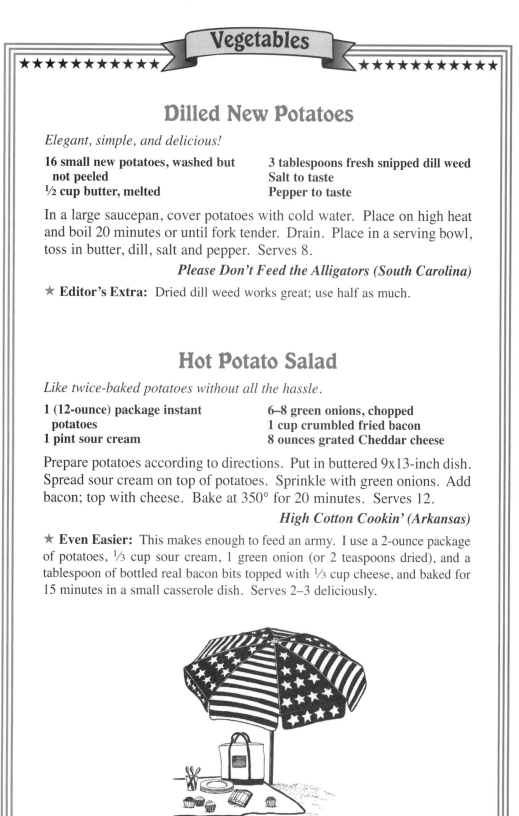

Laredo Potato

So many people love this dish! It's quick to fix, it's very tasty, very low in fat, and it's filled with energy.

1 medium potato
¼ cup chili hot beans
½ tomato, chopped
2 tablespoons chopped green onion

½ ounce (⅓ cup) shredded low moisture, part skim, mozzarella cheese
Salsa

Bake potato in microwave 4 minutes, or till done; split and mash a bit. Top with the beans. Top with tomato, onion, and cheese. Now add salsa for great Mexican flavor. Makes 1 serving. (Pictured on cover.)

Per serving: Cal 320; Fat 3g; Sod 560mg; Fiber 9.5g.

15 Minute, Storage Meals (Oklahoma)

Parmesan Fries

Most kids will love these lowfat fries!

3–4 small baking potatoes (well scrubbed)
1 tablespoon reduced calorie margarine, melted

¼ cup Parmesan cheese
½ teaspoon garlic powder
⅛ teaspoon onion powder
⅛ teaspoon salt

Cut potatoes lengthwise into wedges. Cut into 30 wedges for 3 potatoes or 32 wedges for 4 potatoes. Mix together Parmesan cheese, garlic powder, onion powder, and salt in a large plastic bag. Brush melted margarine onto potatoes. Put 10–11 slices of potato into the bag at a time and shake until potatoes are coated with mixture. Place potatoes on a cookie sheet sprayed with vegetable oil cooking spray. Bake at 400° for 20–25 minutes. Serves 4.

Lowfat, Homestyle Cookbook (Colorado)

★ **Even Easier**: Spray margarine does the job quickly! I usually have to make more seasoning mix.

Thomas Jefferson gets the credit for introducing French fries to America when he served them at a White House dinner. John Adams thought Jefferson was putting on airs by serving "such novelties."

★★★★★★★★★★★   ★★★★★★★★★★★

Spiced Apple and Sweet Potato Casserole

1 (18-ounce) can sweet potatoes,
  sliced
1 (20-ounce) can sliced apples
¾ teaspoon cinnamon

½ teaspoon nutmeg
⅓ cup pineapple juice
¼ cup butter
Parsley flakes

Arrange sweet potato slices and apples in alternating layers in an 8-inch square baking dish. Sprinkle each layer with cinnamon and nutmeg. Add pineapple juice. Dot with butter. Cover and bake at 375° for 15 minutes. Uncover and continue baking 20 minutes. Garnish with parsley flakes. Makes 6 servings.

Incredible Edibles (Ohio)

★ **Editor's Extra:** Top with mini-marshmallows last 20 minutes of baking.

Party Potatoes

1 (2-pound) package frozen Ore-Ida
  Hash Browns
1 can cream of celery soup
8 ounces shredded sharp Cheddar
  cheese

1 small onion, chopped
1 small carton sour cream
1 stick margarine, melted
1 sleeve Hi-Ho (or Ritz) crackers,
  crushed

Mix all ingredients except the margarine and crackers. Put mixture in a 9x13-inch dish. Cover top with melted margarine and crushed crackers. Bake at 350°, uncovered, for one hour. Serves 10–12.

Good Cookin' Cookbook (Illinois)

★ **Editor's Extra:** Quick to fix, it has to bake for an hour . . . and worth every minute!

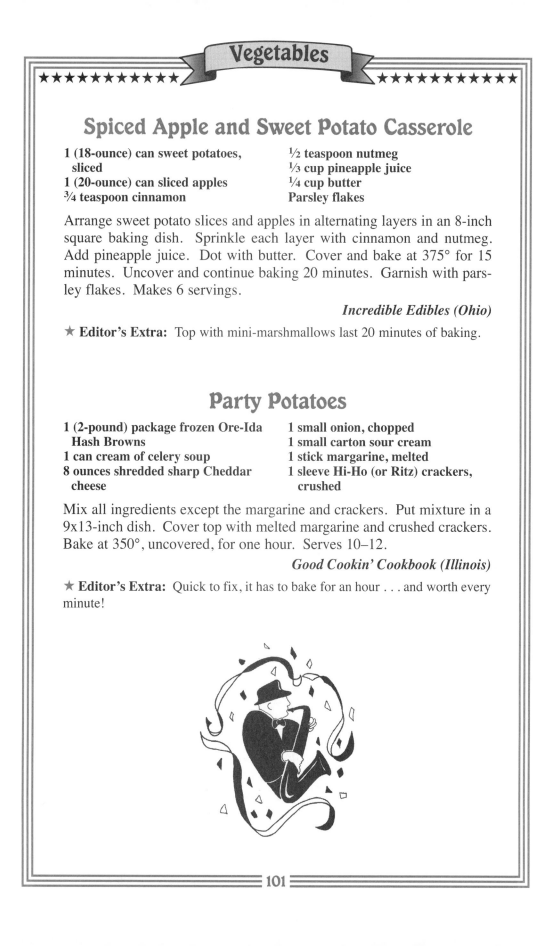

★★★★★★★★★★★   ★★★★★★★★★★★

Potato Pancakes

Potatoes always were and still are one of my favorite foods. They were served at most dinners as we were growing up. I remember making potato pancakes by grating the potatoes on a hand grater, trying not to scratch my knuckles. It took a long time to grate enough for our whole family, but it was well worth it. I sure am glad that food processors and blenders were invented—they save time and fingers.

We were able to store potatoes and carrots all winter in special bins that Dad made in our cellar. They were large bins with ventilated bottoms covered with old rugs. By allowing ventilation under the vegetables, rotting and sprouting were prevented, which helped them stay fresh all winter.

3 cups peeled, grated potatoes	2 tablespoons flour
3 eggs	½ teaspoon salt
1 tablespoon minced onion	

Blot potatoes on a clean dish towel or paper towel to remove excess moisture. Preheat griddle on medium heat. Beat eggs, onion, flour, and salt together. Add grated potatoes and stir until well blended. Fry ⅓-cup portions on a preheated greased griddle for about 2–3 minutes on each side or until golden brown. Serve with butter, applesauce, syrup, or fruit. Good for breakfast, lunch, or dinner. Serves 4.

Grandma's Home Kitchen (Wisconsin)

Baked Potato Sauce

A great alternative to sour cream.

1 cup Hellmann's Mayonnaise	¼ cup butter, softened
½ cup grated Parmesan cheese	½ teaspoon hot pepper sauce
¼ cup grated onion	

Combine all ingredients. This mixture will keep indefinitely under refrigeration. Yields 2 cups.

A Dash of Down East (North Carolina)

According to the Idaho Potato Commission, you should NEVER bake potatoes in aluminum foil, as the foil seals in moisture, making the texture pasty instead of fluffy. The best way is to place scrubbed potatoes directly on oven rack at 425° for 45-60 minutes. It is said that the microwave bakes a more nutritious potato because it is exposed to nutrient-draining heat for a shorter period of time. Pierce the potato and bake one at a time for 4-5 minutes on HIGH.

Barbecued Butter Beans

¾ cup brown sugar
⅓ cup dark corn syrup
2 or 3 drops hot pepper sauce
3 cans large lima beans, well
  drained

½ cup ketchup
2 teaspoons liquid smoke
1 medium diced onion
4 strips raw bacon

Combine all but bacon; mix well. Turn into a 1½-quart casserole. Arrange bacon strips on top. Bake at 325° for one hour. Serves 6–8.

Our Daily Bread (Great Plains)

Barbecue Beans

Fifteen minutes prep, then let these flavors "marry" in the oven.

1 can dark red kidney beans
1 can baked beans
1 garlic clove, mashed
1 medium onion, chopped
3 tablespoons bacon drippings

½ cup catsup
1 tablespoon dark brown sugar
1 tablespoon dry mustard
Salt and pepper to taste

Mix all ingredients and bake in 350° oven for 1 hour. Serves 6.

San Antonio Cookbook II (Texas)

Green Beans Supreme

2 (16-ounce) cans French-cut green
  beans, drained
1 (4-ounce) can water chestnuts,
  drained and diced

1 can cream of mushroom soup
¼ cup water
1 (3½-ounce) can French fried
  onions

Layer beans in small casserole with water chestnuts until all are used. Spoon mushroom soup that has been thinned with water over top. Bake at 350° for 25–30 minutes. Top with onions and brown at 400° for 10 minutes. Serves 6.

Company Fare I (Oklahoma)

Swiss Green Bean Casserole

2 tablespoons margarine
2 tablespoons flour
1 (8-ounce) carton French onion
  dip
2 tablespoons milk

2 (15½- to 16-ounce) cans whole
  green beans, drained (or cooked
  fresh)
¼ pound grated Swiss cheese
Paprika

Melt margarine in a small heavy saucepan; add flour and stir until smooth. Add onion dip and milk, stirring until smooth. Layer beans and ⅔ of sauce in 1½-quart, lightly buttered casserole. Top with cheese. Pour remaining sauce over all. Sprinkle with paprika. Cover and bake in 325° oven for 20 minutes or until cheese melts. Makes 8 servings.

In the Kitchen with Kate (Great Plains)

Marinated Green Beans

This is always a favorite. I usually double it.

4 slices bacon
½ cup sugar
½ cup vinegar

1 (16-ounce) can cut green beans,
  drained

Brown bacon in pan, remove and set aside. Add sugar and vinegar to bacon grease and stir. Add green beans. Simmer about 20 minutes. Then add crumbled bacon and simmer about 5 minutes.

Flaunting Our Finest (Tennessee)

★★★★★★★★★★★★ ★★★★★★★★★★★★

Green Bean Revenge

Hot! And very cheesy!

**3 (16-ounce) cans green beans,
  drained**
**1 (8-ounce) can sliced water
  chestnuts, drained and chopped**

**2 (8-ounce) jars jalapeño Cheez
  Whiz**
1 cup cracker crumbs
2 (3½-ounce) cans onion rings

Place green beans in 9x13-inch baking dish and cover with water chestnuts. Heat both jars of Cheez Whiz in dish in the microwave just until they can be poured. Pour over green beans and water chestnuts. Sprinkle cracker crumbs over green beans, water chestnuts, and Cheez Whiz. Arrange onion rings over casserole and bake at 350° for 25–30 minutes. Serves 12.

A Little Taste of Texas (Texas II)

★ **Editor's Extra:** For the "faint of heart," you might want to use 1 jar of the jalapeño Cheez Whiz and 1 jar of the regular Cheez Whiz.

Sweet and Sour Beets

1 tablespoon cornstarch
3 tablespoons vinegar
**3 tablespoons sugar (or sugar
  substitute)**

1 teaspoon salt
½ cup beet juice (from beets)
1 can beets, drained

Combine all ingredients except beets in a medium saucepan. Heat until thickened. Cool. Add beets. Serve warm or cold. Serves 4.

L'Heritage Du Bayou Lafourche (Louisiana II)

Over 100,000 acres of sugar beets are planted in Michigan each year. The beets are stored outside before being processed and are kept cool naturally by cooler fall temperatures. The storage piles are 20 feet high, 120 feet wide and can be up to ¼ mile in length. One beet is processed into about 5 ounces of pure beet sugar.

★★★★★★★★★★★   ★★★★★★★★★★★

Great Corn on the Cob

6 ears fresh or frozen sweet corn
1 tablespoon parsley flakes
½ teaspoon garlic powder
1 teaspoon oregano

Salt to taste
Pepper to taste
¼ cup butter
Parmesan cheese

Add corn to boiling water and cook 15 minutes. Remove from water and place in rectangular dish. Sprinkle with spices and add butter. Sprinkle corn with Parmesan cheese. Cover dish with foil and place in warm oven until ready to serve. Serves 6.

Note: Remember when salting corn that Parmesan cheese is also salty.

A Dash of Down East (North Carolina)

Baked Corn on the Cob

So simple—so good!

6 ears fresh corn
1 (4-ounce) package whipped cream
  cheese with chives

4 tablespoons butter, softened
¼ teaspoon salt
Dash pepper

Remove husks and silk from ears. Stir cream cheese into butter, add salt and pepper, and blend. Place ears of corn on individual large squares of foil. Spread each ear with some of mixture. Fold up foil and seal. Bake in a 350–400° oven for 30–45 minutes until corn is tender. Carefully open each ear and spoon hot chive butter over ears to serve.

Note: May be done on an outdoor grill. Cooking time is approximately the same. Serves 6.

Three Rivers Cookbook III (Pennsylvania)

The world's only Corn Palace is an a-*maize*-ing *ear*-chitecture. Built in Mitchell, South Dakota, around 1892 to encourage settlement and prove the richness of eastern South Dakota soil, the palace is decorated inside and out with thousands of bushels of native corn, grain, and grasses.

★★★★★★★★★★★ ★★★★★★★★★★★

Deluxe Corn Dish

1 (16½-ounce) can cream-style corn
1 (16½-ounce) can whole-kernel corn
2 eggs, slightly beaten
1 cup sour cream
½ cup melted butter
½ box Jiffy Corn Muffin Mix
Salt and pepper
1 cup grated Cheddar cheese

Combine all ingredients, except cheese. Mix and put in buttered (8x8-inch) casserole. Bake at 350° for one hour. (Do not cover.) Before serving, top with cheese and put foil over it, so it melts. Serves 6.

Our Heritage Cookbook (Minnesota)

Corn, Green Chiles, and Cheese

1 onion, chopped
1 can diced green chiles, drained
2 tablespoons butter
1 can whole-kernel corn, drained
½ pound grated Monterey Jack
  cheese
Salt and pepper
½ cup sour cream

Sauté onion and chiles in 2 tablespoons butter or enough to cover bottom of skillet. Add corn. Fold cheese into mixture until it melts. Add salt and pepper to taste. Just before serving, mix in sour cream. Serve immediately.

Down-Home Texas Cooking (Texas II)

Escalloped Corn

Microwave quick!

1 (17-ounce) can cream-style corn
1 (17-ounce) can whole-kernel corn,
  drained
1 cup cracker crumbs
1 (5¾-ounce) can evaporated milk
1 egg, slightly beaten
2 tablespoons butter

Combine corns, crumbs, and milk in 1-quart casserole. Mix well. Stir in egg. Dot with butter. Cover. Microwave 7½ minutes on "8" or until set. Let stand 3–5 minutes covered. Garnish with paprika, if desired. Serves 6.

Cookbook 25 Years (Illinois)

★★★★★★★★★★★ ★★★★★★★★★★★

Broccoli-Corn Bake

1 (16-ounce) can cream-style corn
1 (10-ounce) package frozen chopped
  broccoli, thawed and well drained
1 egg, beaten
2 teaspoons dehydrated onion

¾ cup coarsely crumbled Ritz
  Crackers (18), divided
3 tablespoons melted butter, divided
Salt and fresh ground pepper

Preheat oven to 350°. Combine corn, broccoli, egg, onion, ½ cup cracker crumbs, and 2 tablespoons butter in a large bowl and mix thoroughly. Spoon into a 1-quart baking dish and season with salt and pepper. Combine 1 tablespoon butter and ¼ cup Ritz Crackers. Mix thoroughly. Sprinkle this mixture over top of casserole. Bake uncovered until golden brown, about 30 minutes. Serves 6.

Gourmet: The Quick and Easy Way (Oklahoma)

★ **Even Easier**: Put crackers on a sheet of wax paper, fold over and roll with a heavy glass to crush. No clean-up! Or easy to use a food processor.

Broccoli Casserole

This can be made a day ahead, stored in refrigerator and cooked the next day.

2 (10-ounce) packages frozen
  chopped broccoli
2 eggs, beaten
¾ cup mayonnaise
1 can cream of mushroom soup

18 Ritz Crackers, crushed
1 (8-ounce) package grated Cheddar
  cheese
¼ cup butter

Thaw and put broccoli in 9x13-inch baking dish. Mix eggs, mayonnaise, and mushroom soup, and pour over broccoli. Put Ritz Cracker crumbs and cheese on top. Dot with butter. Bake at 350° for 30–40 minutes.

The Centennnial Society Cookbook (Minnesota)

★ **Even Easier**: Halve the recipe and use ½–¾ cup bread crumbs instead of Ritz Cracker crumbs.

★★★★★★★★★★★★ ★★★★★★★★★★★★

Artichoke Heart Quiche

2 (6-ounce) jars marinated
  artichoke hearts
½ cup sliced green onion
1 tablespoon oil
4 eggs

Salt, pepper
½ pound sharp Cheddar cheese,
  shredded
6 Ritz Crackers, crushed
2 dashes Tabasco

Drain artichokes; cut in sixths. Sauté onions in oil. Beat eggs; add artichokes, onion and remaining ingredients. Pour into a greased 8x12-inch pan. Bake at 350° for 30–35 minutes. Cut into squares; serve warm. Serves 8 or makes 40 pieces for an appetizer.

Grand Detour Holiday Sampler (Illinois)

Artichoke Casserole

2 (14-ounce) cans artichokes,
  drained
4 tablespoons butter or margarine
4 tablespoons flour

½ cup milk
½ cup Parmesan cheese
½ teaspoon celery salt
4 tablespoons bread crumbs

Cut artichokes in quarters; place in greased casserole. Reserve. Melt butter in a small pot, stir in flour, milk, cheese, and celery salt, stirring and cooking until thick. Pour over artichokes and mix; sprinkle bread crumbs on top. Bake 30 minutes at 350°. Serves 4–6.

The Prima Diner (Florida)

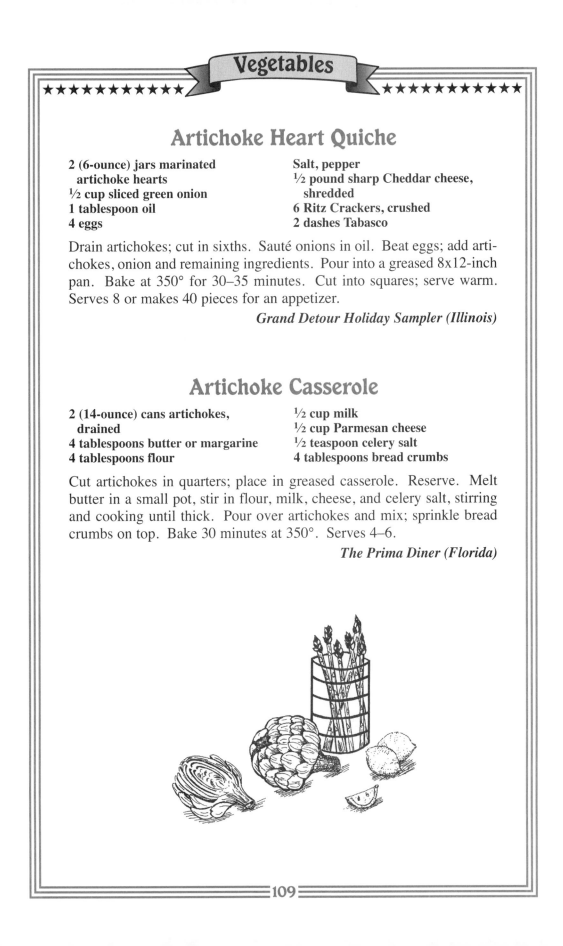

★★★★★★★★★★★ ★★★★★★★★★★★

Darrell's Baked Onions

Onions	Salt
Margarine	Pepper

Clean onions, remove top of center core with knife in a spiral "V". Place onions in a pan and fill center with margarine. Sprinkle generously with salt and pepper. Bake, covered, at 350° for (up to) 1½ hours or until tender.

Note: May substitute Lawry's seasoned salt for regular salt.

Recipes & Remembrances / Courtland Covenant Church (Great Plains)

★ **Even Easier**: So easy to cook these in microwave. Cook 2 medium onions as directed in one tablespoon of water, covered, 5–6 minutes on HIGH, till softened.

Vidalia Onion Pie

1 cup crushed saltine crackers	2 eggs
5 tablespoons butter, melted	¾ cup milk
2½ cups thinly sliced Vidalia onions	Salt and pepper
2 tablespoons oil	¼ pound grated Cheddar cheese

Combine crackers and butter and press into 8-inch pie pan. Bake at 350° for 8–10 minutes.

Sauté onions in oil until tender; put in the pie shell. Mix remaining ingredients except cheese and pour over onions. Top with Cheddar cheese. Bake 350° for 45 minutes. Serves 8.

Champions: Favorite Foods of Indy Car Racing (Indiana)

★ **Even Easier**: Boil the milk and this will bake in 30 minutes. Good subbing Swiss cheese, too. If you don't have Vidalia onions, don't let this keep you from making this yummy dish with whatever onions you have.

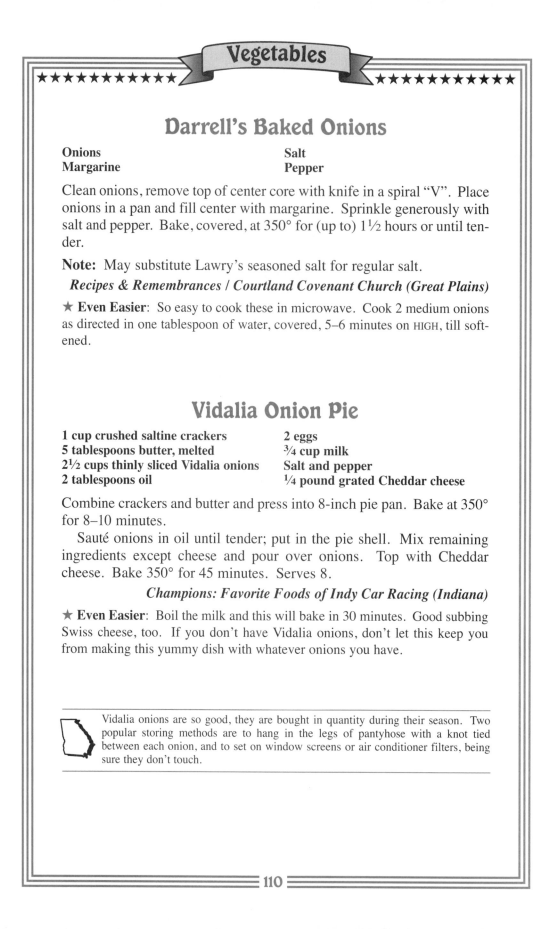

Vidalia onions are so good, they are bought in quantity during their season. Two popular storing methods are to hang in the legs of pantyhose with a knot tied between each onion, and to set on window screens or air conditioner filters, being sure they don't touch.

★★★★★★★★★★★ ★★★★★★★★★★★

Onion Patties

Tastes just like onion rings!

¾ cup flour
1 tablespoon sugar
1 tablespoon cornmeal
2 teaspoons baking powder

2 teaspoons salt (or less)
¾ cup milk
2½ cups finely chopped onions

Mix dry ingredients together; then add milk. Batter should be fairly thick. Add onions and mix thoroughly. Drop by tablespoons into ½ inch of oil in skillet. Flatten slightly when you turn them. Brown on both sides until crisp. Serves 6.

The Amish Way Cookbook (Ohio)

Zucchini (Mock) Crab Cakes

2 cups coarsely grated zucchini
  (drain liquid)
1 cup seasoned bread crumbs
2 tablespoons grated onion
2 tablespoons mayonnaise

2 eggs
2 teaspoons Old Bay Seasoning
½ teaspoon salt
1 tablespoon chopped parsley

In a mixing bowl combine all ingredients, mix, and shape into cakes. Fry in Crisco (a few tablespoons), browning each side. Serves 6.

The Best of Zucchini Recipes (Pennsylvania)

Zucchini Pie

3 small zucchini, cubed (about
  1–1¼ pounds)
1 small onion, chopped
1 cup Bisquick
½ cup oil

½ cup grated sharp cheese
4 eggs, beaten
Pinches of salt, pepper, parsley, and
  basil

Mix together all ingredients. Pour into a lightly greased 10-inch pie plate. Bake at 350° for 30–40 minutes, until golden. Serves 4.

Think Healthy (Virginia)

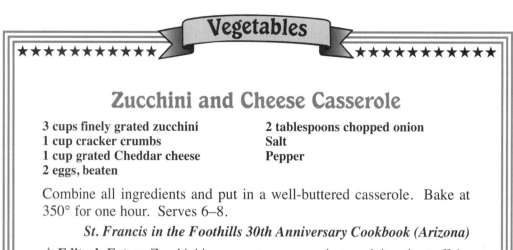
Zucchini and Cheese Casserole

3 cups finely grated zucchini
1 cup cracker crumbs
1 cup grated Cheddar cheese
2 eggs, beaten

2 tablespoons chopped onion
Salt
Pepper

Combine all ingredients and put in a well-buttered casserole. Bake at 350° for one hour. Serves 6–8.

St. Francis in the Foothills 30th Anniversary Cookbook (Arizona)

★ **Editor's Extra:** Zucchini is so easy to prepare—just scrub it and cut off the ends. Throw chunks in a food processor, or chop finely or grate—it's a very colorful, nutritious, "easy" vegetable. And good!

Crispy Parmesan Zucchini

Serve these as an appetizer, too.

3 large zucchini (about 1½ pounds)
⅓ cup melted butter
½ cup grated Parmesan cheese

Seasoned salt
Minced fresh herb, like marjoram
  or basil (optional)

Preheat broiler. Cut zucchini into ½-inch thick diagonal slices. Dip one cut surface of each slice into melted butter, then cheese, coating well. Place zucchini slices, cheese-side up, on greased pan(s) with shallow sides. Sprinkle with seasoned salt and herb, if desired. Broil 4–6 inches from heat until crisp and golden, about 6–8 minutes. Serve immediately. Makes 6–8 servings.

Palates (Colorado)

★ **Even Easier:** A toaster oven works well for ½ recipe.

Zucchini is an incredibly versatile food. This squash can be steamed, grilled, sauteed, deep-fried, or baked. The usually dark green skin is tender and most often doesn't have to be peeled. Common market length is 4–8 inches, but some specimens are as tiny as a finger, while some (mostly home-grown) can reach 2 feet long and 6 inches in diameter! Zucchini is used in salads, vegetable dishes, casseroles, and even desserts. And it's good for you.

★★★★★★★★★★★ ★★★★★★★★★★★

Stir-Fry Zucchini with Cheese

1 medium (or 2 small) zucchini
2 tablespoons salad oil
1 medium onion, sliced

Dash pepper
¼ pound American or Cheddar
  cheese

If zucchini is tender, wash only, and use the skin, too. Slice in thin slices. Put oil and onion in frying pan and cook until clear. Add zucchini. Reduce heat and cook only until zucchini is tender. Stir as needed. Cut cheese in thin pieces or grate. Add to zucchini. Cover and heat only until cheese melts. Serves 2–3.

Our Favorite Recipes (Pennsylvania)

Okra and Tomatoes Creole

½ small onion, chopped
1 tablespoon bacon grease or salad
  oil
½ cup fresh okra, washed and sliced

1 teaspoon flour
1 tomato, cut in pieces
½ teaspoon sugar
Salt and pepper to taste

In heavy medium-size saucepan or skillet, slightly brown onion in bacon grease, about 1 minute on medium heat. Dredge okra in flour and add to onion. Continue cooking until okra is slightly brown, about 5 minutes. Add tomato to mixture. Add sugar. Cook partly covered over slow heat about 25 minutes, stirring occcasionally to keep from sticking. Season. Serves 1–2.

Quickies for Singles (Louisiana)

Steamed Cauliflower

1 head cauliflower

1 jar Cheez Whiz, melted

After removing leaves, rinse cauliflower, giving 1–2 shakes to remove excess water. Place on plate, cover with plastic wrap, leaving a 1-inch vent opening. For each pound the cauliflower weighs, microwave on HIGH for 7 minutes. When done, carefully remove plastic wrap and pour melted Cheez Whiz over top. Garnish as desired.

Gardener's Delight (Ohio)

Asparagus Casserole

48 ounces canned asparagus, whole
  or cut-style
1–2 tomatoes
3 slices red onion

8 slices (or more) crisp bacon,
  crumbled
1 cup grated Cheddar cheese

Place drained asparagus in a 8x8-inch buttered casserole dish. Place enough sliced tomatoes on top of asparagus to cover. Next layer onion slices (separate into rings), crumbled bacon, and cheese. Bake in 325° oven for 20 minutes or until hot. This casserole is good served cold. Serves 6.

San Angelo Junior League Cookbook (Texas)

Baked Asparagus

1 (16-ounce) can asparagus or 2
  cups fresh, cut into 1-inch lengths
2 hard cooked eggs, sliced
½ cup slivered almonds

2½ cups grated Cheddar cheese
1 can cream of mushroom soup
1 cup Ritz Cracker crumbs

Preheat oven to 350°. Layer drained asparagus, eggs, almonds and cheese in greased baking dish; cover with soup. Sprinkle with crumbs. Bake for 25–35 minutes until thick and bubbly. Yields 4–5 servings.

Miss Daisy Entertains (Tennessee)

★ **Editor's Extra**: A good cream sauce can substitute quite well for cream soups. Melt 2 tablespoons butter in a saucepan; stir in 2 tablespoons flour. Now whisk in a cup of milk and season it. For variety, add some chopped mushrooms and/or onions, or maybe some grated cheese. Simmer a little while, then add to the recipe.

Asparagus are considered gourmet vegetables, and rightfully so. It takes years (2–5) to cultivate the land, grow the seedlings, transfer the crowns to the field, and finally to reap the harvest . . . and much of it is done by hand, including selecting and cutting the mature spears. Asparagus roots grow deep—at least six feet and up to 20! At the pinnacle of their growth stage, when the weather is appropriately warm, you can almost watch the shoots grow—sometimes six inches in just a couple of days. Asparagus are green or white, and mostly grown in California, Washington, and Michigan.

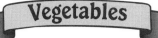
★★★★★★★★★★★ ★★★★★★★★★★★

Quesadillas with Morels

1 cup small morels
6 tablespoons butter

6 small flour tortillas
6 slices Monterey Jack cheese

Sauté morels in butter until golden, about 5 minutes. In a sauté pan, heat tortillas, one at a time, turning with a spatula. Place a slice of cheese on each tortilla, fold in half and continue to turn until cheese begins to melt. Top each cheese-filled tortilla with 3 tablespoons sautéed morels. Cut each tortilla in 3 pie-shaped sections and serve immediately. Yields 6 servings.

One Magnificent Cookbook (Illinois)

★ **Editor's Extra:** This works with most any sliced mushrooms of your choice. Good for brunch or lunch.

Mushrooms Florentine

¼ cup butter
¼ cup chopped onion
1 pound fresh mushrooms, sliced
2 (10-ounce) packages frozen
  chopped spinach, cooked and
  drained

1 cup grated Mozzarella, Monterey
  Jack, or Romano cheese
1 teaspoon salt
¼ teaspoon garlic salt

In a medium skillet, melt the butter. Add the onion and mushrooms, and sauté for 5 minutes. Stir in the remaining ingredients and transfer the mixture to a 9x9-inch baking dish. Bake the casserole at 350° for 20 minutes. Serves 6–8.

La Bonne Cuisine (Louisiana)

Vegie-Melt

1 cup sliced fresh mushrooms
1 cup sliced zucchini
1 tablespoon butter
4 pita or pocket breads

1 firm tomato, sliced
4 slices Monterey Jack cheese
Alfalfa sprouts (optional)

Sauté mushrooms and zucchini in butter for 5–10 minutes. Split pita bread and divide mushroom mixture evenly among 4 breads. Top each with a slice of tomato and cheese. Run under broiler just long enough to melt cheese. Can top with sprouts, if desired. Top with other half of pita bread. Can also add sliced, cooked chicken breast, or a big slice of sweet onion. Serves 4.

Three Rivers Cookbook II (Pennsylvania)

Swiss Vegetable Medley

1 (16-ounce) bag frozen broccoli,
  carrots and cauliflower
1 can cream of mushroom soup
1 cup shredded Swiss cheese, divided

⅓ cup sour cream
¼ teaspoon black pepper
1 can French fried onions, divided

Combine vegetables, soup, ½ cup cheese, sour cream, pepper and ½ can onions. Pour into 1-quart casserole. Bake covered at 350° for 40 minutes. Top with remaining cheese and onions. Bake uncovered for 5 more minutes.

Cooking with Mr. "G" and Friends (Louisiana II)

★ **Even Easier**: After mixing ingredients, cook in microwave 10 minutes on BAKE (#7 power). Stir, then bake in regular oven as directed to melt cheese and crisp onions.

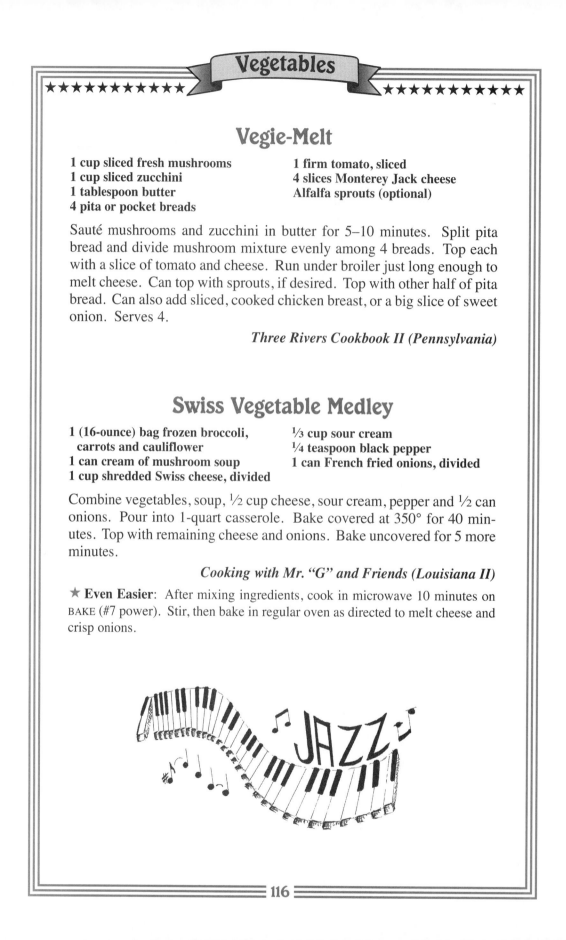

Vegetable Casserole

1 onion, chopped
½ stick butter
1 can sliced water chestnuts,
  chopped slightly

1 cup Hellmann's Mayonnaise
1 cup grated cheese
2 cans Veg-All, drained
½ cup crushed potato chips

Sauté chopped onion in butter. Mix all ingredients except potato chips, and pour in casserole. Top with potato chips last 10 minutes of baking time. Bake 30 minutes at 350°.

A Bouquet of Recipes (Louisiana II)

Vegetable Casserole

1 (16-ounce) can French-cut green
  beans, drained
1 can shoepeg corn
½ cup onion, chopped

½ cup sour cream
1 can cream of chicken soup
½ cup cheese, shredded
Salt and pepper to taste

Mix all together and pour in buttered baking dish.

TOPPING:
1 stack Ritz Crackers, rolled fine
1 stick margarine

½ cup slivered almonds (optional)

Place crackers, margarine and almonds in fry-pan and stir until margarine is melted; do not brown. Spread on top of vegetables and bake at 350° for 45 minutes. Serves 6.

500 Favorite Recipes (South Carolina)

★ **Even Easier**: Cut the cook time by microwaving for 15 minutes or so on #7 power.

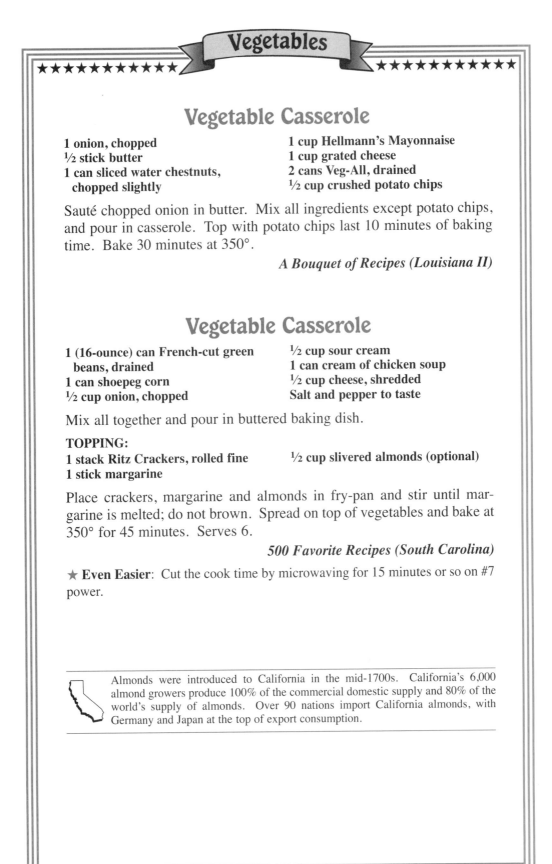

Almonds were introduced to California in the mid-1700s. California's 6,000 almond growers produce 100% of the commercial domestic supply and 80% of the world's supply of almonds. Over 90 nations import California almonds, with Germany and Japan at the top of export consumption.

★★★★★★★★★★★ ★★★★★★★★★★★★

Glazed Carrots

1 (14-ounce) package frozen baby
  carrots or 2 cups fresh
¼ cup unsweetened apple juice or
  apple cider

¼ cup apple jelly
1½ teaspoons Dijon mustard

Place carrots and apple juice in medium nonstick skillet. Bring to a boil. Reduce heat; cover and simmer 7–9 minutes or until carrots are crisp-tender. Uncover; cook over medium heat until liquid evaporates. Stir in jelly and mustard; cook and stir over medium heat until jelly melts and carrots are glazed. Serves 4.

Per Serving: Cal 85 (6.1% from fat); Fat 0.6g (Sat 0.1g); Chol 0mg; Fiber 2.5g; Sod 78.8mg. Diabetic Exchange: Not recommended.

Here's To Your Heart: Cooking Smart (Wisconsin)

Cousin Patty's Carrot Soufflé

Extra good and colorful.

¾ cup sugar
3 tablespoons flour
¼ teaspoon salt
¼ teaspoon black pepper
1 teaspoon baking powder

1 stick (¼ pound) butter, softened
1 teaspoon vanilla
2 tablespoons rum (optional)
1 (16-ounce) can carrots, drained
3 eggs

Preheat oven to 350°. Whisk together sugar, flour, salt, pepper, and baking powder. Combine all ingredients in blender and blend thoroughly. Pour into greased casserole dish and bake for 45 minutes. Serve hot. Serves 4–6 hungry hogs!

The Hungry Hog (Louisiana II)

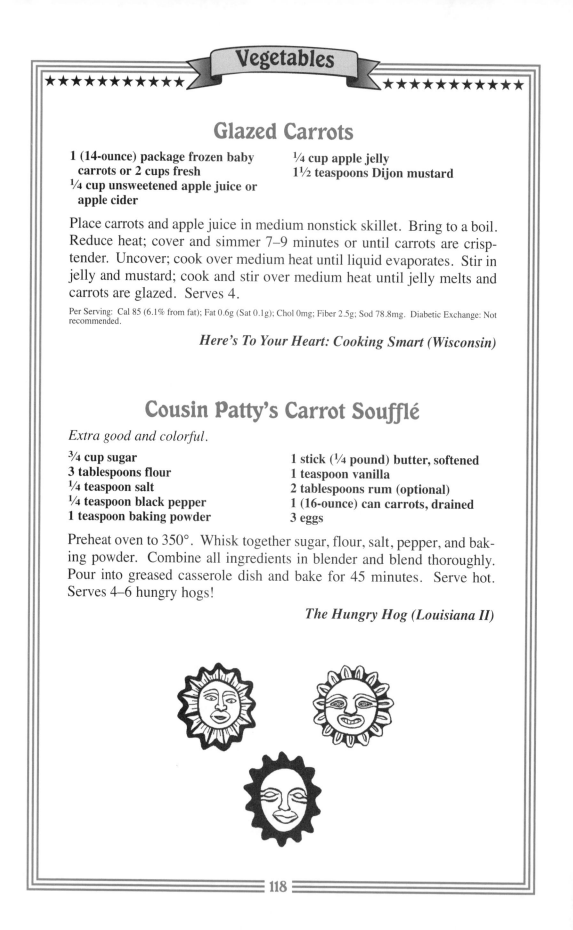

Zippy Glazed Carrots

No one will know that you did not take the time to peel, slice, and cook these delicious carrots.

1 tablespoon butter
1 tablespoon brown sugar
1 teaspoon mustard

¼ teaspoon salt
1 (15-ounce) can sliced carrots, drained

Combine butter, brown sugar, mustard and salt in a 12-inch nonstick skillet. Cook until blended. Add carrots. Fry until carrots are heated and glazed. Yields 1½ cups or 4 servings.

The Give Mom a Rest (She's on Vacation) Cookbook (Great Plains)

Sunshine Carrots

Tangy and quick!

5 medium carrots
2 tablespoons water
1 tablespoon sugar
1 teaspoon cornstarch

¼ teaspoon salt
¼ teaspoon ginger
¼ cup orange juice
2 tablespoons butter

Slice carrots diagonally, about 1-inch thick. Place in covered 1½-quart glass casserole with water. Cook on HIGH in microwave for 8 minutes. Stir halfway through cooking time. Drain.

Meanwhile, combine sugar, cornstarch, salt and ginger in a small saucepan. Add orange juice; cook, stirring constantly until mixture thickens and bubbles. Boil 1 minute. Stir in butter. Pour over hot carrots, tossing to coat evenly.

If you do not have a microwave, cook carrots covered in a small amount of boiling salted water until just tender, about 20 minutes. Drain. Serves 4.

Gulfshore Delights (Florida)

★ **Even Easier**: I also tried this with 2 cans of carrots. Micro only 2 minutes to warm, then drain and add sauce. Beta carotene never tasted so good.

Carrots weren't always used strictly as a food source. During the reign of England's King James I, the wearing of carrot leaves in sprays became very fashionable, particularly during the autumn months when the leaves took on a reddish coloration. Flowers and leaves were used to adorn hats, and ladies wore sprigs of carrot leaves in their hair.

★★★★★★★★★★★ ★★★★★★★★★★★

Poz Noz

Unbelievable that something that's good for you can be so good!

6 eggs
2 pounds cottage cheese
1 (16-ounce) package frozen
  chopped spinach, well drained
2 tablespoons margarine, melted

⅓ cup flour
½ cup chopped onion
1 teaspoon salt
½ cup grated Cheddar cheese

Beat eggs. Add cottage cheese and well drained spinach (press water out of spinach). Into margarine, stir flour and onion. Put all together; add salt and grated cheese. Bake at 350° for 1 hour. Serves 8–10.

College Avenue Presbyterian Church Cookbook (Illinois)

★ **Even Easier**: I halve the recipe (use a 10-ounce package spinach) and microwave 9–13 minutes, till firm. There's never any left!

Microwave Spinach and Tomatoes

1 (10-ounce) package frozen
  spinach, chopped
¾ cup ricotta cheese, drained
½ teaspoon garlic powder
¼ teaspoon nutmeg

Salt and pepper, to taste
2 tomatoes, thinly sliced
½–¾ cup mozzarella cheese, grated
Parmesan cheese

Defrost spinach and drain to remove all liquid. Mix with ricotta cheese, garlic powder, nutmeg, salt and pepper. Spread half of mixture in bottom of 1-quart casserole. Cover with half of tomato slices and sprinkle with half of mozzarella cheese. Repeat layers; sprinkle top with Parmesan cheese. Cover with wax paper and cook on MEDIUM power in microwave until cheese is melted and heated throughly, approximately 8–10 minutes. Yields 6 servings.

Note: May be baked in conventional oven at 350° for 20 minutes.

Upper Crust: A Slice of the South (Tennessee)

★★★★★★★★★★★ ★★★★★★★★★★★

Spinach Everyone Likes

2 (10-ounce) packages spinach,
  (1 chopped, 1 whole leaf)
1 cup low-fat sour cream

½ package onion soup mix
½ cup bread crumbs or herbed
  stuffing mix

Cook spinach according to package directions. Drain well. Add remaining ingredients except bread crumbs. Mix well. Pour into ungreased 2-quart casserole. Top with bread crumbs. Bake at 350° for 35 minutes. Serves 6.

Think Healthy (Virginia)

Broiled Tomatoes

Tomatoes
Margarine
½ teaspoon salt
⅛ teaspoon pepper
¼ teaspoon basil

¼ teaspoon thyme
¼ teaspoon oregano
¼ teaspoon sugar
Parmesan cheese, grated

Purchase firm ripe tomatoes according to how many you are going to feed. Slice in fairly thick slices and place on foil-lined baking sheet. Dot with a little margarine.

Combine the salt, pepper, spices and sugar. Sprinkle mixture on tomatoes, then Parmesan cheese on top. Grill or bake at 300° for about 20 minutes. Check frequently.

Gazebo I Christmas Cookbook (Alabama)

★ **Even Easier**: Here's a good time to use spray margarine.

★★★★★★★★★★★ ★★★★★★★★★★★

Raisin Sauced Beets

1 (1-pound) can sliced beets (reserve
  ⅓ cup liquid, drain the rest)
⅓ cup light or dark raisins
¼ cup sugar

1 teaspoon cornstarch
3 tablespoons lemon juice
2 tablespoons butter

In medium saucepan, combine ⅓ cup beet liquid and raisins. Cover; simmer until raisins are plumped, about 5 minutes. Combine sugar and cornstarch; stir into raisins. Add lemon juice and butter. Cook and stir over medium heat until slightly thickened. Stir in beets and simmer until mixture is heated through, about 5 minutes. If desired, garnish with a twist of lemon. Makes 5 servings.

Nutritional analysis: Cal 136; Carbo 24g; Vit E 2mg; Sod 208mg; Potas 198mg.

REC Family Cookbook (Great Plains)

★ **Editor's Extra:** For variation, deluxe these yummy beets with a small can of crushed pineapple, drained.

Marian's Sweet Pickles from Dill

Good, quick, and easy!

1 quart commercially prepared
  hamburger dill slices, drained

2 cloves garlic, sliced
3 cups sugar

Drain hamburger dill slices. Discard vinegar solution. Place the well drained pickles in bowl. Add sliced garlic and sugar. Stir. Continuing stirring until all sugar is absorbed by the pickles and a sweet syrup is made. Rinse out the pickle jar and return pickles to the jar with the sweet syrup. Refrigerate.

Home Cookin' is a Family Affair (Illinois)

Our country's namesake, Amerigo Vespucci, was a pickle peddler in Seville, Spain. He supplied ships with pickled vegetables to prevent sailors from getting scurvy on long voyages. Way to go, Amerigo.

★★★★★★★★★★★ ★★★★★★★★★★★

English Pea Casserole

Goddess green good!

1 (10¾-ounce) can cream of
  mushroom soup
¼ cup margarine
1 (16-ounce) can English peas,
  drained

1 (10-ounce) can asparagus,
  drained
1 (8½-ounce) can sliced water
  chestnuts, drained

Warm soup and margarine until margarine melts. Add vegetables and
bake in 350° oven for 30 minutes.

Prairie Harvest (Arkansas)

Apple-Cheese Casserole

1 can unsweetened apples
¾ cup sugar
¾ cup self-rising flour

8 ounces sharp Cheddar cheese,
  grated
1 stick butter

Place apples with juice in dish. Mix sugar, flour, cheese and butter that
has been chopped in small pieces. Pour over apples and bake 30–35
minutes at 350°. Serves 4–6.

Traditionally Wesleyan (Georgia)

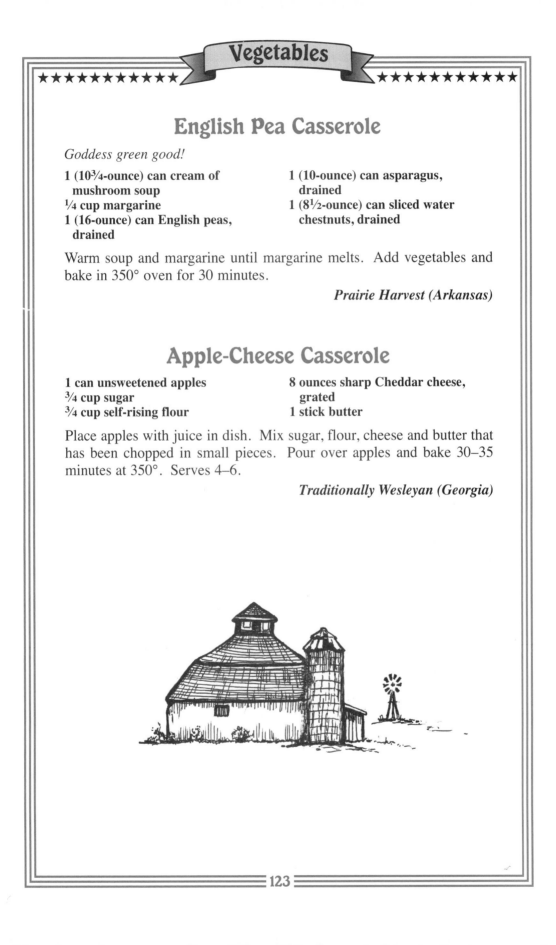

★★★★★★★★★★★   ★★★★★★★★★★★

Broiled Grapefruit

½ grapefruit per serving   Brown sugar

Slice grapefruit in half; cut out center, remove seeds; run knife around edge to loosen membrane. Sprinkle brown sugar on top. Broil until sugar melts. Serve warm with cherry in center.

Home Cooking in a Hurry (Tennessee)

★ **Even Easier**: Or microwave about 30 seconds on HIGH.

Broiled Peaches

Good with cured ham or pork.

FOR EACH SERVING:
1 peach   Dash cinnamon
1 teaspoon brown sugar   ½ teaspoon margarine

Peel fresh peaches, halve and remove pits. Place in shallow baking dish. To each half add 1 teaspoon brown sugar, sprinkle with cinnamon and top with ½ teaspoon of margarine. Broil until mixture bubbles and peaches are lightly browned. Serve warm.

The Peach Sampler (South Carolina)

Hot Fruit Salad

1 (17-ounce) can fruit for salad,   1 (16-ounce) can applesauce
  drained   ½ cup light brown sugar
1 (17-ounce) can apricots, drained   3 tablespoons butter or margarine

Slightly stir above ingredients and place in 350° oven for about one hour. Delicious with meats. Serves 10–12.

Kitchen Prescriptions (Missouri)

★ **Editor's Extra:** Add a teaspoon of curry powder if you want to spice it up.

★★★★★★★★★★★★ ★★★★★★★★★★★★

Baked Pineapple

This is a long-time family favorite to go with ham, especially at Easter.

**1 (14½-ounce) can crushed
   pineapple**
½ cup sugar
2 tablespoons cornstarch

2 eggs
½ teaspoon cinnamon
1–2 tablespoons butter

Mix first 4 ingredients well. Place in greased casserole. Sprinkle with cinnamon; dot with butter. Bake until firm, 30 minutes at 350°. Easy to make and delicious. Serves 6.

Fabulous Favorites (California)

Baked Pineapple

**1 (20-ounce) can pineapple chunks,
   drained (reserve juice)**
1 cup semi-sharp cheese, grated
1 cup sugar

2 tablespoons flour
1 cup dry bread crumbs
2 tablespoons butter

Put pineapple and cheese into a glass baking dish. Combine pineapple juice, sugar and flour in a saucepan. Heat to near boiling. Pour over cheese and pineapple. Blend crumbs with butter; sprinkle on top. Bake in 350° oven for 20–25 minutes. Serves 6–8.

Blew Centennial Bon-Appetit (Great Plains)

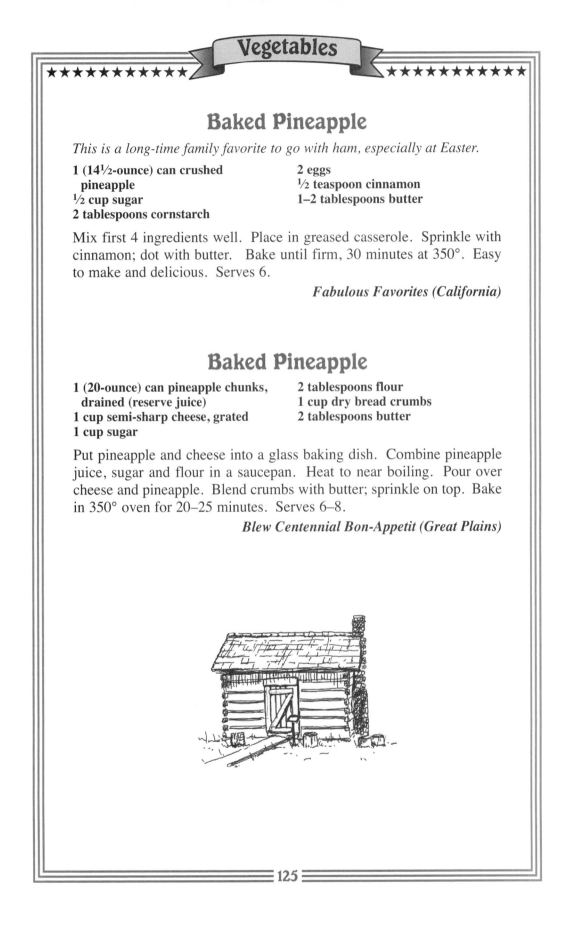

★★★★★★★★★★★   ★★★★★★★★★★★

Holiday Cran-Apples

3 cups apples, peeled and chopped   **⅓ cup white sugar**
2 cups fresh cranberries   **⅓ cup brown sugar**

TOPPING:
1 stick margarine, melted   **⅓ cup flour**
1 cup brown sugar   **⅓ cup chopped nuts**
1 cup oatmeal

Combine apples, cranberries and sugars; pour into a greased 9x13-inch Pyrex dish. Combine topping ingredients and pour over cranberry-apple mixture. Bake in a 350° oven for 45 minutes. Delicious with turkey and ham. Serves 8–10.

Seasoned with Sunshine (Florida)

This bronze cowboy (titled "Welcome Sundown") at the National Cowboy and Western Heritage Museum in Oklahoma City seems to hide his head at the pitiful renditions Barbara and Gwen are doing of his pose.

★★★★★★★★★★★★   ★★★★★★★★★★★★

15-Minute Creamy Fettucine Alfredo

Cook the fettucine first, the rest is a snap!

**1 (8-ounce) package cream cheese,
    cubed**
¾ cup Parmesan cheese

½ cup margarine
½ cup milk
8 ounces fettucine, cooked, drained

In large saucepan, stir together cream cheese, Parmesan cheese, margarine, and milk over low heat until smooth. Add fettucine; toss lightly. Serves 4.

A Taste of Twin Pines (Indiana)

Fettuccine Alfredo

3 tablespoons butter
2 tablespoons flour
Cayenne pepper, to taste (optional)
2 minced garlic cloves

1½ cups whole milk
¾ cup grated Parmesan cheese
½ cup grated Romano cheese
1 (7-ounce) package noodles, cooked

In saucepan, heat butter until melted. Add flour to make roux. Add cayenne pepper, garlic, milk, and cheeses. When mixture becomes thick and creamy, pour over hot noodles. Serves 6.

Titonka Centennial Cookbook (Iowa)

Macho Fettucine

8 ounces fettucine
1 pound Italian sausage

1 can cream of chicken soup
2 cups sour cream

Cook fettucine and drain. Cut up Italian sausage into small pieces. Brown sausage over medium-high heat for about 8 minutes. Place on paper towel to drain grease. Mix all ingredients together. Put into a large Pyrex dish. Bake 30 minutes at 350°. Serves 4–6.

The College Cookbook FOR Students BY Students (Texas II)

★ **Editor's Extra:** Fettuccine can be spelled several different ways, but all of these recipes spell it "delicious."

★★★★★★★★★★★ ★★★★★★★★★★★

Garlic Spaghetti with Broccoli

½ pound (2 sticks) butter
1 box frozen chopped broccoli or
  ½ bunch broccoli, washed and cut
  in pieces
1 teaspoon salt

½ teaspoon pepper
2 tablespoons garlic powder
1 (16-ounce) package thin spaghetti
Parmesan cheese, grated (optional)

Melt butter in large skillet. Add broccoli, salt, pepper, and garlic powder, and simmer until broccoli is cooked, but firm.

Cook spaghetti in boiling water according to package directions. After spaghetti is cooked, drained and rinsed, add to the broccoli mixture and stir. Add more salt, pepper or garlic powder if desired. Top with Parmesan cheese. Serves 6–8. (Pictured on cover.)

College Survival Cookbook (Pennsylvania)

★ **Even Easier**: Try spraying your colander with vegetable spray—pasta slips right out, and colander is lots easier to clean.

Zucchini with Noodles & Basil

4 ounces egg noodles
1 clove garlic, minced
2 medium zucchini, thinly sliced

2 tablespoons margarine or butter
1 teaspoon crushed basil
¼ teaspoon pepper (optional)

Cook noodles. Sauté garlic and zucchini in butter or margarine until zucchini is tender, about 5–10 minutes. Stir in basil and pepper. Drain noodles and toss with zucchini. Serve immediately. Serves 4.

The Parkview Way to Vegetarian Cooking (New England)

Omelets with Ramen

1 package any flavor Ramen noodles	½ cup ham, chopped
1 tablespoon margarine	¼ cup onion, chopped
3 eggs, beaten	¼ cup green peppers, chopped

Cook noodles and drain. Add seasoning packet. Melt margarine in skillet and add beaten eggs. Fold in other ingredients. Cook until lightly brown. Serves 2–4.

101 Ways to Make Ramen Noodles (Colorado)

Easy Pasta Bake

1 pound ground beef	½ cup Parmesan cheese
1 (8-ounce) package mostacciolli, cooked	1 (8-ounce) package shredded mozzarella cheese
1 (30-ounce) jar spaghetti sauce	

Brown ground beef in large skillet; drain. Stir in cooked pasta, spaghetti sauce, and Parmesan cheese. Spoon into 9x13-inch baking dish. Top with mozzarella cheese. Bake at 375° for 20 minutes. Serves 8–10.

Taste of Coffeyville (Great Plains)

Vermicelli

So easy and always a big hit.

1 small (7- to 8-ounce) package
  vermicelli
1 stick butter (not margarine)
2 cans beef broth

1 can mushrooms
1 tablespoon soy sauce
1 or 2 chopped green onions

Lightly brown broken pieces of vermicelli in butter. Add beef broth, mushrooms, and soy sauce. Simmer until liquid is absorbed. Add green onions just before noodles are done.

If It Tastes Good, Who Cares? I (Great Plains)

Tarragon Shrimp Spaghetti

1 clove garlic, minced
1½ tablespoons olive oil
½ cup white wine
½ cup chicken broth
½ teaspoon lemon juice

¼ teaspoon tarragon
2 teaspoons butter
1 cup uncooked shrimp
Cooked spaghetti or linguini

Sauté garlic in olive oil. Add wine, broth, lemon juice, and tarragon. Blend together, then add butter and shrimp. Cover and cook for about 3 minutes or until shrimp have just turned pink. Do not overcook or the delicate flavor will be lost. Serve shrimp sauce over spaghetti or linguini. Serves 2.

Apalachicola Cookbook (Florida)

Tarragon is one of the most distinguished culinary herbs, known for its distinctive anise-like flavor. Tarragon has two varieties: Russian and French tarragon. French tarragon is the variety cultivated in the U.S. Freshly cut leaves are dried within hours to preserve their color. Care should be taken when using tarragon since its assertiveness can easily dominate other flavors.

Sausage-Rice Casserole

1 pound hot pork sausage
¼ teaspoon pepper
1 cup chopped celery
1 cup chopped green pepper
1 cup chopped onion

2 (11-ounce) cans chicken rice soup
1 soup can water
1 (8-ounce) can mushrooms and
   liquid
1¼ cups uncooked rice

Cook sausage until crumbly. Add pepper and chopped celery, green pepper, and onion. Cover and steam until tender. Add remaining ingredients and bake in a large casserole dish for 45–60 minutes at 350°. Stir once while baking so top will not dry out. Makes 8 large portions.

Cook Book (California)

★ **Even Easier**: Use a bag of frozen sauté vegetables (chopped onion, celery, and green pepper) for a hastier fix.

Infallible Rice

Serve this and listen to the compliments.

1 medium onion, minced
2 tablespoons butter

1 cup long grain raw white rice
2 cups chicken broth (hot)

Sauté onion in butter until transparent. Add rice and hot broth. Bring to a boil on top of range. Cover and place in 325° oven for 20 minutes. Serves 4 hungry or 6 polite people.

Pulaski Heights Baptist Church Cookbook (Arkansas)

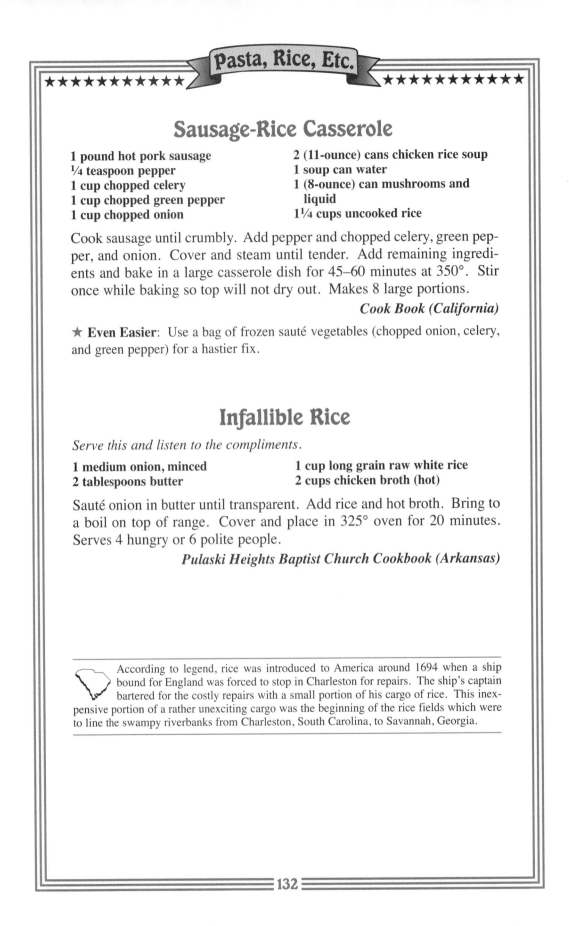

According to legend, rice was introduced to America around 1694 when a ship bound for England was forced to stop in Charleston for repairs. The ship's captain bartered for the costly repairs with a small portion of his cargo of rice. This inexpensive portion of a rather unexciting cargo was the beginning of the rice fields which were to line the swampy riverbanks from Charleston, South Carolina, to Savannah, Georgia.

Rice and Sour Cream Casserole

3 cups sour cream
2 cans green chiles, drained and chopped
3 cups cooked rice (measure exactly)
Salt and pepper
¾ pound Monterey Jack cheese, sliced
½ cup Cheddar cheese

Mix sour cream and chopped chiles. Layer rice, salt, pepper, sour cream mixture and Jack cheese (two layers of each) in buttered casserole. Top with Cheddar cheese. Bake in 350° oven until hot and bubbly, 30 minutes to one hour. Serves 6.

Our Daily Bread (Great Plains)

★ **Editor's Extra:** One regular size boil-in-bag rice packet yields 2 cups cooked; one extra large bag yields 3 cups cooked.

Rice with Raisins and Pine Nuts

Very nice side dish with chicken and veal.

2 tablespoons butter, divided
3 tablespoons chopped green onion
½ teaspoon finely minced garlic
1 cup rice
½ cup golden raisins
1½ cups chicken broth
¼ cup pine nuts

Melt one tablespoon butter in saucepan and add onion and garlic. Cook, stirring until soft. Add the rice and stir. Add raisins and chicken broth and bring to boil. Cover and let simmer exactly 17 minutes. Stir to fluff rice while blending in the pine nuts and remaining butter. Serves 4.

Some Enchanted Eating (Michigan)

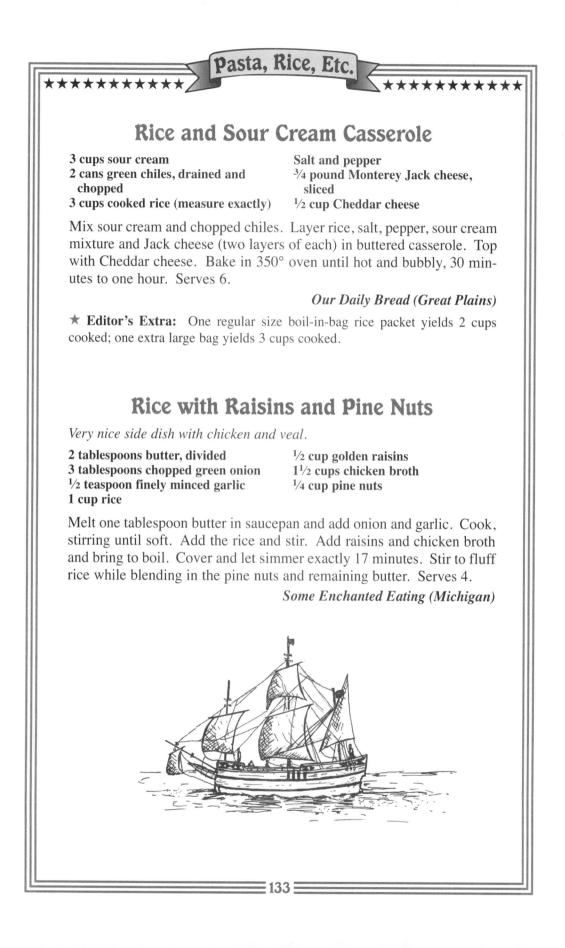

Baked Rice

½ cup raw rice
⅛ cup chopped green pepper
⅛ cup chopped onion

1 (4-ounce) can mushrooms
½ cup melted butter
1 (10¾-ounce) can beef consommé

Add all ingredients in order into a 1½-quart casserole. Stir and bake uncovered at 350° for one hour. Serves 4.

A Heritage of Good Tastes (Virginia)

Tuna and Rice Quickie

Filling, pretty and good!

1 (10¾-ounce) can cream of
  mushroom soup
1 (5-ounce) can evaporated milk
2½ cups cooked rice
2 (7-ounce) cans tuna, drained and
  flaked

¼ pound processed American
  cheese, grated
¼ cup finely chopped onion
¼ cup finely chopped pimiento
2 dashes Tabasco

In large mixing bowl, combine all ingredients, mixing well. Turn into greased 1½-quart baking dish. Bake 30 minutes at 350° or until hot throughout. Yields 6 servings.

Cook 'em Horns: The Quickbook (Texas II)

Easy Rice Casserole

1 cup Uncle Ben's long-grain rice
1 (7-ounce) can sliced mushrooms
  (do not drain)

1 can French onion soup
1 can sliced water chestnuts, drained
⅔ stick butter

Mix first 4 ingredients. Top with butter pats and bake uncovered for one hour at 350°.

Palate Pleasers (Tennessee)

LeaRaye's Mushroom Rice

2 cups uncooked rice
4 cups chicken or beef broth
1 stick butter

½ cup chopped green onions
1 clove garlic, minced
1 pound mushrooms, sliced

Cook rice in broth. While rice is cooking, sauté green onions and garlic in butter in a large skillet until tender. Add mushrooms and continue to cook until mushrooms are tender. Add mushroom mixture to warm rice and mix well. Cover and let stand 10–15 minutes to let flavor develop before serving. Serves 6–8.

Nun Better (Louisiana II)

Rice and Chile Bake

Great as a dip—pass the Tostitos!

1 cup rice
2 cups sour cream
1 cup green chile, chopped

1 cup Monterey Jack cheese, cubed
1 teaspoon salt

Cook rice according to package directions, undercooking slightly. Combine all ingredients and place in a greased casserole. Bake at 350° for 15–20 minutes or until cheese melts and mixture is thoroughly heated. Serves 6–8.

Fiesta Mexicana (New Mexico)

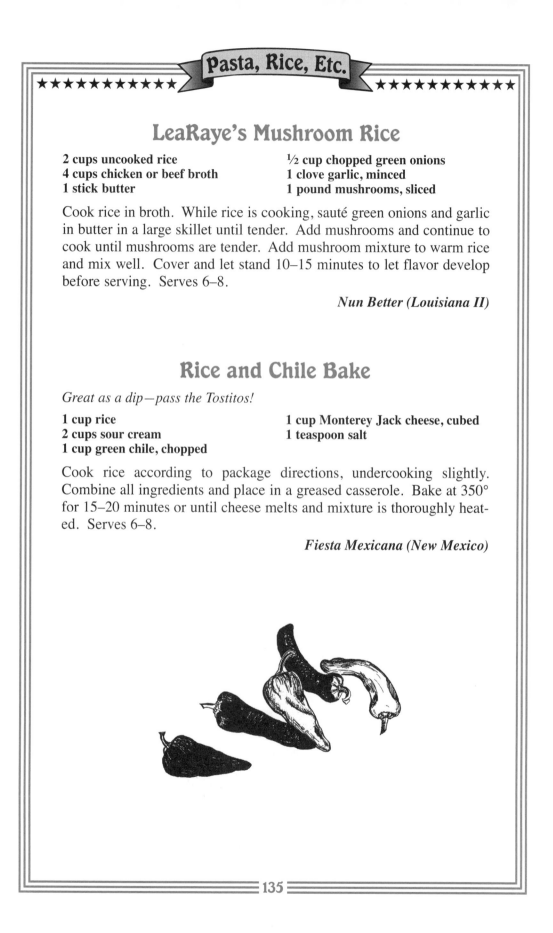

Hot Pepper Rice

You may omit the jalapeño pepper if you desire a milder dish.

3 cups cooked long-grain rice
1 cup sour cream
1 (4-ounce) can chopped green
  chiles, drained
1 medium fresh jalapeño pepper,
  seeded and diced (optional)

1 (8-ounce) package Monterey Jack
  cheese, shredded and divided
½ cup shredded Cheddar cheese

Combine rice, sour cream, green chiles, and jalapeño pepper. Layer half of rice mixture in a lightly greased 7x11x2-inch baking dish; top with half of the Monterey Jack cheese. Repeat procedure and sprinkle with Cheddar cheese. Bake at 350° for 15 minutes or until cheese melts and casserole is heated through. Yields 6–8 servings.

Cooking with Mr. "G" and Friends (Louisiana II)

★ **Even Easier**: Try substituting hot pepper cheese for the jalapeño pepper and Jack cheese. Olé spicy!

Shrimp Fried Rice

3 green onions, tops included,
  chopped
1 onion, chopped
½ cup butter
3 cups cold cooked rice
2 eggs, beaten

4 ounces water chestnuts, drained
  and sliced
Soy sauce, to taste
1 (7¾-ounce) can tiny shrimp,
  drained and rinsed

Sauté onions in butter in wok or large frying pan over moderately high heat. Stir in rice, mixing until heated and coated with butter. (Add more butter, if necessary.) With wooden spoon, make a path to bottom of pan; pour in eggs and gently scramble. Mix throughout rice. Add water chestnuts and sprinkle liberally with soy sauce to taste. Gently fold in shrimp and heat. Serves 4.

Company's Coming (Missouri)

Brown, white, short, long, wild, cultivated . . . did you know there are nearly 80,000 varieties of rice? Rice is mankind's largest food crop. Each of us in the U.S. eats about 18 pounds of rice per year. It grows once a year and mostly in Texas, Arkansas, Louisiana, Mississippi, Missouri, and California.

★★★★★★★★★★★★   ★★★★★★★★★★★★

Easy Brown Rice

1 stick butter or margarine
1 cup raw rice

2 (10½-ounce) cans beef consommé
¼ cup Parmesan cheese

Melt butter or margarine in 3-quart casserole dish. Add raw rice. Pour 2 cans beef consommé over rice. Sprinkle with generous amount of Parmesan cheese on top. Bake 45 minutes at 350°. Check at baking time; may need more moisture if baked longer.

Quasquicentennial / St. Olaf of Bode (Iowa)

Spanish Rice

2 tablespoons oil
1 large onion, chopped
½ medium bell pepper, chopped
2 cups long grain rice

1 (16-ounce) can tomatoes
3 cups water
1 teaspoon vinegar
Salt and pepper, to taste

Sauté onion and bell pepper in oil until tender. Add rice and fry until lightly brown, stirring occasionally. Add tomatoes and fry a little longer. Add water, vinegar, salt and pepper, and cover. Let cook over low fire until fluffy, stirring occasionally. Serves 8.

Variation: Add 2 tablespoons capers in liquid.

Recipes and Reminiscences of New Orleans II (Louisiana)

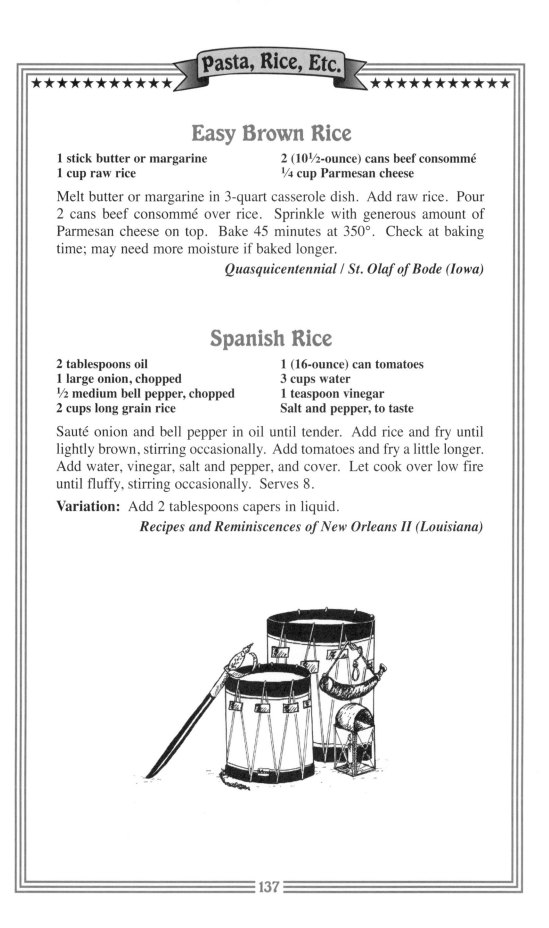

Ham Casserole

1 (12-ounce) package noodles
1 cup whole kernel corn, drained
½ cup chopped green pepper
⅓ cup milk

1 cup chopped cooked ham
¾ cup diced cheese
1 can cream of mushroom soup

Cook noodles according to package directions. Combine well with remaining ingredients. Turn into greased baking dish. Bake covered at 375° for 45 minutes. Serves 6–8.

Celebrating Iowa (Iowa)

★ **Even Easier**: Instead of baking in the oven, microwave it in a fraction of the time. Spoon out a 2-serving portion into a small covered container and it only takes 5 minutes. Microwaving the whole casserole will take a bit longer, stirring at minute intervals.

Chicken Quiche

The word is . . . yum!

1 box Stove Top Stuffing Mix
1 chicken breast, cooked and diced
  (1 cup)
½ pound Swiss cheese, grated (1 cup)

4 eggs, beaten
1 (5½-ounce) can evaporated milk
Salt and onion to taste

Prepare stuffing mix as directed. Press into a 9-inch pie plate and pre-bake at 400° for 10 minutes until brown. Spread onto stuffing the chicken and cheese. Mix and add eggs, milk, salt, and onion. Bake at 350° for 25–30 minutes or until center is set. Serves 4.

The Bloomin' Cookbook (Pennsylvania)

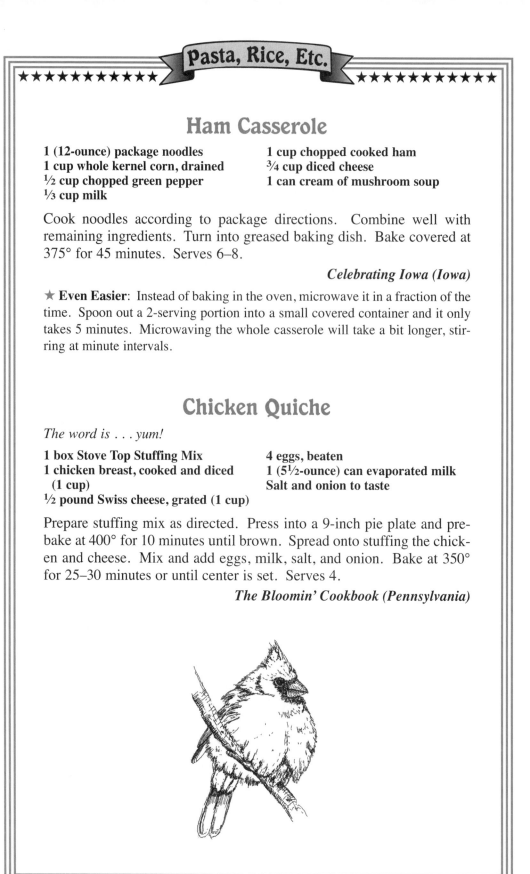

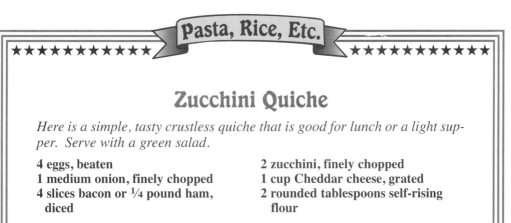

Zucchini Quiche

Here is a simple, tasty crustless quiche that is good for lunch or a light supper. Serve with a green salad.

4 eggs, beaten
1 medium onion, finely chopped
4 slices bacon or ¼ pound ham,
  diced

2 zucchini, finely chopped
1 cup Cheddar cheese, grated
2 rounded tablespoons self-rising
  flour

Preheat oven to 375°. In a bowl, combine all ingredients. The mixture will be fairly thick. Grease a 9-inch quiche or pie dish. Pour the mixture into the dish and smooth over. Bake in oven for 30 minutes. Serves 4.

The Original Philadelphia Neighborhood Cookbook (Pennsylvania)

Chile Pie

Not really a "pie," this is more like a quiche without a crust. Delectable as a main dish for lunch, it could also make a light supper. And how about doubling the recipe, making it in a rectangular baking dish, and cutting in small squares to serve at a party?

4–6 whole mild green chiles
1 cup grated Jack or longhorn cheese
4 eggs

1 cup scalded half-and-half or
  evaporated milk
½ teaspoon garlic salt

Line a buttered 8- or 9-inch pie pan with chiles (fresh, canned or frozen). Sprinkle with the cheese. Beat eggs and combine with half-and-half and garlic salt. Pour over cheese. Bake at 325° for about 40 minutes or until the custard has set. Cut in wedges and serve. Serves 4.

The Best from New Mexico Kitchens (New Mexico)

Around 1900, Wilbur Scoville invented a test to rate the heat level of chiles. The habanero is the hottest chile pepper known to date with a SHU (Scoville Heat Unit) rating of about 250,000. The popular jalapeño is mild in comparison, with a rating of only 9,000 SHU.

Cheese Enchiladas, Pronto!

1 dozen corn tortillas
1 pound shredded Cheddar cheese
  (4 cups)

½ cup chopped onion
2 (10-ounce) can enchilada sauce or
  chili hot dog sauce

Wrap 6 tortillas in a damp paper towel. Sandwich between two salad plates and microwave on HIGH 45 seconds. Place ⅓ cup cheese and a sprinkle of onions on each tortilla and roll up. Place seam-side down in a 2-quart rectangular dish. Repeat for remaining tortillas. Pour enchilada sauce over all. (If using chili hot dog sauce, microwave on HIGH 3 minutes so it will pour over enchiladas.) Sprinkle with any remaining cheese and onions. Cover and microwave on 70% (MEDIUM-HIGH) 5–6 minutes. Serves 4–6.

Note: If making half of a recipe, microwave 3 minutes on 70% power.

Microwave Know-How (Texas)

Quick Enchilada Casserole

1 (9-ounce) package corn chips
1 large onion, peeled and chopped

1 (1-pound) can chili without beans
Grated American cheese

Place corn chips in bottom of a greased casserole. Top with onions. Pour in chili. Cover with cheese, using as much as desired. Bake at 375° for 15–20 minutes, or until cheese is melted and casserole is well heated. Serves 2–4.

Down-Home Texas Cooking (Texas II)

Sausage Pilaf

A meal in a dish!

1 pound hot pork sausage
1 cup chopped celery
½ cup chopped onion
½ cup chopped bell pepper

1 cup cream of mushroom soup
3 cups cooked rice
½ cup chopped cashew nuts or
   peanuts (optional)

Brown sausage, drain; add celery, onion, and pepper. Cook 3 to 5 minutes. Stir in soup and rice. Pour into a 1-quart casserole. Cover. Bake 20 minutes at 350°. Remove from oven, sprinkle nuts on top and return to oven uncovered for 10 minutes longer. Serves 6.

Prairie Harvest (Arkansas)

★ **Even Easier:** This is quicker with boil-in-a-bag or Minute Rice.

Instant Pizza

6 English muffins
1 (4-ounce) can tomato sauce
½ cup Parmesan cheese, grated

1 teaspoon oregano
48 thin slices pepperoni
12 thin slices mozzarella cheese

Slice muffins in half. Toast muffins until light brown. Spread tomato sauce on each half. Sprinkle with Parmesan cheese and oregano. Place 4 slices pepperoni on each. Top with mozzarella cheese. Place on cookie sheet or aluminum foil and bake at 350° until cheese bubbles, approximately 10 minutes. Makes 12.

Note: Bagels may be substituted for English muffins.

College Survival Cookbook (Pennsylvania)

Red Beans and Rice

Easy-do, all-in-a-pan delicious!

1 pound ground beef
1 large onion, chopped
1 large bell pepper, chopped
1 tablespoon chili powder
2 teaspoons salt

1 (16-ounce) can tomotoes or
 tomato juice
1 cup water
1½ cups uncooked rice
1 can red kidney beans, undrained

Brown meat with onion and pepper. Add remaining ingredients except rice and beans, and simmer for 15 minutes. Remove from heat and pour into 9x13-inch pan. Evenly distribute 1½ cups uncooked rice and 1 can red kidney beans in mixture. Cover and bake at 350° for 1 hour. Take out and stir, cover, and return to oven for another 15 minutes. Serves 8.

Note: If you use a smaller can of tomatoes than 16 ounces, (can sizes sometimes "shrink" from when the recipe was conceived), add ¼ cup water.

The Farmer's Daughters (Arkansas)

★ **Editor's Extra:** This is more like a red beans and rice pilaf, but call it what you will, I call it a pan full of flavor!

Poultry

★★★★ ★★★★

Little towns and places are always so fascinating, begging us to pull off the highway. We stopped in Possum Trot, Kentucky, and were directed to this quaint little gift shop in Aurora on the Land Between the Lakes. We are never disappointed in local culture and the people we meet.

★★★★★★★★★★★★ ★★★★★★★★★★★★

Chicken Squares

1 (3-ounce) package cream cheese,
  softened
1 teaspoon melted margarine
1 tablespoon milk

1 teaspoon onion flakes
2 cups cooked and cubed chicken or
  ham
2 tubes refrigerated crescent rolls

Mix together cream cheese and next 4 ingredients; add to chicken. Put one tablespoon chicken mixture on each crescent square and press. Roll up and bake at 350° about 18 minutes. Serves 8.

Look What's Cooking at C.A.M.D.E.N. (Wisconsin)

★ **Even Easier**: Canned chicken or ham works just fine!

Broiled Apricot Chicken

Tantalizing taste.

1 cup apricot nectar
3 tablespoons brown sugar
1 teaspoon grated orange peel
2 tablespoons catsup
2 tablespoons cornstarch

1 tablespoon horseradish mustard
½ teaspoon salt
6 boneless chicken breasts
1 can apricot halves (drained)

Preheat broiler. Combine apricot nectar, brown sugar, orange peel, catsup, cornstarch, horseradish mustard, and salt in saucepan. Stir until cornstarch is fully dissolved. Bring to a boil and hold for 1 minute. Remove from heat.

Broil chicken breasts 4–5 minutes on each side. Brush often with apricot sauce during broiling and before serving. Garnish with apricot halves. Makes 6 servings.

The French-Icarian Persimmon Tree Cookbook (Illinois)

★ **Editor's Extra:** A little on the "y" side of easy, but once you taste it, you'll know "y" we included it.

A recent study at the University of Massachusetts found that recipes using canned ingredients are comparable in nutritional value and taste appeal to those made with fresh or frozen items. The findings send a strong message to people looking for convenient ways to eat healthy.

Lemon Teriyaki Glazed Chicken

½ cup lemon juice
½ cup soy sauce
¼ cup sugar
3 tablespoons brown sugar
2 tablespoons water

4 cloves garlic, minced
¾ teaspoon ground ginger
6–8 chicken breasts, strips, or
  chicken thighs

In skillet, combine all ingredients except chicken. Cook over medium heat 3–4 minutes. Add chicken. Simmer 30 minutes or until thoroughly cooked.

To Tayla with TLC (Great Plains)

★ **Editor's Extra:** This is so tasty, you'll want to serve it over rice or angel hair pasta to get every bit of this terrific flavor.

Hawaiian Chicken

10 ounces frozen breaded chicken
  tenders
1 (10-ounce) jar sweet and sour sauce

1 (8¾-ounce) can pineapple tidbits
1 (16-ounce) package frozen
  oriental vegetables

Prepare chicken tenders according to package directions. Place tenders in large skillet. Add sweet and sour sauce, pineapple, and vegetables. Heat, cover and simmer 25 minutes or until vegetables are tender. Serve over rice.

More of the Four Ingredient Cookbook (Texas II)

Lo Mein Ramen

1 tablespoon oil
1 tablespoon soy sauce
1 package chicken Ramen noodles
1 pound chicken breast strips

½ cup sliced onions
½ cup chopped green peppers
¼ cup chopped carrots

In skillet mix oil, soy sauce and ½ seasoning packet. Add chicken; brown. Boil noodles and drain. Add vegetables to chicken; cook until tender. Add noodles and cook on medium for 5 minutes, stirring constantly. Serves 2–4.

101 Ways to Make Ramen Noodles (Colorado)

Stir-Fry Chicken and Rice

3 tablespoons margarine
1 pound stir-fry chicken
1 medium onion, chopped
1 pound fresh mushrooms, sliced or
  1 (8-ounce) can, drained
1 (14-ounce) can tomato chunks

2 tablespoons Worchestershire
  sauce
1 teaspoon salt
¼ teaspoon black pepper
2 cups Minute Rice
2 cups water

In large skillet, heat margarine, chicken, onion, mushrooms, and tomatoes. Cook on medium heat until chicken is tender (20 minutes). Add Worcestershire sauce, salt, and pepper.

In a separate pan, prepare 2 cups of rice with 2 cups of water. Add cooked rice to chicken mixture. Heat for 2 minutes. Serves 6.

CEASRA of Slippery Rock Cookbook (Pennsylvania)

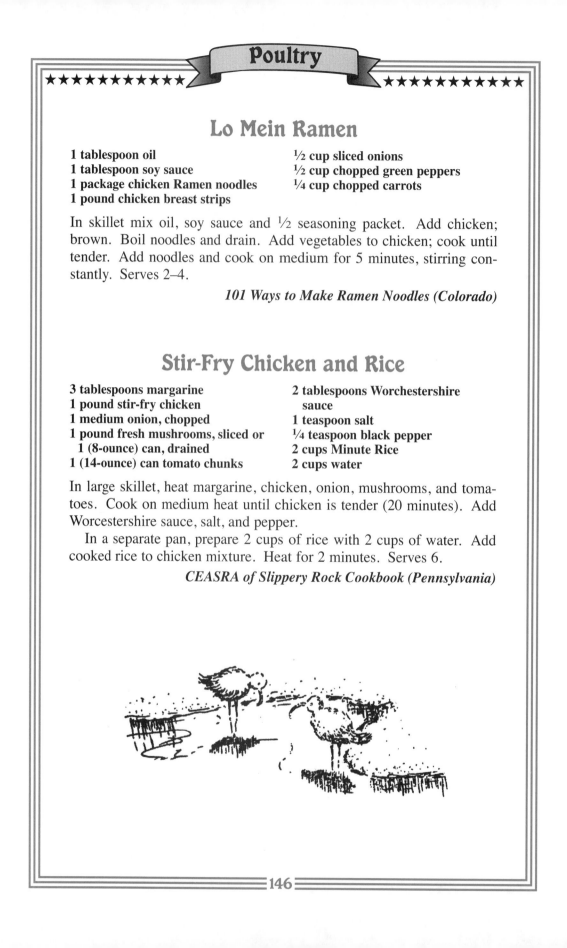

Orange and Chicken Cashew

Superbly simple . . . simply superb!

4 chicken breasts (6 ounces)　　　¼ cup butter
¼ cup flour　　　　　　　　　　1 cup orange juice
1 teaspoon salt　　　　　　　　　¼ cup toasted cashews or almonds
1 teaspoon paprika

Dust chicken lightly in flour mixed with salt and paprika. Sauté in butter until golden brown (turn only once). Add orange juice; cover and cook over low heat for 20 minutes. Uncover, remove chicken to a serving dish. Reduce liquid to a thickened sauce. Pour over chicken, sprinkle with nuts, and serve at once with rice. Serves 4.

Dixie Cook Book V (Arkansas)

★ **Even Easier**: If you don't want to wait for the liquid to reduce, remove chicken and stir a teaspoon of cornstarch into the sauce to thicken.

Spicy Gazebo Springs Chicken

1 pound boneless chicken breasts,　　¼ cup slivered orange peel
　skinned　　　　　　　　　　　1 clove garlic, minced
2 tablespoons corn oil　　　　　　¾ teaspoon ground ginger

Thinly slice chicken. In a wok or large skillet, heat corn oil over medium-high heat. Add chicken, a few slices at a time. Stir-fry 3 minutes or until browned, removing slices that are cooked. Return all chicken to wok. Add orange peel, garlic, and ginger. Stir-fry one minute.

SAUCE:
2 tablespoons cornstarch　　　　　⅓ cup orange marmalade
½ cup dry sherry　　　　　　　　¾ teaspoon dried crushed red
1 cup chicken broth　　　　　　　　pepper
⅓ cup soy sauce

Stir together sauce ingredients in a small bowl. Stir into chicken. Stirring constantly, bring to a boil over medium heat and boil several minutes. Serve over rice or pasta. Serves 4.

Steamboat Entertains (Colorado)

★ **Even Easier**: For quicker fixin', use boneless chicken tenders.

Lemony Chicken

Easy and always good.

3 whole boneless, skinless chicken
  breasts (6 halves)
¼ cup flour
½ teaspoon salt
⅛ teaspoon pepper

3 tablespoons butter or margarine
1 chicken bouillon cube
1 cup water
1 large lemon, halved

Pound chicken to ¼-inch thick. Mix flour, salt and pepper; pat onto both sides of chicken. Reserve remaining flour mixture.

In large skillet over medium-high heat in margarine, cook 3 chicken pieces at a time until lightly browned on both sides. Remove chicken to a plate. Reduce heat to low. Into drippings in skillet, stir reserved flour mixture; add bouillon, water and juice of half lemon, stirring to loosen bits.

Return chicken to skillet. Thinly slice lemon half and top chicken with slices; cover and simmer 5 minutes. Serves 6.

The Marlborough Meetinghouse Cookbook (New England)

Chicken Provençal

Definitely a family favorite!

¼ cup Italian-style bread crumbs
2 tablespoons Parmesan cheese
2 skinless, boneless chicken breasts,
  cut in half
1 tablespoon cornstarch

1 (14-ounce) can Italian-style
  tomatoes (with onion and green
  pepper), chopped
1 cup mushrooms, sliced and
  sautéed (optional)

Mix together bread crumbs and Parmesan cheese. Spread mixture on a plate. Roll chicken breasts in mixture until coated. Spray large skillet with vegetable oil cooking spray and heat to medium. Cook chicken for 5 minutes, then turn and cook another 5 minutes, or until thoroughly cooked. Remove chicken from skillet and keep warm.

Mix together cornstarch and tomatoes in skillet; cook on medium heat and stir constantly for about 4 minutes. Place chicken breasts on individual plates and spoon over tomato mixture. Top with sautéed mushrooms, if desired. Serve with a green salad and a side dish of pasta. Serves 4.

Lowfat, Homestyle Cookbook (Colorado)

Pecan Chicken

This recipe is a real winner!

1 cup flour
1 cup ground pecans
¼ cup sesame seeds
1 tablespoon paprika
1½ teaspoons salt
⅛ teaspoon pepper

1 egg, beaten
1 cup buttermilk
8 (5-ounce) chicken breasts, boned
  and skinned
⅓ cup butter
¼ cup coarsely chopped pecans

Combine first 6 ingredients. Mix together egg and buttermilk. Dip breasts in egg mixture and then coat well in flour mixture. Melt butter in baking dish. Place breasts in dish, turning once to coat with butter. Sprinkle with coarsely chopped pecans. Bake in a preheated 350° oven for 30 minutes. Do not overcook. Serve with cream sauce, if desired. Serves 8.

The Peach Tree Tea Room Cookbook (Texas II)

Coca-Cola Chicken

1 chicken, cut-up
Salt and pepper
1 cup ketchup

1 cup Coca-Cola
1 tablespoon Worcestershire sauce

Place chicken in large frying pan or electric skillet; add salt and pepper. Mix ketchup, Coca-Cola, and Worcestershire sauce together and pour over chicken. Simmer for one hour covered, turning once during cooking time. Serve with rice. Serves 6–8.

Canopy Roads (Florida)

★ **Editor's Extra:** This works beautifully in a slow-cooker on low for 6–8 hours. Great for appetizer wings—add Tabasco or red pepper if you like hot wings.

Coca-Cola was invented in Atlanta, Georgia, in 1886. The name "Coca-Cola" was suggested by inventor Dr. John S. Pemberton's bookkeeper, Frank Robinson, who penned the name in the flowing script that is so famous today. During the first year, sales at Jacob's Pharmacy in Atlanta averaged nine drinks a day, totaling fifty dollars for the year. Since expenses were seventy dollars, Dr. Pemberton took a loss. Today Coca-Cola products are consumed at the rate of one billion drinks per year.

★★★★★★★★★★★ ★★★★★★★★★★★

Chicken Piccata

An extraordinary dish made from ordinary ingredients.

1 egg	**4 chicken breast halves, skinned**
3 tablespoons lemon juice, divided	**and boned**
¼ cup all-purpose flour	**¼ cup butter or margarine, melted**
⅛ teaspoon garlic powder	**2 chicken bouillon cubes dissolved**
Dash paprika	**in ½ cup boiling water**

Beat egg with 1 tablespoon lemon juice. Combine flour, garlic powder and paprika. Dip chicken in egg mixture, then in flour. Brown both sides of chicken in butter. Add bouillon and 2 tablespoons lemon juice to chicken. Cover and simmer 20 minutes or until tender. Serves 4. Freezes well.

Stir Crazy! (South Carolina)

Chicken Piccata

The low-fat version of a classic dish.

1 pound boneless chicken breasts,	**Butter Buds Mix equivalent to 6**
thinly sliced	**tablespoons butter**
¼ cup flour	**3 tablespoons lemon juice**
½ teaspoon salt	**½ cup white wine**
¼ teaspoon pepper	**2 tablespoons chopped fresh parsley**

Coat chicken with flour and pan-fry quickly in large nonstick skillet, turning once. Season with salt and pepper. Combine Butter Buds, lemon juice, and white wine, and add to skillet. Tilt skillet to distribute liquid evenly. Add a small amount of water, if necessary, to prevent juices from becoming too thick. Cover and simmer 20 minutes. Uncover and sprinkle with chopped parsley during the last minute of cooking time. Serves 4.

Per Serving: Cal 217; Fat: 3.8g; Chol: 66mg.

Italian Cooking for a Healthy Heart (Pennsylvania)

Chicken should be kept in the coldest part of the refrigerator, sealed as it comes from the market, and used within 2 or 3 days of purchase. When freezing chicken, it is important to wrap it tightly with the wrap close to the skin, and in this way, no ice crystals will form, and it will maintain top quality for up to a year.

★★★★★★★★★★★ ★★★★★★★★★★★

Chicken á la King in Toast Cups

1 (4-ounce) can mushrooms, drained
¼ cup chopped green pepper
¼ cup butter
¼ cup flour
1 teaspoon salt
⅛ teaspoon pepper
1 cup chicken broth
1 cup milk
1 cup diced cooked chicken
¼ cup chopped pimento

Sauté mushrooms and green pepper in butter. Blend in flour, salt, and pepper. Let bubble. Slowly stir in chicken broth and milk; bring to boiling over low heat, stirring constantly. Boil 1 minute. Add chicken and pimento; heat through. Serve in Toast Cups. Serves 6.

TOAST CUPS:
Cut crusts from day-old bread; brush lightly with melted butter. Press into muffin pans or custard cups. Toast in oven (350°) for 15–30 minutes.

Talk About Good III (Missouri)

Chicken with Lime Butter

3 whole chicken breasts, boned,
  skinned and halved
½ teaspoon salt
½ teaspoon pepper
⅓ cup vegetable oil
Juice of 1 lime
½ cup butter
1 teaspoon minced chives
½ teaspoon dill

Sprinkle chicken with salt and pepper. Heat oil in large skillet over medium heat. Sauté chicken until light brown, about 3 minutes per side. Cover; reduce heat to low. Cook 10–15 minutes or until chicken is tender. Remove chicken to serving platter. Drain oil from skillet. Add lime juice. Cook over low heat until juice begins to boil, about one minute. Add butter, one tablespoon at a time, until butter becomes opaque and forms a thick sauce. Remove from heat. Stir in chives and dill. Spoon sauce over chicken. Serve immediately. Serves 4–6.

A Cleveland Collection (Ohio)

★ **Even Easier**: Boneless, skinless chicken breast halves also come flash frozen. Their advantage is that you can easily remove individual pieces, without thawing the entire package.

Ramen Fajitas

So tasty and easy, this will get lots of encores.

1 package any flavor Ramen noodles	**1 tablespoon oil**
1 skinned chicken breast, cut in strips	**1 cup sliced onions**
½ cup sour cream	**1 cup salsa**

Cook noodles, add flavoring packet, and drain. Brown chicken in skillet in oil. Add onions and salsa; cook over medium heat until onions are tender. Serve over noodles and top with sour cream.

101 Ways to Make Ramen Noodles (Colorado)

Lazy Man's Fried Chicken

2–3 pounds frying chicken, cut up	**1 teaspoon salt**
¼ cup shortening	**1 teaspoon paprika**
¼ cup butter	**¼ teaspoon pepper**
½ cup flour	

Preheat oven to 350°. Wash and dry chicken. In oven, melt shortening and butter in 9x13x2-inch pan. Mix flour, salt, paprika and pepper. Coat chicken thoroughly with flour mixture. Place chicken, skin-side-down, in melted shortening. Bake, uncovered, for 30 minutes. Turn chicken and cook 30 minutes more. Serves 4.

Ship to Shore I (North Carolina)

★ **Editor's Extra:** This "fried chicken" doesn't need constant attention, and my favorite part is that there are no messy spatters to clean up.

Cajun Fried Chicken

⅓ teaspoon red pepper
1 tablespoon yellow mustard
3 ounces Tabasco
4 tablespoons water

1 (2 to 3-pound) fryer, cut up
Salt to taste
1 cup self-rising flour

Combine red pepper, yellow mustard, Tabasco, and water to make a sauce. Salt chicken pieces. Dip chicken in sauce and roll in flour. Fry in hot oil at 400° for about 10 minutes on each side until golden brown. Drain on paper towels. Serves 4.

Louisiana Largesse (Louisiana)

Golden Chicken Nuggets

3 whole chicken breasts, skinned
  and boned
½ cup all-purpose flour
¾ teaspoon salt

2 teaspoons sesame seeds
1 egg, slightly beaten
½ cup water
Hot vegetable oil

Cut chicken into 1–1½-inch pieces. Set aside. Combine the next 5 ingredients. Dip chicken into batter and fry in hot oil (375°) until golden brown. Drain on paper towels. Yields 6–8 servings.

Thoroughbred Fare (South Carolina)

Baked Chicken Nuggets

7–8 boneless chicken breasts,
  uncooked
2 cups fine breadcrumbs
1 cup grated Parmesan cheese

1½ teaspoons salt
1½ tablespoons dried thyme
1½ tablespoons dried basil
1 cup butter, melted

Cut chicken into 1½-inch pieces. Combine next 5 ingredients. Dip chicken in butter, then in breadcrumb mixture. Place on baking sheet. Bake at 400° for 20 minutes. Makes 14–16 pieces.

Easy Does It Cookbook (Texas)

Chicken Nuggets

How can something this fast be this good?

4 chicken breasts   **½ cup melted butter**

CRUMB MIXTURE
½ cup bread crumbs   **¼ cup finely grated Cheddar cheese**
¼ grated Parmesan cheese   **1 teaspoon basil**
¼ teaspoon pepper   **½ teaspoon salt**

Cut chicken into 1½-inch pieces or smaller. Dip chicken in melted butter, then roll in crumb mixture. Place on a cookie sheet covered with lightly greased aluminum foil. Bake in 400° oven for 10–15 minutes.

175th Anniversary Quilt Cookbook (Ohio)

Quick Marinated Chicken

8 chicken breasts   **1 package dry onion soup mix**
Salt and pepper   **1 (10-ounce) jar apricot, peach, or**
1 (8-ounce) bottle dark Wish-bone   **orange marmalade**
** Russian Dressing**

Season breasts with salt and pepper. Combine rest of ingredients. Mix well. Layer half of sauce on bottom of baking dish; layer chicken on top. Pour remaining sauce over chicken. Marinate overnight, or at least 4–5 hours. Bake uncovered at 325° for one hour or until tender. (Pictured on cover.)

The Bonneville House Presents (Arkansas)

★ **Editor's Extra:** Marinating makes it a bit tastier, but if you're ready to cook it, just do it!

★★★★★★★★★★★★ ★★★★★★★★★★★★

Chicken and Stuffing Casserole

4 whole chicken breasts, split,
  skinned and deboned
8 slices Swiss cheese
1 (10¾-ounce) can cream of
  chicken soup (undiluted)

¼ cup white wine
1 cup herb-seasoned stuffing mix
¼ cup melted butter

Place chicken in lightly greased 9x13-inch baking dish. Top with cheese slices. Combine soup and wine; mix well. Spoon sauce over chicken and sprinkle with stuffing mix. Drizzle butter over crumbs. Bake at 350° for 45 minutes, uncovered.

What's Cooking at Trinity (Pennsylvania)

★ **Editor's Extra:** Okay to omit the wine—good either way.

Lazy Day Chicken

2–3 pounds chicken breasts
⅓ cup flour
1 package dry onion soup mix
2–3 sliced carrots
2–3 stalks sliced celery

1 can mushrooms, drained (optional)
½ cup sherry
1 can cream of chicken soup
Paprika

Oil large baking dish. Dredge chicken in flour and place in dish. Sprinkle onion soup over top. Place sliced vegetables on soup. Combine sherry and cream soup. Spread over chicken and vegetables. Dot with paprika. Cover with foil and bake at 350° for at least 1 hour 15 minutes.

A Southern Lady's Spirit (Virginia)

★ **Even Easier:** This only takes 13 minutes to assemble with boneless chicken breasts and canned or baby carrots, and is ready in one hour. The sherry gives it a unique flavor. The sauce is so good, you'll want to serve it over rice. Put some whole potatoes or sweet potatoes in the oven to bake at the same time. Come back in an hour for a super meal.

The average American ate about 81 pounds of chicken in 2000, compared to 28 pounds per person in 1960. At 81 pounds, chicken enjoys the highest per-capita consumption of any of the major meats, with beef in second place at 69 pounds per person on a retail weight basis. Pork is in third place with 52 pounds.

Margaret's Chicken

4–6 chicken breasts, boned and
  skinned
4–6 slices Swiss cheese

1 can cream of chicken soup
½ soup can dry white wine
½ cup slivered almonds

Place chicken breasts in greased baking dish. Cover each breast with a slice of Swiss cheese. Mix soup and wine. Spoon over chicken. Top with slivered almonds. Bake at 350° for one hour.

The What in the World Are We Going to Have for Dinner? Cookbook
(Virginia)

Homemade Shake & Bake

Great on chicken, fish, chops, tenderized steak, etc.

2 cups flour
2 cups cracker meal
2 tablespoons sugar
1 teaspoon garlic salt

1 teaspoon onion salt
1 tablespoon paprika
¼ cup vegetable oil

Blend ingredients with a fork and store in airtight container (marked). When using, preheat oven to 325°–350°. Place ½ cup in bag, adding more as needed. Moisten meat evenly with water or milk. Shake meat to cover and mix (1 piece at a time). Place meat in a greased pan. Bake about 1 hour or until tender.

Come Grow With Us (Oklahoma)

★ **Editor's Extra:** You can buy cracker meal, or crush about 24 single crackers in a food processor, or roll a heavy glass or rolling pin over crackers in a Ziploc bag.

★★★★★★★★★★★★   ★★★★★★★★★★★★

Easy Chicken

4 chicken legs and thigh quarters,   **1 (8-ounce) bottle Italian dressing**
   skinned

Place chicken in baking dish. Pour Italian dressing over the chicken. Bake at 350° for 30 minutes. Turn chicken over and bake another 30 minutes. Serves 4.

Amish Country Cookbook III (Indiana)

Chinese Chicken

Stir, pour, and let it bake. Great flavor.

4 tablespoons soy sauce   **1½ tablespoons vinegar**
¾ cup ketchup   **1 medium onion, diced**
½ cup brown sugar   **1 dash of garlic powder**
1 cup water   **6 skinless chicken breasts**

Mix together all but chicken. Salt and pepper to taste; pour over chicken. Bake at 375° for 45–60 minutes, until tender. Serve over rice.

Recipes and Memories (Minnesota)

Parmesan Chicken

1 cup crushed herb-seasoned   **¾ cup butter**
   stuffing mix   **1 large clove garlic, crushed**
⅔ cup grated Parmesan cheese   **1 (3-pound) frying chicken, cut up**
¼ cup chopped, fresh parsley

Preheat oven to 375°. Mix crumbs, cheese, and parsley together in small bowl. Melt butter in small skillet. Add garlic while butter is melting, so flavors can blend. Dip chicken pieces in butter. Roll in crumbs. Place in baking dish. Sprinkle remaining crumbs and butter over chicken. Bake at 375° for 45 minutes, or until chicken is done. May be refrigerated several hours before baking. Makes 4 servings.

Elsah Landing Heartland Cooking (Illinois)

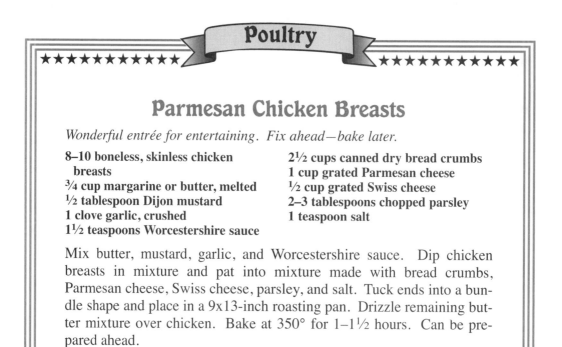

Parmesan Chicken Breasts

Wonderful entrée for entertaining. Fix ahead—bake later.

8–10 boneless, skinless chicken
  breasts
¾ cup margarine or butter, melted
½ tablespoon Dijon mustard
1 clove garlic, crushed
1½ teaspoons Worcestershire sauce

2½ cups canned dry bread crumbs
1 cup grated Parmesan cheese
½ cup grated Swiss cheese
2–3 tablespoons chopped parsley
1 teaspoon salt

Mix butter, mustard, garlic, and Worcestershire sauce. Dip chicken breasts in mixture and pat into mixture made with bread crumbs, Parmesan cheese, Swiss cheese, parsley, and salt. Tuck ends into a bundle shape and place in a 9x13-inch roasting pan. Drizzle remaining butter mixture over chicken. Bake at 350° for 1–1½ hours. Can be prepared ahead.

Our Favorite Recipes (Minnesota)

★ **Editor's Extra:** As a rule of thumb, if not specified, go ahead and spray pans with vegetable oil spray—makes clean-up easier.

Chicken Parmigiana

4 boneless, skinless, chicken breast
  halves
2 eggs, beaten
1 cup Progresso Italian Style Bread
  Crumbs
¼ cup olive oil

1 (15½-ounce) jar meat flavored
  spaghetti sauce
½ cup grated Parmesan cheese
1 cup (4-ounces) shredded
  mozzarella cheese

Preheat oven to 400°. Dip chicken in eggs, then bread crumbs. Coat thoroughly. In medium skillet, heat olive oil. Cook chicken in oil until done and well browned. Pour spaghetti sauce in 11x17-inch pan. Place chicken on sauce and top with cheeses. Bake 15 minutes or until cheese is melted and lightly browned. Makes 4 servings.

Favorite Recipes of Collinsville Junior Service Club (Illinois)

Quick Chick Trick

4 boneless chicken breasts or
  1 whole chicken
1 can cream of chicken soup

8 ounces sour cream
40 Ritz Crackers, crushed
1 stick margarine, melted

Boil and debone chicken; tear into small pieces and line bottom of baking dish. Mix together soup and sour cream. Pour over chicken. Put cracker crumbs on top; pour melted margarine over crumbs. Bake 30 minutes at 350° until bubbly. May be reheated in microwave.

Heavenly Food II (Ohio)

★ **Even Easier:** Use canned chicken or chicken you have cooked earlier and frozen. My favorite "chicken thing" is to buy boneless, skinless chicken tenders, then boil or stir-fry in minutes! Or buy fully cooked, ready-to-eat roasted chicken—you can also use the carcass for making broth.

Chicken Pot Pie

How wonderful! Chicken pot pie you can make without deboning a chicken and peeling vegetables.

2 (9-inch) deep dish frozen pie shells
1 (10-ounce) can chunk chicken,
  drained
1 (15-ounce) can mixed vegetables,
  drained

1 (2.8-ounce) can French fried
  onion rings
2 (11-ounce) cans condensed cream
  of chicken soup
¼ teaspoon salt

Prick bottom of one pie shell all over with a fork. Bake, uncovered, at 375° for 10 minutes. Combine chicken, vegetables, onion rings, soup, and salt. Fill bottom pie shell with mixture. Place second pie shell on top. Prick with fork in 6 places. Set on foil-covered oven rack to catch spills. Bake, uncovered, at 375° for 40 minutes. Yields 6 servings.

Give Mom a Rest (She's on Vacation) Cookbook (Great Plains)

★ **Editor's Extra:** A meal in itself! Great with a fruit salad. Put pineapple, peach or pear slices on lettuce leaves, sprinkle with grated cheese and top with a dollop of mayo.

Dijon-Grilled Chicken Cutlets

3 tablespoons Dijon-style mustard
2 teaspoons fresh lime juice
1 teaspoon low-sodium teriyaki
  sauce

1 garlic clove, finely minced
Pinch ground red pepper
4 (4-ounce) skinless, boneless
  chicken breasts

In medium bowl with wire whisk, combine mustard, lime juice, teriyaki sauce, garlic, and ground red pepper. Dip chicken breasts into mixture, one at a time, coating both sides. Spray an indoor ridged grill pan with nonstick cooking spray. Place on prepared pan. Grill chicken, brushing with any remaining mustard mixture, 4 minutes on each side, until cooked through and juices run clear when pierced with a fork. Serves 4.

Centennial Cookbook (California)

Sour Cream Chicken

This one is easy and will bring raves from guests.

12 skinned chicken breast halves
1 large carton sour cream
¼ cup lemon juice
2 teaspoons Worcestershire
1 teaspoon salt
¼ teaspoon pepper
1 teaspoon celery salt

1 teaspoon paprika
1 teaspoon garlic powder
1 clove crushed garlic
Ritz Crackers and/or cheese
  crackers
2 tablespoons butter, melted

Mix sour cream, lemon juice, Worcestershire, and seasonings together and marinate chicken overnight. Roll in cracker crumbs, (½ cheese crackers and ½ Ritz Crackers or all Ritz Crackers.) Drizzle butter over chicken. Bake at 350° for 1 hour on a cookie sheet. Serves 6–8.

Cooking on the Fault Line—Corralitos Style (California)

★ **Editor's Extra:** A great do-ahead dish. Put it in the fridge the night before, or first thing in the morning—then it's just a pop in the oven away from those rave reviews. If the chicken breasts halves are on the small side, this will cook in 40 minutes. Okay, we admit this one is borderline easy, but we love it, and we think you will, too.

★★★★★★★★★★★★ ★★★★★★★★★★★★

Chicken Casserole Amandine

8 chicken thighs
½ cup honey
½ cup prepared mustard
1 tablespoon chopped onion

1 tablespoon lemon juice
½ teaspoon curry powder
½ cup slivered almonds

Place chicken thighs, single layer, in baking dish. Combine remaining ingredients (except almonds) and pour over meat. Cook, covered, 30 minutes at 350°. Remove cover, sprinkle slivered almonds over the top, and bake another 10 minutes, uncovered. Serves 4–6.

Durham's Favorite Recipes (California)

Turkey and Broccoli Casserole

Great way to use leftover turkey.

1 package frozen broccoli
2 cups chopped cooked turkey
1 can cream of chicken soup
½ cup mayonnaise
1 teaspoon lemon juice

1 teaspoon curry powder
½ cup shredded cheese
½ cup Ritz Crackers, crumbled
¼ cup margarine

Cook broccoli, drain. Arrange in buttered 1½-quart baking dish. Spread turkey on top. Mix soup (undiluted), mayonnaise, lemon juice, and curry powder. Spread over turkey. Sprinkle cheese, then cracker crumbs on top. Dot with margarine. Bake in preheated oven 30 minutes at 350°.

Atlanta Natives' Favorite Recipes (Georgia)

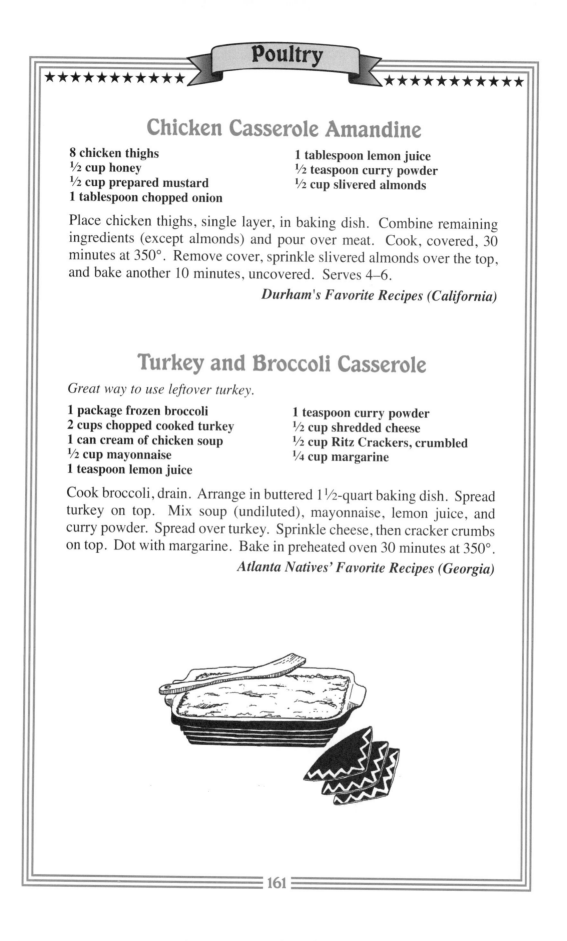

Chicken South of the Border

4 whole chicken breasts
12 corn tortillas
1 can cream of chicken soup
1 can cream of mushroom soup
1 soup can milk

1 onion, minced
1 (4-ounce) can diced green chiles
1 pound sharp Cheddar cheese,
  shredded

Cut chicken into large pieces. Cut tortillas into 1-inch strips. Mix soups, milk, onion, and chiles. Add 3 tablespoons water to mixture. Place ½ of cut tortilla strips into bottom of a 9x13-inch greased baking dish, then layer ½ of chicken pieces, then ½ of soup mixture. Repeat. Top with cheese. Bake at 300° for 1½ hours. Cool 15 minutes. Serves 8.

Treasured Recipes (California)

Seafood

★★★★ ★★★★

When you go to Maine, you have to eat lobster. We chose a checkered-tablecloth eatery rather than a fancy restaurant, so that we could enjoy the cracking, dipping, dripping, and schlurping. And we did. These were fresh out of the traps, and every bit as scrumptious as they look.

Baked Crab Casserole

1 pound crabmeat	½ teaspoon cayenne
1 cup Pepperidge Farm Stuffing	1 cup mayonnaise
Milk	1 teaspoon Worcestershire
4 hard-boiled eggs, chopped	1 teaspoon lemon juice

Pick over crab to remove any shell. Put dry stuffing in a measuring cup and add milk over stuffing to the 1-cup line. Mix with the remaining ingredients and put in a buttered casserole. Top with bread crumbs and dot with butter, if desired. Bake at 350° for 20–30 minutes. Serves 8.

Seafood Sorcery (North Carolina)

★ **Editor's Extra:** For perfect boiled eggs, place eggs in pot with cold water to cover. Bring to a full boil, cover, take off heat, and let sit for 15 minutes. Run cold water over eggs, drain, and shake the pot. Eggs will practically peel themselves!

Vince's Crab Cakes

These all-meat crab cakes are outstanding!

2 tablespoons chopped onion	½ teaspoon mustard
2 tablespoons cooking oil	Salt and pepper to taste
1 pound claw crabmeat	½ cup seasoned bread crumbs
1 egg, beaten	

Sauté onion in oil until tender. Combine all ingredients except bread crumbs. Shape into 6 or 8 cakes, then roll in crumbs. Fry at moderate heat until golden brown on both sides, about 5–7 minutes. Drain on absorbent paper. Serves 3–4.

Vincent Russo's Seafood Cookbook (Georgia)

Crabs are noted for their sweet, succulent meat and are the second most popular shellfish (after shrimp) in the U.S. There are fresh and saltwater crabs, the latter being the most plentiful. The major catch on the Pacific coast is Dungeness crab, from the North Pacific come the King crab and snow crab, along the Atlantic and Gulf coasts it's Blue crab, and Florida waters give us the Stone crab. Hard-shell crabs are sold whole (cooked or live), and in the form of cooked lump meat (whole white meat pieces) or flaked meat (small bits of light and dark meat). Soft-shell crabs are always sold whole. Live crabs should be used on the day they're purchased.

Hot Crab Open Faces

7½ ounces flaked crabmeat,
  canned or fresh
¼ cup mayonnaise
3 ounces cream cheese
1 egg yolk
1 teaspoon finely chopped onion

¼ teaspoon prepared mustard
⅛ teaspoon salt
6 English muffin halves
Hard-boiled eggs, tomatoes or
  avocados (optional)

Mix the crabmeat, mayonnaise, cream cheese, egg yolk, onion, mustard, and salt together in a bowl. Spread the mixture on the muffin halves. Arrange the halves on a broiler pan and broil 2–3 minutes, until the top is golden brown. Garnish with sliced hard-boiled eggs, tomatoes or avocados, depending on whether it is being served for brunch or lunch. Makes 6 servings.

Recipe from Abriendo Inn, Pueblo.
Best of the Historic West (Colorado)

Creamed Crab

1 pound fresh crabmeat
¼ cup margarine
¼ cup all-purpose flour
2 cups milk or half-and-half

Salt and pepper to taste
Worcestershire sauce to taste
Herbed toast points

Remove and discard shell from crabmeat; set aside. Melt margarine in a large saucepan over low heat. Add flour; cook, stir in milk, crabmeat and seasonings. Transfer to a chafing dish. Serve over herbed toast points. Yields 8–10 servings.

Seafood Sorcery (North Carolina)

★ **Editor's Extra:** Stir a little basil or mixed herbs into soft butter and spread on hot toast cut on the diagonal. I like to make these first so they get dry and crusty—sooo good with Creamed Crab on top.

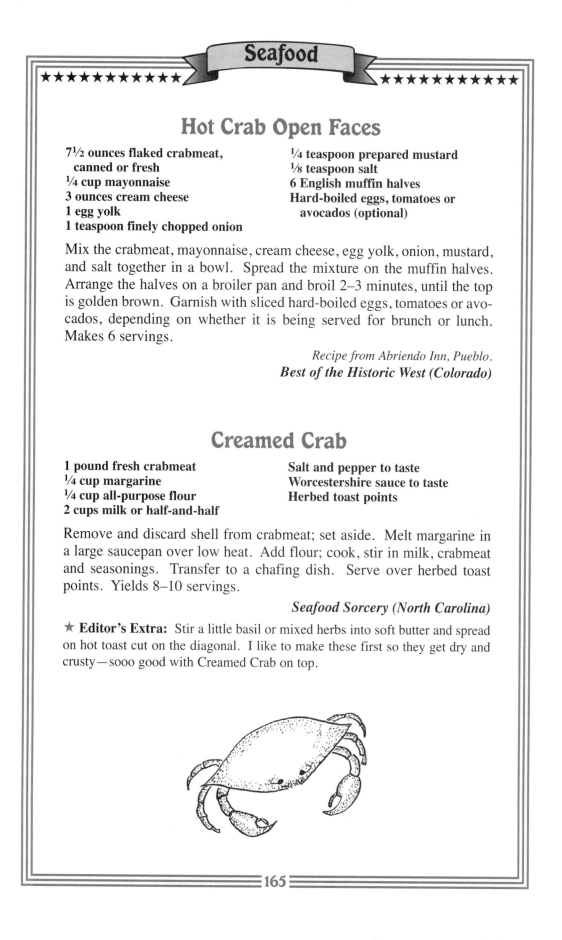

Meeting Street Crabmeat

4 tablespoons butter
4 tablespoons flour
½ pint cream
Salt and pepper to taste

4 tablespoons sherry
1 pound white crabmeat
¾ cup grated sharp cheese

Make a cream sauce with butter, flour, and cream. Add salt, pepper, and sherry. Remove from fire and add crabmeat. Pour the mixture into a buttered casserole or individual baking dishes. Sprinkle with grated cheese and cook in a hot oven (400° for 2 or 3 minutes) or until cheese melts. Do not overcook. Serves 4.

Variation: 1½ pounds shrimp may be substituted for the crab.

Charleston Receipts (South Carolina)

Elly's Shrimp Spaghetti

1 pound mushrooms, sliced
2 cloves garlic, crushed
5 sprigs parsley, chopped
1 stick butter
1 pound shrimp, cooked and cleaned

¼ cup sherry
½ teaspoon salt
3 cups cooked spaghetti
Parmesan cheese

In a large skillet, sauté mushrooms, garlic, and parsley in butter until tender. Add shrimp, sherry, and salt, and toss until heated through. Pour over spaghetti and toss with Parmesan to taste. Serves 4–6.

Heavenly Hostess (Alabama)

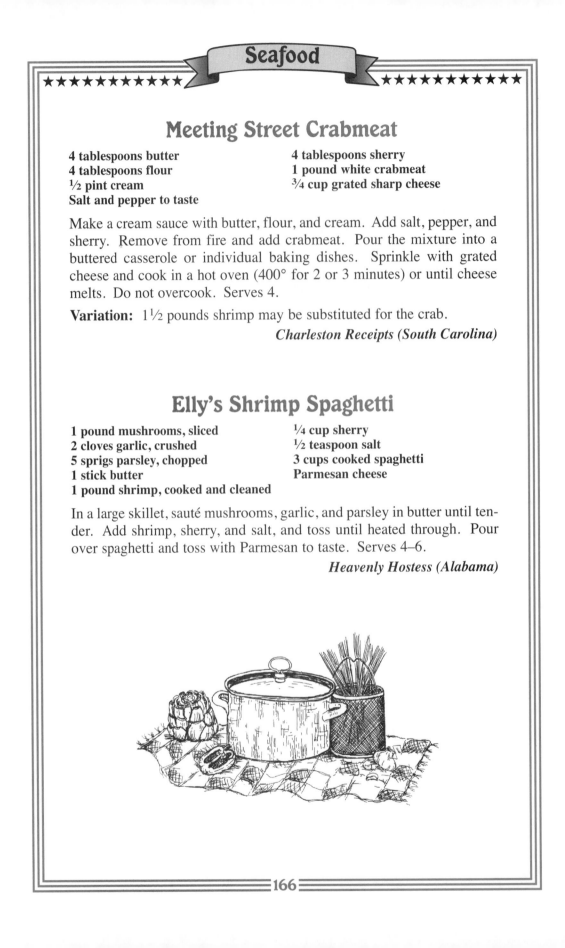

★ ★ ★ ★ ★ ★ ★ ★ ★ ★ ★   ★ ★ ★ ★ ★ ★ ★ ★ ★ ★ ★

Hot Shrimp

1 stick margarine
2–5 pounds shrimp in shells
Salt

Minced garlic
1 (8-ounce) bottle Italian dressing

Melt margarine in large roasting pan. Put in shrimp and seasoning to taste. Pour dressing over. Cover tightly and bake at 350° until done—about 45 minutes to 1 hour.

More Fiddling with Food (Alabama)

★ **Editor's Extra:** Spread the newspaper on the table and start peeling! And better have some hot French bread for sopping up this tasty sauce.

Nevie's Stove-Top Scampi

This may be used as an appetizer, first course, or main dish. Quick and easy!

3 tablespoons olive oil
3 tablespoons butter
1 clove garlic, finely minced
1½ pounds jumbo shrimp, peeled,
   deveined and butterflied

3 tablespoons lemon juice
Seasoned salt, to taste
White pepper, to taste
3 tablespoons vermouth

Heat olive oil in large skillet over medium-high heat; add butter and turn to medium heat. Add garlic and sauté for 2 minutes, carefully coating pan. Place shrimp into pan; lightly brown on one side and turn. After turning, sprinkle with lemon juice, seasoned salt, and pepper. Turn heat up to medium high for quick browning. Sprinkle with vermouth evenly. Swirl shrimp and seasonings together. Turn off heat, cover, and set off to side. Serve immediately. Yields 6 appetizer or 2 main-course servings.

Mississippi Memories (Mississippi)

★ **Editor's Extra:** Want a great go-with? Split a loaf of French bread or hoagie bun down the middle, brush with olive oil and sprinkle with Parmesan cheese. Broil 2–3 minutes. Open a bag of pre-mixed salad and you've got a super supper.

Shrimp is the most popular seafood in the United States. Shrimp are sized by count (number of shrimp per pound)—the smaller the count, the larger the shrimp.

Baked Shrimp

½ cup grated onion
4 tablespoons butter
½ pound grated Cheddar cheese
½ teaspoon dry mustard
½ teaspoon salt

½ teaspoon crushed garlic
1 pound cooked shrimp
6 tablespoons sherry
Grated coconut

Simmer onion in butter; add other ingredients except shrimp, sherry and coconut. Stir until cheese has melted; add sherry, pour over shrimp arranged in individual ramekins. Broil for 5 minutes under low heat; when almost done, sprinkle with grated coconut and let brown. Serve very hot. Serves 6.

Woman's Exchange Cookbook I (Tennessee)

★ **Editor's Extra:** Most ovens only have one broil setting, so you can regulate the heat by lowering the shelf. This should be about 5–6 inches away from the heat source.

Lemon-Garlic Broiled Shrimp

2 pounds shrimp (medium, peeled)
2 cloves garlic, halved
¼ cup butter (½ stick)
3 tablespoons lemon juice
½ teaspoon salt

¼ teaspoon black pepper
½ teaspoon hot sauce
1 tablespoon Worcestershire sauce
3 tablespoons chopped parsley

Place shrimp in single layer in a large flat pan; set aside. Sauté garlic in butter until garlic is brown; remove and discard garlic. Add next 5 ingredients, stirring well; pour mixture over shrimp. Broil shrimp 4 inches from heat source for 8–10 minutes, basting once. Sprinkle with parsley; serve immediately. Serves 6.

Gardeners' Gourmet II (Mississippi)

Crawfish Etouffée

So fast, so typically, terrifically Cajun.

1 bunch green onions, chopped
1 bell pepper, chopped
4 tablespoons butter
1 can Ro-Tel tomatoes

1 can tomato sauce
1 can cream of mushroom soup
1 pound crawfish tails

Sauté green onions and bell pepper in butter until wilted. Add Ro-Tel tomatoes, tomato sauce, and mushroom soup. Over low heat, bring to a boil; add crawfish and let cook only until thick. Serve over rice. Serves 6.

In the Pink (Louisiana II)

★ **Editor's Extra:** Buy packaged frozen, cleaned, and peeled crawfish tails in the seafood section of your supermarket. They can go from freezer to pot!

Crawfish Dog

Good on crackers as a Cajun hors d'oeuvres.

3 tablespoons shortening
3 tablespoons flour
1 medium onion, chopped
½ pound crawfish tails, peeled
  and ground

½ cup crawfish fat
¼ cup water
1 teaspoon red pepper
2 teaspoons salt
8 hot dog buns

Make roux with shortening and flour; cook, stirring, over medium heat until light brown. Add onion; cook until done. Add crawfish (with fat), water and seasonings. Cook 20 minutes and serve on open-face hot dog buns.

Cajun Cooking (Louisiana II)

★ **Editor's Extra:** Use a (12-ounce) package of frozen crawfish tails "with fat" which isn't like "fat" fat—read the label. Cajun cooking tends to be hot, so you might want to use less red pepper to start. A food processor will grind the crawfish—just give it a few pulses.

A Cajun fable: It is said some of the lobsters in Nova Scotia wanted to relocate with the Acadians to Louisiana, but the trip was so hard and long that they lost a lot of weight. Hence, crawfish!

★★★★★★★★★★★ ★★★★★★★★★★★

Spanish Rice-a-Roni Crawfish

1 pound crawfish tails
½ cup onion, chopped
¼ cup bell pepper, chopped
4 cloves garlic

⅛ teaspoon red pepper
½ teaspoon salt
2 tablespoons butter
1 package Spanish Rice-a-Roni

Sauté crawfish, onion, bell pepper, garlic, red pepper, and salt in butter until crawfish are done (about 2 minutes). Use package directions for preparing Rice-a-Roni. Fold in crawfish mixture. Serve hot.

The Louisiana Crawfish Cookbook (Louisiana)

Tuna Burgers

1 (6-ounce) can tuna
1 cup chopped celery
½ cup Cheddar cheese, diced
½ cup ripe olives, chopped

¼ cup mayonnaise
Salt and pepper, to taste
1 small onion, minced
6 hamburger buns

Combine tuna, celery, cheese, olives, mayonnaise, salt, pepper, and onion. Spread on buns and wrap in foil. Bake at 350° for 10–15 minutes. May freeze. May also use chopped chicken or turkey.

Cook of the Week Cookbook (Iowa)

Seafood Cocktail Sauce

⅔ cup catsup
3 tablespoons chili sauce
2 tablespoons horseradish

3 tablespoons fresh lemon juice
Hot pepper sauce, to taste

Mix all ingredients well; refrigerate until ready to serve. This is served with any fried or boiled seafood.

Variation: Minced onion may be added.

Cajun Cuisine (Louisiana II)

One of the laws regulating oysters prohibited their taking during the months without an "R." Although this was done as a conservation measure during spawning, people erroneously came to believe that oysters were inedible in May, June, July, and August.

★★★★★★★★★★★ ★★★★★★★★★★★

Poor Man's Lobster

This is delicious—I serve it with rice.

1 pound haddock, skinned and boned
½ cup butter, melted

1 stack-pack round buttery
crackers, crushed

Cut haddock into bite-size pieces. Dip in melted butter, then dredge in cracker crumbs. Place in a lightly greased 1½-quart shallow baking dish. Cover. Bake at 350° for 10 minutes. Uncover. Bake 10 minutes longer. Serves 4.

Note: Do not substitute any other fish for haddock.

Cuisine á la Mode (New England)

★ **Editor's Extra:** Haddock probably tastes a bit like lobster, but I have to confess I did substitute other kinds of fish, and granted, the tastes were all different . . . but all good.

Trent Shores Panned Oysters

Great!

1 pint oysters, drained
¼ cup butter
2 tablespoons dry white wine
1 tablespoon lemon juice
1 teaspoon Worcestershire sauce

½ teaspoon salt
Toast points, or rounds of
  Holland Rusk
Lemon wedges

Sauté oysters gently in butter for 8–10 minutes. Remove oysters; add wine and seasonings; heat to a boil. Pour over oysters. Serve on toast with lemon wedges. Yields 6 servings.

Pass the Plate (North Carolina)

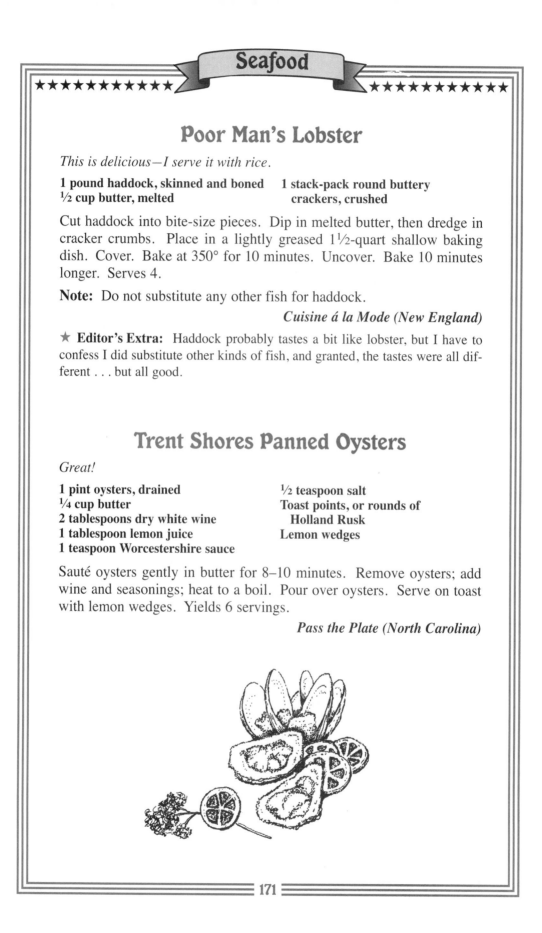

★★★★★★★★★★★ ★★★★★★★★★★★

Baked Crunchy Trout

Easy and good.

2 pounds trout fillets
1 onion, chopped
1 (8-ounce) bottle creamy Italian
  dressing

2½ cups crushed potato chips

Lay trout fillets in the bottom of a buttered 3-quart baking dish. Sprinkle with chopped onion. Spread dressing over onion to cover fish. Put crushed potato chips on top to cover completely. Bake at 350° for 35 minutes. Yields 4 servings.

From A Louisiana Kitchen (Louisiana)

Baked Trout with Lemon Sauce

2 pounds trout fillets
Salt and pepper, to taste
4 green onions, chopped

1 tablespoon chopped parsley
Paprika

Place fillets on baking sheet lined with foil. Sprinkle with salt and pepper, green onions, and parsley. Then sprinkle with paprika. Cover with Lemon Sauce. Bake at 375° for 20–25 minutes. Baste with Lemon Sauce during cooking. Serves 6.

LEMON SAUCE:
¼ cup light margarine, melted
2 tablespoons lemon juice

2 cloves garlic, minced

Combine all ingredients and pour over prepared fish.

L'Heritage Du Bayou Lafourche (Louisiana)

The lemon is a lovely thing. Its name is synonymous with freshness. Its tart juice brings fish and seafood to life, keeps fruits from turning brown, and with a little help from sugar, makes all sorts of delicious desserts and beverages. When purchasing, choose lemons that are firm, plump, and heavy. They can be refrigerated in a plastic bag for 2 to 3 weeks. You can buy juice in a bottle, but it bears little resemblance to fresh; the frozen kind is passable, but there's no substitute for the real thing. An excellent source of vitamin C, the simple lemon adds flavor magic like few things can.

Baked Fish with Shrimp-Parmesan Sauce

3 tablespoons butter
2 tablespoons flour
½ teaspoon salt
1 cup milk

2 pounds white fish fillets (ocean
perch, flounder, sole, etc.)
½ pound small cooked shrimp
¼ cup Parmesan cheese (optional)

Make a medium white sauce: melt butter in skillet, add flour and cook until bubbly, add salt and milk, stirring constantly. Remove from heat. Layer fish in a buttered flat baking dish. Spread shrimp and white sauce over fish. Sprinkle with Parmesan cheese. Bake for 20–25 minutes in a 325° oven.

Recipes from Miss Daisy's (Tennessee)

Glazed Salmon

4 salmon steaks or fillets
¼ cup butter
¼ cup brown sugar, firmly packed

2 tablespoons lemon juice
Salt and pepper to taste
Crushed red pepper flakes (optional)

In small saucepan, combine all ingredients except salmon, and melt. Marinate salmon in glaze for one hour. Arrange salmon on lightly greased broiler pan. Brush with glaze. Broil 5–6 inches from heat, 8–10 minutes on each side or until fish flakes easily, brushing occasionally with remaining glaze. Place salmon on serving platter and spoon over any leftover glaze. Serve with lemon wedges. This dish is also great when cooked on a grill. Serves 4.

Steamboat Entertains (Colorado)

★ **Even Easier**: You can marinate this for less time—I even tried it immediately, and it's pretty darn good!

★★★★★★★★★★★ ★★★★★★★★★★★

Salmon Patties

1 (16-ounce) can salmon
2 eggs
½ teaspoon salt
⅛ teaspoon pepper

1½ tablespoons grated onion
3 tablespoons sour cream
½ cup bread crumbs

Drain salmon, remove skin. Mash with fork. Add remaining ingredients. Divide into 8 patties (flouring your hands makes it easier), and fry until golden brown in hot oil. Serves 6–8.

C-U in the Kitchen (Illinois)

Grilled Salmon with Sweet Onion Relish

4 salmon steaks
2 large sweet onions (Walla Walla
  or Vidalia), chopped
¼ cup olive oil

1 tablespoon sugar
1 bay leaf
1 sprig fresh thyme
1 tablespoon balsamic vinegar

Grill salmon steaks 12–15 minutes, depending on thickness. Sauté onions in olive oil until transparent. Add sugar and herbs. Cook until mixture is caramelized. Add vinegar to taste. Serve sauce over grilled salmon steaks. Serves 4.

When Friends Cook (Minnesota)

★ **Even Easier**: Grill steaks on a 2-sided contact grill (George Foreman-type) for 3–5 minutes, depending on thickness.

Flounder Parmesan

A microwave swift fish dish!

1 pound fillet of flounder
½ cup sour cream
2 tablespoons grated Parmesan
  cheese
1 teaspoon lemon juice

1 tablespoon grated onion
½ teaspoon salt
Dash hot pepper sauce
Paprika
Chopped parsley

Cut fish into serving-size portions. Arrange in baking dish with thickest portions to the outside. Mix remaining ingredients except paprika and parsley; spread mixture on fish; sprinkle with paprika. Cook uncovered on HIGH 5–7 minutes until done. Garnish with parsley. Serves 4.

Simply Scrumptious Microwaving (Georgia)

★ **Editor's Extra:** Fish is so good for you. For some reason, many people shy away from buying fresh fish, perhaps not knowing what to buy or how much to buy or how long it will keep or freeze. I try to make a practice of buying fish the same day I want to cook it to ensure peak freshness. Don't be afraid to ask your seafood market manager if you're unsure.

Seasoned Catfish

1 teaspoon onion powder
1 teaspoon garlic salt
1 teaspoon ground red pepper
1 teaspoon dried basil
½ teaspoon thyme

¼ teaspoon sage
4 catfish fillets
¼ cup margarine or butter
Lemon slices

In a shallow dish, combine all seasonings. Brush both sides of fish with some of the melted margarine or butter. Coat both sides of fish with the seasoning mixture.

Grill fish or use a nonstick frying pan with 2 teaspoons margarine or butter, and quick-fry them. Garnish with lemon slices.

Arizona Small Game and Fish Recipes (Arizona)

"The Catfish Capital of the World" is located in Humphreys County, Mississippi, It is the largest catfish producing county in the world with annual production of catfish exceeding 150 million pounds.

Baked Fish with Sour Cream

A succulent way to love fish!

1 (4-pound) flounder, red snapper or other large fish Paprika	Butter 2 cups sour cream Sliced almonds

Preheat oven to 350°. Scale, clean, split and remove bones from fish. Flatten it out. Rub inside and out with butter and paprika. Place on ovenproof dish. Cover with sour cream; sprinkle with almonds. Cover the dish. Bake about 45 minutes or until done. Garnish with chopped parsley. Serves 4–6.

Sawgrass and Pines (Florida)

★ **Even Easier**: I used fish fillets that were smaller, so cooked in 30 minutes or less.

Oven-Fried Red Snapper

1 tablespoon oil 2 (8-ounce) fillets red snapper ½ cup seasoned bread crumbs	½ teaspoon paprika ½ teaspoon garlic powder Fresh lemon

Preheat oven to 400°. Oil bottom of baking dish very lightly. Wet fillets. Roll in combined dry ingredients. Place in baking dish. Squeeze on fresh lemon. Bake 20–30 minutes without turning. Fish is done when flaky. Serves 2.

Serve with whipped potatoes and broccoli. (Don't forget the tartar sauce.)

The Fishlady's Cookbook (Illinois)

★ **Even Easier:** Foil is my friend where baked or broiled fish is concerned. I spray it with Pam so that the fish lifts off easily. And of course, the clean-up is throw-away quick.

★★★★★★★★★★★ ★★★★★★★★★★★

Fish Fillets Elegante

1 (1-pound) package frozen or fresh
  fish fillets (sole, haddock, halibut,
  flounder, cod or trout)
½ teaspoon pepper
2 tablespoons butter or margarine

1 (10½-ounce) can condensed
  cream of shrimp soup
¼ cup Parmesan cheese, grated
½ teaspoon paprika
1 lemon, cut into wedges

Preheat oven to 400°. Butter a 9x13-inch baking dish. Separate fillets.
Place in baking dish. Dash with pepper; dot with butter. Spread soup
over fillets; sprinkle with Parmesan cheese and paprika. Bake for 25
minutes. Garnish with lemon wedges. Serves 2–4.

A Cook's Tour of the Azalea Coast (North Carolina)

Butter-Herbed Baked Fish

Heavenly—absolutely melts in your mouth.

½ cup butter or margarine
⅔ cup finely crushed saltines
½ teaspoon each: basil, oregano
  and salt

¼ teaspoon garlic powder
¼ cup Parmesan cheese
1 pound white fish fillets such as
  halibut or orange roughy

Preheat oven to 350°. Melt butter or margarine. Mix crumbs, herbs, and
Parmesan cheese. Dip fish in butter or margarine, then in crumbs.
Arrange in baking dish and bake 25–30 minutes. Serves 3–4.

Still Gathering (Illinois)

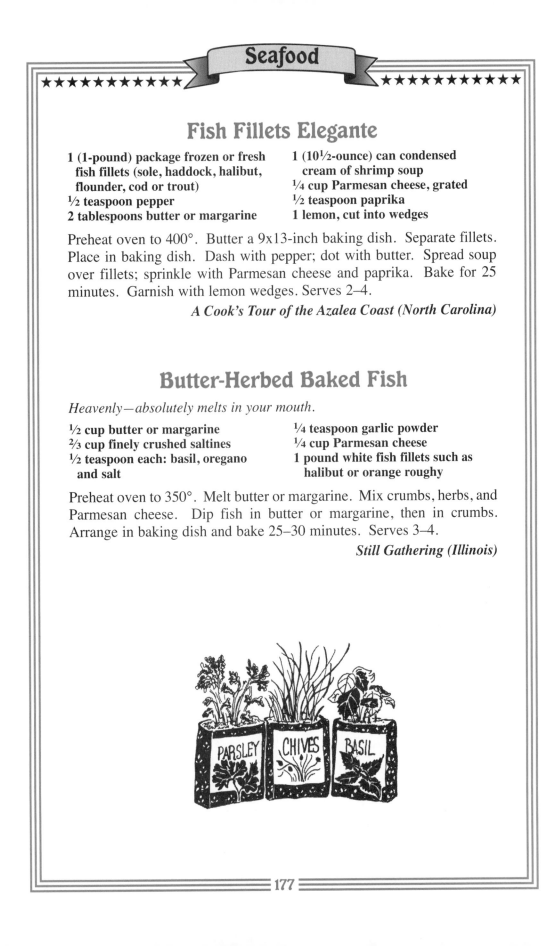

Oven-Fried Fish Fillets

¾ pound fish fillets
¼ cup frozen orange juice
  concentrate
Salt and lemon pepper to taste

¼ cup dry bread crumbs
1 tablespoon melted butter
Parsley and lemon slices

If the fillets are large, cut them into small portions. Preheat the oven to 500°. Combine the orange juice concentrate with salt and lemon pepper. Dip the fish in it, then roll in bread crumbs, coating well.

Place the fish in a single layer in a greased baking dish. Drizzle on melted butter. Bake for 10 minutes. Reduce the heat to 350° and continue cooking for 5 minutes, or until the fish flakes when pierced with a fork. Serve on a heated platter, garnished with parsley and lemon slices. Makes 2 servings.

Love Yourself Cookbook (North Carolina)

★ **Even Easier**: Spray margarine makes this a snap.

Home-Fried Fish

1–1½ pounds white fillets
  (scrod, haddock, sole, cod)
1 egg, beaten

2–3 tablespoons milk
Cornflake crumbs

Cut fish into serving sizes. Dip in egg wash of egg and milk. Coat with crushed cornflakes on both sides. Fry in a thin layer of hot corn oil in a skillet until brown on both sides. Or put in a metal fish platter which has just a little oil on bottom and bake at 350° until coating is brown and fish is flaky.

Note: May use egg substitute for egg wash.

The Island Cookbook (New England)

Meats

★★★★   ★★★★

Pete Jones proclaims to have the world's best barbecue. You have to drive a little to get to Ayden, North Carolina, but you have no trouble spotting the Skylight Inn with a replica of our nation's capitol on the roof! Pete packed us some of his famous barbecue for the road— we had no arguments with his claim!

Italian Steak

2 eggs
2 cups bread crumbs
½ cup Parmesan or Romano cheese, grated
2 cloves garlic, chopped fine
2 tablespoons parsley

Salt and pepper to taste
2 (12.25-ounce) packages sandwich steaks (like Steak-umm), cut in serving pieces
Hot oil (2 tablespoons or more)

Beat eggs in flat dish. In a separate container, combine the bread crumbs, cheese, garlic, parsley, salt and pepper. Dip meat in eggs and then in bread crumb mixture. Fry in hot oil until brown, about 2 minutes on each side. Don't overcook. Drain steaks on paper towels. Serve hot with pasta or cold in a sandwich.

Cooking with Daisy's Descendants (Illinois)

French Dip

An easy-do crockpot all-day-er!

½ cup soy sauce
1 beef bouillon
1 bay leaf
1 teaspoon thyme
1 teaspoon garlic powder

3–4 peppercorns
Water
1 (3-pound) rump roast
French bread rolls

Put soy sauce, bouillon, bay leaf, thyme, garlic powder, and peppercorns in crockpot. Mix with 1 cup water. Put rump roast in and cover with water. Cook on low 8–10 hours; put sliced meat on rolls and use juice for dipping. Serves 8–10.

St. Joseph's Table (Great Plains)

★ **Editor's Extra:** Here are some general oven-to-crockpot cooking time conversions: 15–30 minutes in the oven equals 1½–2½ hours on high or 4–6 hours on low; 35–45 minutes in the oven equals 2–3 hours on high or 6–8 hours on low; 50 minutes–3 hours in the oven equals 4–5 hours on high or 8–18 hours on low.

Crockpot Barbecued Beef

Easy and super good for sandwiches.

1 (3- to 4-pound) roast
1 (24-ounce) bottle catsup
⅓ cup barbecue sauce
½ cup chopped onion

¼ cup brown sugar
Salt to taste
Pepper to taste
Chili powder to taste

Trim all fat from roast; pat dry and place roast in crockpot. Mix all other ingredients and pour over roast. Cook on low for 10–12 hours. Shred with 2 forks.

Taste & See (Indiana)

Beef Roast (Mock Prime Rib)

Ready when you get home.

1 (5-pound) boneless rump roast
1 can beef broth
1 (1-ounce) package au jus mix

1 package Good Seasons Italian
   Dressing Mix

Place roast in slow cooker. Mix beef broth, au jus mix, and dressing mix. Pour over roast. Cover and cook 8–10 hours on low setting. Broth may be thickened for gravy.

Applause Applause (Iowa)

After Opera Special

Good as a late night supper or appetizer.

½ pound beef, chopped in small
   cubes (any tender cut)
2 tablespoons butter
1 (16-ounce) can artichoke hearts,
   drained, thinly sliced
1 pint sour cream

½ cup dry white wine (or sherry)
1 tablespoon grated Parmesan
   cheese
English muffins or toast points
Paprika to garnish

Brown beef in butter in skillet. Stir in artichoke hearts, sour cream, white wine, and Parmesan cheese. Cook until well blended and heated thoroughly. (If thin, thicken with a little cornstarch.) Serve on toasted English muffins or toast points. Sprinkle with paprika. Yields 4–6 servings.

Unbearably Good! (Georgia)

★★★★★★★★★★ ★★★★★★★★★★

No Peek Stew

Small on prep . . . large on tender results.

2 pounds chuck roast (cut up in
  chunks) or stew meat
1 package dry onion soup mix
1 can cream of mushroom soup

1 (2½-ounce) can mushrooms,
  drained
1 cup ginger ale

Throw all ingredients into a pot with a tight-fitting lid and bake at 350°
for 2½–3 hours. Do not peek. Makes 6 servings.

Home Cookin' is a Family Affair (Illinois)

Wiener Schnitzel

Breaded veal cutlets Vienna-style—perfectly prepared!

4 boneless veal cutlets (pork may
  be used)
Paprika
Salt and pepper to taste
Flour

1 egg
Milk or water (1–2 tablespoons)
Bread crumbs
Butter for frying (2 tablespoons)
Lemon slices

If there is a skin around meat, cut it in several places so it won't curl up
while frying in the pan. Pound meat a little. Sprinkle with paprika, salt
and pepper. Coat with flour. Beat egg and water (or milk) and dip cutlets in it. Coat with bread crumbs on both sides. Heat butter in fry pan
and add meat. Let cook to a golden brown over medium heat, about 5
minutes on each side. Serve with lemon slices.

Guten Appetit (Indiana)

Veal Piccata

1 pound thin veal scallopini	2 tablespoons margarine or butter
2 tablespoons flour	½ lemon
½ teaspoon salt	½ cup dry white wine
¼ teaspoon pepper	Parsley

Wipe veal scallopini with damp paper towels. Combine flour, salt, and pepper. Use flour mixture to coat veal well. Heat margarine in a medium skillet until it sizzles. Add half of veal slices, and cook over high heat until well-browned on both sides; remove. Repeat with remaining slices of veal.

Return all veal to skillet. Slice lemon and add, along with dry white wine, to veal. Cook over low heat, covered, for 5 minutes. Arrange veal on serving platter. Garnish with parsley sprigs. Makes 4 servings.

Italian Dishes et cetera (Colorado)

★ **Editor's Extra:** To keep sautéed meat from tasting boiled and having a gray look when you turn it over, dry it first with a paper towel or flour it before sautéing. Be sure the pan is hot, and don't crowd pieces in the skillet—this will help to keep it crisp.

Veal or Round Steak Lausanne

This is great!

2 pounds veal cutlets or beef round steak	1 cup sliced raw onion rings
Flour for coating	1 (4-ounce) can button mushrooms, drained
Salt and pepper to taste	⅓ cup light cream
3 tablespoons shortening, melted, or bacon drippings	3 tablespoons dry white wine

Coat the meat in the flour and sprinkle with salt and pepper. Brown meat in shortening. Arrange in a shallow baking dish. Sauté onions in the same skillet; pour over meat. Garnish with mushrooms. Add cream and wine. Bake covered at 375° approximately 40 minutes or until tender. Yields 4–6 servings.

A Pinch of Sunshine (Florida)

★ **Editor's Extra:** Never cook with wine you wouldn't drink. If it doesn't taste good, it's not going to make the recipe taste good either.

★★★★★★★★★★★ ★★★★★★★★★★★

Mandarin Beef

This holds nicely in the oven till you're ready to serve.

2 pounds round steak, cut into
  ½x3-inch strips
¼ cup salad oil
2 (4-ounce) cans mushrooms and
  liquid
1 cup chopped onion

2 cups sliced celery
½ cup water
¼ cup soy sauce
1 (10-ounce) can cream of chicken
  soup

Brown steak in oil. Pour remaining ingredients over. Cover and bake one hour at 350°. Serve on baked or cooked rice. Serves 6–8.

Note: Recipe is good to use when dinner hour is uncertain. Turn oven low, 325° or lower, depending on when ready to eat.

Kitchen Keepsakes (Minnesota)

Cheeseburger Pie

Pizza-flavored meatloaf pie! Can be made ahead.

2 pounds hamburger
1 cup chopped onions
3 eggs
1½ cups milk

1 cup Bisquick
1 pint pizza sauce
2 cups mozzarella cheese, shredded

In a saucepan, brown hamburger, and onions. Season slightly. Drain and pour in 2 loaf pans. Mix eggs, milk, Bisquick and pour over hamburger mixture. Pour pizza sauce on and top with cheese. Bake at 350° for 30–40 minutes. Serves 8–10.

500 Favorite Recipes (South Carolina)

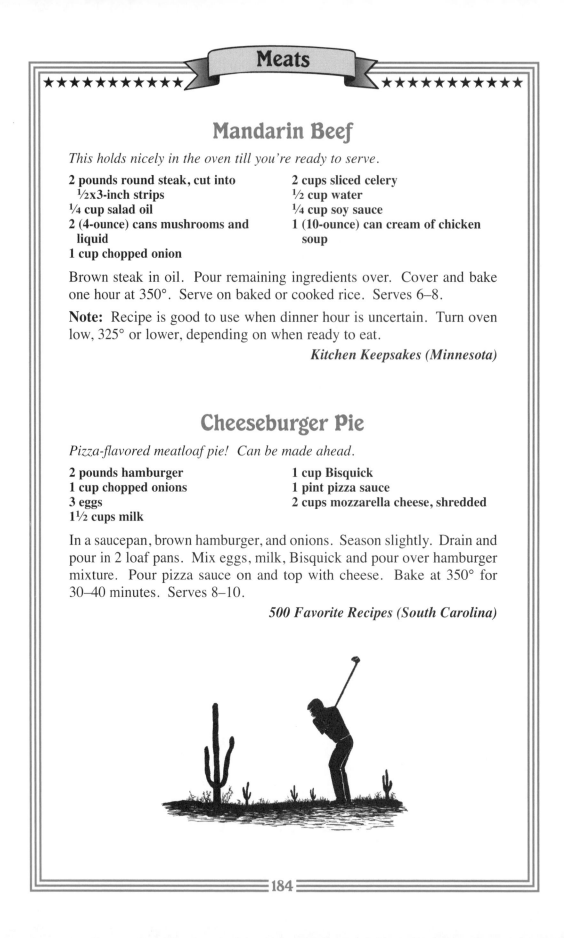

Easy Enchilada Pie

1 pound lean ground beef	1 (10¾-ounce) can condensed
1 small onion, chopped	cream of chicken soup
1 (8-ounce) can tomato sauce	½ cup milk (can use skim milk)
1 (1¼-ounce) package taco	12 (6-inch) corn tortillas
seasoning mix	8 ounces shredded Cheddar cheese

In a large skillet, brown ground beef and chopped onion. Drain off fat. Stir in tomato sauce and taco seasoning. Bring mixture to a boil. Reduce heat and simmer, uncovered, 5 minutes. Remove skillet from heat. Stir together soup and milk. Spoon ½ soup mixture into a 9x13x2-inch baking dish. Cut tortillas in half. Use 12 halves to place over soup in dish. Spoon meat mixture over tortillas. Layer remaining tortillas and soup, then top with cheese. Bake in a 350° oven for 30 minutes or until heated through. Serves 6–8.

Nuggets, Nibbles and Nostalgia (California)

Taco Pie

Not just pretty good . . . it's pretty and good!

1 pound ground beef	¾ cup Bisquick Baking Mix
½ cup chopped onion	3 eggs
1 envelope taco seasoning mix	2 tomatoes, sliced
1 envelope chili mix	1 cup shredded Monterey Jack
1 can chopped green chiles	cheese
1¼ cups milk	

Sauté ground beef. Add the next 4 ingredients and sauté for a few minutes. Pour into greased baking dish. Blend milk, Bisquick, and eggs together. Pour over ground beef mixture and bake at 400° for 25 minutes. Place tomato slices on top and sprinkle with cheese. Place in oven for 10 minutes.

CDA Angelic Treats (Louisiana II)

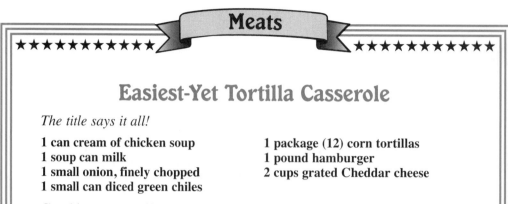

Easiest-Yet Tortilla Casserole

The title says it all!

1 can cream of chicken soup
1 soup can milk
1 small onion, finely chopped
1 small can diced green chiles

1 package (12) corn tortillas
1 pound hamburger
2 cups grated Cheddar cheese

Combine soup, milk, onion, and chiles in large pan and bring to a slow boil. Tear tortillas into small pieces and add to soup mixture. Brown hamburger in another skillet and drain. Add to soup mixture. Alternate layers of soup mixture and grated cheese in greased casserole dish, ending with cheese. Bake at 350° for 30 minutes. Serves 5–7.

Rehoboth Christian School Cookbook (New Mexico)

Soft Tacos

2½ pounds hamburger
2 tablespoons garlic salt
2 teaspoons pepper
½ cup diced onions
18-count package flour tortillas

16 ounces shredded longhorn
  cheese
½ head lettuce, shredded
2 diced tomatoes
Salsa

In a skillet, brown hamburger; season during browning. Last 5 minutes, add onions. Heat flat skillet. In one side of the tortilla, add a couple of spoonfuls of meat mixture and sprinkle with cheese. Fold plain side over. Grill each side until lightly brown. Remove to plate and place lettuce and tomatoes inside of each. Top with salsa.

Cooking with Cops (Arizona)

A definitive element of Mexican cuisine is the tortilla, a simple, round flatbread eaten with just about every meal in Mexican households. These delicious discs come in two basic varieties—corn and flour. Both are common in Tex-Mex cooking, although corn tortillas are much more traditional in Mexico. Corn tortillas begin with a type of specially treated corn flour called masa harina. Flour tortillas are different from corn tortillas in that they contain wheat flour rather than corn flour, and include the additional ingredients of baking powder and shortening or lard. These pale cousins of the corn tortilla are usually larger and thinner because the gluten in the wheat flour allows the dough to be stretched without falling apart.

★★★★★★★★★★★★   ★★★★★★★★★★★★

Picadillo

Probably Spanish explorers introduced this delicious blend of meat, spices, and fruit in a pastry turnover.

½ pound ground beef
½ pound ground pork
1 onion, minced
1 clove garlic, minced
2 cups stewed tomatoes

½ teaspoon cinnamon
¼ teaspoon ground cumin
⅛ teaspoon cloves
1 cup white (golden) raisins
Salt and pepper to taste

Brown meats in skillet; drain off fat. Add onion and garlic. Add tomatoes, spices, and raisins with salt and pepper to taste. Simmer 5 minutes. Serve in a heated flour tortilla or empanada, or use as a taco filling.

Iola's Gourmet Recipes in Rhapsody (Great Plains)

★ **Editor's Extra:** In a small fondue pot, this is an excellent appetizer with Tostitos or Frito Scoops.

Sun Devil Surprise

1 pound ground beef
2 tablespoons soy sauce
2 tablespoons teriyaki sauce
Dash onion powder

Pepper
4 flour tortillas
Grated cheese
1 tablespoon picante sauce

Brown beef on high heat, drain, lower heat to medium. Mix in soy sauce, teriyaki sauce, onion powder, and pepper. Put mixture on a warm flour tortilla, top with cheese and picante sauce and eat it. Makes 4 servings, takes 15 minutes.

The College Cookbook FOR Students BY Students (Texas II)

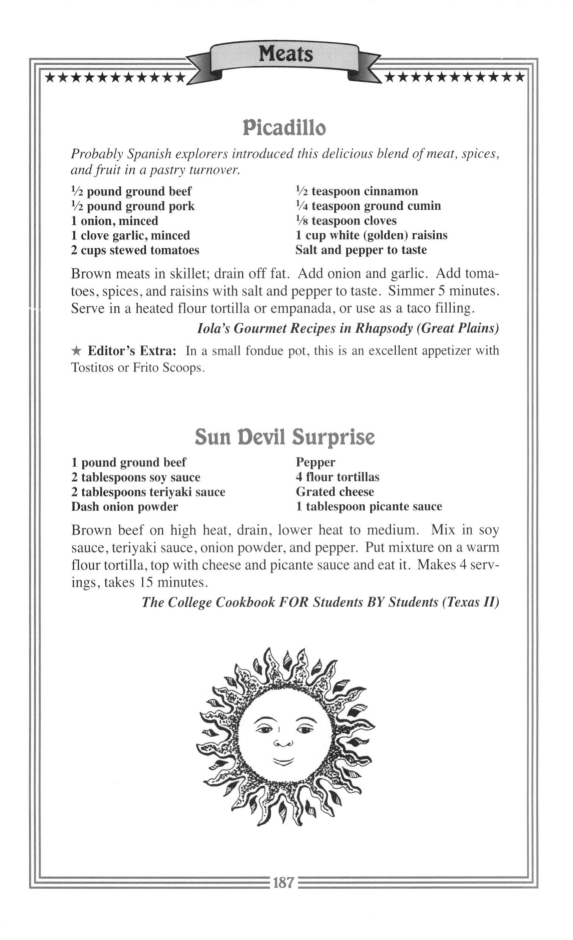

★★★★★★★★★★★   ★★★★★★★★★★★

Hobo Stew

As quick a stew as you'll ever do.

1 cup thinly sliced onion
1 cup green pepper, coarsely chopped
¼ cup olive oil
1 pound ground beef
1 (15¼-ounce) can red kidney
  beans, drained
1 (15¼-ounce) can whole kernel
  corn, drained

1 (28-ounce) can Italian style
  tomatoes
2 (8-ounce) cans tomato sauce
1 tablespoon steak sauce
Dried basil, dry mustard, salt and
  pepper to taste

Cook onion and green pepper in oil in large skillet (or Dutch oven) until golden brown. Add beef and cook, stirring. Add rest of ingredients and mix well. Cover and simmer 15–20 minutes. Serves 8–10.

Jarrett House Potpourri (North Carolina)

Beef and Potato Casserole

A superb meal-in-a-dish!

1 pound ground beef
1 medium chopped onion
1 can mushroom stems and pieces
1 can cream of mushroom soup
1 can ranch-style beans

1 (16-ounce) package frozen
  O'Brien potatoes (hash browns)
1 (8-ounce) package grated
  Cheddar cheese

Brown meat; drain and add onion; cook until done. Add mushrooms, soup, and beans. Pour mixture into a greased 9x13-inch pan over the O'Brien potatoes. Top with grated cheese and bake 25–30 minutes in 375° oven until heated through or cheese is melted. Serves 8–10. Very good!

Seasoned With Love (Oklahoma)

Green Chile Goulash

1 cup chopped green chiles
1 cup chopped onions
3 tablespoons cooking oil
1 pound ground beef

4 cups whole grain corn
2 (8-ounce) cans tomato sauce
1 teaspoon salt

Brown the chiles and onions in oil. Add the ground beef and stir until browned. Drain. Add the remaining ingredients and simmer slowly for 20 minutes. Serves 4.

Variation: Use 1 (16-ounce) can peeled tomatoes instead of the sauce and add ¼ teaspoon cumin and ½ cup chopped celery. Stir in one cup cooked macaroni and lay strips of American cheese over the mixture. Heat until it melts. Or add ½ teaspoon crushed oregano and ¼ teaspoon garlic powder. Serve over rice or macaroni.

Green Chile Bible (New Mexico)

Chili Casserole

Fifteen minutes from start to eat!

1 large bag corn chips
½ head iceberg lettuce
1 can chili with beans

1 can chili without beans
Longhorn cheese, grated
1 small can diced green chiles

Spread corn chips in the bottom of a 9x13-inch pan. Shred lettuce over corn chips. In a saucepan, heat the 2 cans of chili and pour over the corn chips and lettuce. Cover with grated cheese and chiles. Bake in oven at 400° until cheese melts (6 minutes or so). Serve hot.

Pioneer Family Recipes (Arizona)

When you bite into a four-alarm chili, don't wait for the fire trucks. The most soothing thing is milk! Swish it around in your mouth—it's the number one fire-putter-outer. There are a few other remedies including buttermilk, yogurt, fruit syrup, peanut butter, and olive oil.

Beef and Potato Casserole

1½ pounds ground beef
1 (32-ounce) jar spaghetti sauce
⅔ cup water

3 or 4 medium potatoes, peeled and
  thinly sliced
Mozzarella cheese

Cook ground beef. Drain off grease. Add spaghetti sauce and water. Stir and cook for one minute. Put half of this mixture in a greased 9x13x2-inch pan. Layer potatoes over the meat. Put rest of meat mixture over the potatoes. Cover with foil. Bake at 350° for about one hour. Remove foil. Arrange thin slices of mozzarella cheese over casserole (or use 8 ounces shredded cheese). Bake until cheese melts.

Decades of Recipes (Illinois)

★ **Even Easier**: Frozen hash browns would also work.

Quick Tater Tot Bake

1 pound hamburger
1 small onion, chopped
Salt and pepper, to taste
1 (16-ounce) package frozen
  tater tot potatoes

1 can cream of mushroom soup,
  undiluted
½ can milk or water
1 cup (4 ounces) shredded Cheddar
  cheese

Brown hamburger and onion. Drain. Season with salt and pepper. Place in greased 1½–2-quart casserole. Top with potatoes. Combine soup and milk or water. Pour over potatoes. Sprinkle with cheese. Bake at 325° for 30–40 minutes.

Kompelien Family Cookbook (Minnesota)

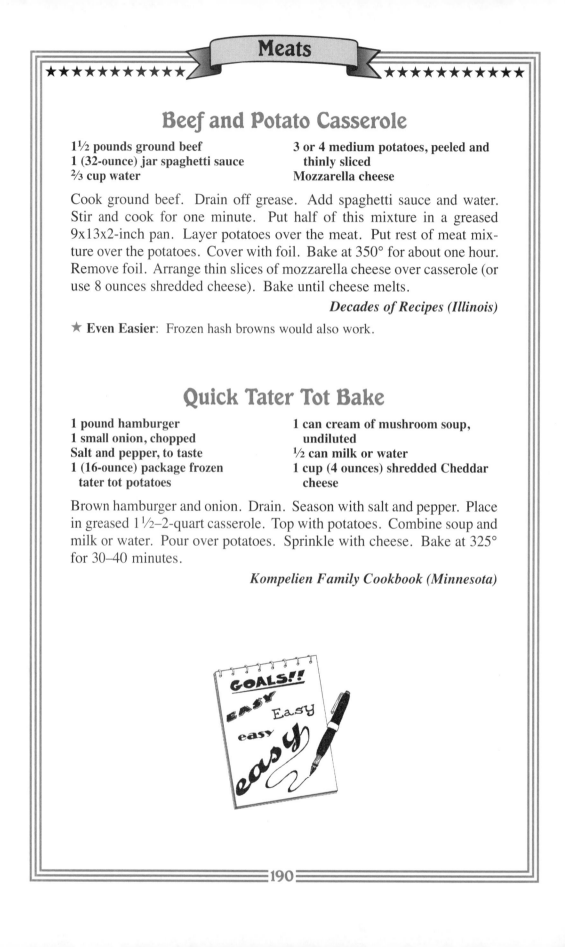

★★★★★★★★★★★   ★★★★★★★★★★★★

Easy Barbecued Hamburger

Prepare a salad, bring out the potato chips, and make this hot sandwich for a quick evening meal.

2½ pounds hamburger	3 tablespoons sugar
2 cups chopped green pepper	2 tablespoons vinegar
2 onions, chopped	1 tablespoon salt
1 cup catsup	12 hamburger buns
1 tablespoon dry mustard	

Cook first 3 ingredients together until meat is browned and vegetables are tender. Add remaining ingredients except buns; cook ½ hour on low heat. Serve on warm hamburger buns. Makes 12.

Sharing Our Best (Indiana)

Mom's Hamburgers

Young people especially like my hamburgers. They always call them Mom's Hamburgers.

1 pound ground beef	2 tablespoons minced onion
1 beaten egg	1½ tablespoons Worcestershire
½ teaspoon salt (or to taste)	sauce
Dash pepper	¼ cup bottled chili sauce
¾ cup cornflakes, crushed	¼ cup barbecue sauce

Combine ingredients. Mix thoroughly. Form into 6 or 7 patties. Broil 4–5 inches from heat. Broil about 8–10 minutes, turn, broil 5–7 minutes. Serve on Roman Meal or white hamburger buns.

Family Favorites by the Miller's Daughters (Tennessee)

★ **Even Easier:** A 2-sided contact grill does these in less than half the time.

Legend has it that in 1885, Charles R. Nagreen invented the hamburger at Seymour, Wisconsin's first fair, when he flattened meatballs into patties and served them between bread to make them more portable. The world's largest hamburger, weighing 5,520 pounds, was grilled at Seymour's Hamburger Hall of Fame in 1989.

Sloppy Joes

2½ pounds hamburger
1 medium onion, chopped
2½ tablespoons Worcestershire sauce
⅓ cup brown sugar

½ cup catsup
1 tablespoon mustard
1 (10¾-ounce) can cream of
   mushroom soup

Brown meat; drain. Add rest of ingredients and cook slowly until thick.
Fills 8–12 hamburger buns.

Recipes & Remembrances (Ohio)

Barbecue Cups

These are popular with everybody, always fun to serve.

¾ pound ground beef
½ cup barbecue sauce
2 teaspoons instant onion
Dash garlic powder

1 (10-ounce) package refrigerator
   biscuits
2 ounces grated Cheddar cheese

Brown ground beef; drain off excess grease. Add barbecue sauce, instant
onion, and garlic powder; mix well. Flatten each biscuit and press into
a muffin tin. Spoon beef mixture into center of each biscuit cup; then top
with grated cheese. Bake at 400° for 10–12 minutes. Makes 10 cups.

People Pleasers (Minnesota)

★ **Editor's Extra:** I use a can of big flaky biscuits which I separate in 2 layers, and form into 12 cups; separate the remaining 2 biscuits and bake alongside. Bakes in only 8 minutes.

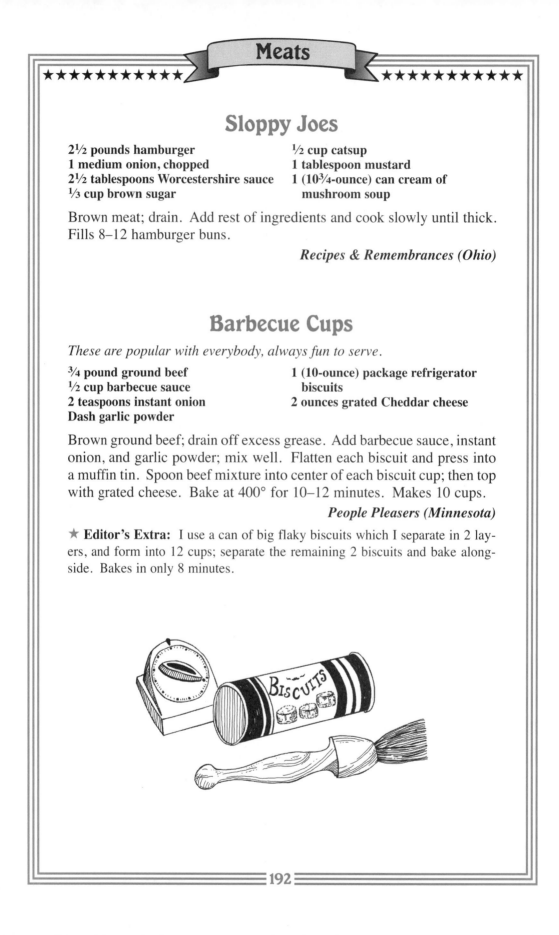

Hot Wheel Burgers

1½ pounds lean ground beef
1 (10¾-ounce) can tomato soup
1½ teaspoons dried minced onion
1 tablespoon prepared mustard
1 tablespoon Worcestershire sauce

1 teaspoon horseradish
1 teaspoon salt
6 hamburger buns
12 tomato slices
12 cheese slices

Combine first 7 ingredients. Spread thinly on 6 hamburger bun halves. Broil about 4–5 inches from heat for 5 minutes, or till lightly browned. Top with tomato slices and cheese slices. Broil until cheese melts (about 2 minutes). Serves 6.

Children's Party Book (Virginia)

★ **Editor's Extra:** I tried tomato sauce instead of tomato soup, and it was good that way, too. (See substitutions, page 291.)

Pizza Burger

Serve on buns or eat it with a fork—good!

1 pound ground meat
½–1 teaspoon salt

¼–½ cup pizza sauce
4 slices mozzarella cheese

Combine the meat, salt, and ½ of the pizza sauce. Mold into 4 patties and pan-fry over medium heat for 5–6 minutes on each side. Just before burgers are done, top each with a spoonful of pizza sauce and a slice of cheese. Continue cooking until cheese melts.

Look Mom, I Can Cook (Georgia)

Hot Dog!

A simple supper dish—not just for kids!

8 hot dogs
8 cheese slices

1 (8-ounce) package crescent rolls

Split hot dogs and fill them with a folded cheese slice. Wrap this in a crescent dough roll and bake 10–13 minutes in 375° oven. Serve with mustard to dip them in. Yummy!

The Indiana Kid's Cookbook (Indiana)

★★★★★★★★★★★ ★★★★★★★★★★★

Sugar Shack Cookout

You can teach an old "dog" new tricks!

2 tablespoons shortening
1 teaspoon soy sauce
1 teaspoon mustard
¾ cup maple syrup

1 tablespoon vinegar
1 teaspoon cornstarch
1 package hot dogs
1 package hamburger buns

Simmer first 6 ingredients in a saucepan for 8–10 minutes or until sauce is smooth and thick. Cut hot dogs halfway through in several places along one side only. Place on cookie sheet and grill, basting with sauce several times (as they cook the hot dogs will form circle). Place rounded hot dogs on toasted hamburger buns and fill center with baked beans.

Wisconsin Pure Maple Syrup Cookbook (Wisconsin)

★ **Editor's Extra:** Use the longer weiners and cut each one 10–12 times. These are so cute, kid-friendly, and fun to serve.

Trailer Treat

Good to cook over the fire while camping.

1 medium onion, chopped
3 tablespoons margarine
1 pound franks, quartered
1 teaspoon salt
1 tablespoon flour
1½ teaspoons chili powder

2 (15-ounce) cans kidney beans,
  drained
1 (16-ounce) can stewed tomatoes
1 (12-ounce) can corn kernels,
  drained

Sauté onion in melted margarine. Add franks. Heat until franks are cooked and onions are lightly browned. Add salt, flour and chili powder to onions and franks. Mix in beans, tomatos and corn. Simmer, covered, about 15 minutes.

Variation: May use 1 can kidney beans, drained, 1 can baked beans, 1 can tomato soup, 1 can tomatoes, and 1 can whole-kernel corn, drained.

Home Cookin' (Colorado)

★ **Editor's Extra:** This is good and easy for lunch or supper. Teenagers can do this easily, and proudly serve it when parents get home from work.

Hot Ham Buns

Poppy seeds give them a special flavor; try to use rye buns.

¼ cup soft butter or margarine
2 tablespoons prepared horseradish
  mustard
2 teaspoons poppy seed
2 tablespoons finely chopped onion

4 rye hamburger buns, split
4 thin slices boiled ham (can use
  baked)
4 slices Swiss cheese

Mix butter, mustard, poppy seed, and onion; spread generously on both cut surfaces of buns. Tuck a slice of ham and cheese in each bun. Arrange on baking sheet. Bake at 350° for about 15 minutes or until sandwiches are hot. Makes 4 sandwiches.

Note: Do not wrap in foil. Baking the sandwiches unwrapped results in a deliciously crisp outside with a tasty filling.

Singing in the Kitchen (Iowa)

Honey-Glazed Ham Slice

This will bring them buzzing 'round the table . . .

¼ cup orange juice
¼ cup honey
1 teaspoon prepared mustard

1 slice smoked (fully-cooked ham),
  cut 1-inch thick

Combine orange juice, honey, and mustard and cook slowly for 10–12 minutes, stirring occasionally. Place ham in broiling pan about 3 inches from heat. Brush with orange glaze. Broil 8 minutes on first side, then turn, brush with glaze, broil 6–8 minutes longer. Serves 2–3.

From My Apron Pocket (Texas)

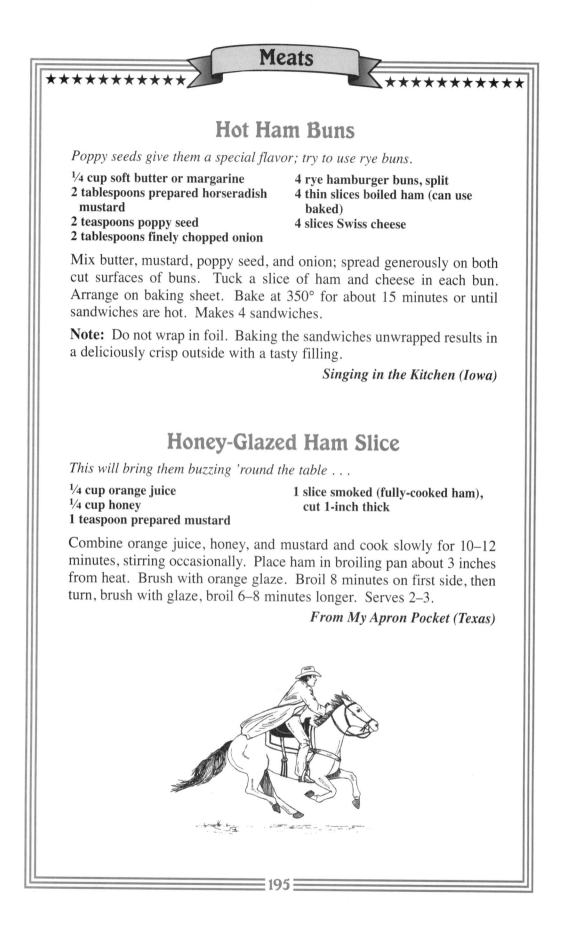

Ham Red Eye Gravy

When you fry ham, leave the "leavings" in the skillet. Take one teaspoon salt and sprinkle over the bottom of the skillet (less, if ham is salty). A sprinkle of sugar may be added. Brown the sugar and salt, then add 1 cup coffee (already made), put lid on so it won't spew on stove. Before adding coffee, make sure the fat and skillet are real hot. Pour off excess fat. Good on hot biscuits.

Seems Like I Done It This A-Way III (Oklahoma)

★ **Editor's Extra:** A thick ham slice is one of the quickest "entrées." Red eye gravy is good on grits, too. Heat a can of sweet potatoes with a few marshmallows and a pat of butter, open a bag of salad . . . there's your meal!

Ham 'N Swiss Pie

A low-fat lovely.

2 cups (8-ounce package) chopped
  Healthy Choice smoked ham deli
  meat
4 fat-free Kraft Swiss cheese slices,
  chopped
⅓ cup chopped onions or green
  onions
1 cup egg substitute
2 cups skim milk
1 cup reduced fat Bisquick baking
  mix
¼ teaspoon pepper
Vegetable spray

Heat oven to 400°. Spray a 10-inch pie plate with vegetable cooking spray. Sprinkle ham, cheese, and onions in pie plate. Beat remaining ingredients until smooth, 15 seconds in blender on high or 1 minute with hand beater. Pour into plate. Bake until golden brown and knife inserted in center comes out clean, 35–40 minutes. Cool 5 minutes. Makes 6 servings.

Nutritional Analysis Per Serving: Cal 135; Fat 2.8g; Cal from fat 19%; Chol 2.3mg; Sod 226mg; Fiber .3g; Exchanges ½ starch, 2 meats.

The Heart of Cooking II (Indiana)

★ **Even Easier**: A food processor does it all—chop ham and spread in pie plate, then cheese slices, then onion, then egg mixture.

Dinner in a Skillet

6 lean pork chops
1 tablespoon shortening or fat
2 tablespoons chopped onion
1 green pepper, sliced in rings

1 can tomatoes (2½ cups)
⅓ cup rice
1 teaspoon salt
¼ teaspoon pepper

Brown the chops in hot fat; pour off any excess. Add onion and green pepper and pour tomatoes over the top. Sprinkle the rice around the chops, also the salt and pepper. Cover; cook over low heat until the chops are tender, about one hour.

St. Joseph's Table (Great Plains)

Birds' Nests

A hearty "tweet."

1 pound ground or chopped beef
1 tablespoon finely chopped onion
1 tablespoon finely chopped parsley

Pepper, salt, nutmeg to taste
2 tablespoons butter or margarine
4 eggs

Mix meat with onion, parsley, and seasonings. Divide into 4 equal portions and shape into rings. Heat butter in large skillet and brown the rings on one side. Turn. Break one egg into each, taking care that the egg whites do not spill over the meat. Cover, and fry over moderate heat until egg whites are firm.

Note: Great served with creamed spinach and strips of bread, fried golden brown.

Dutch Touches (Iowa)

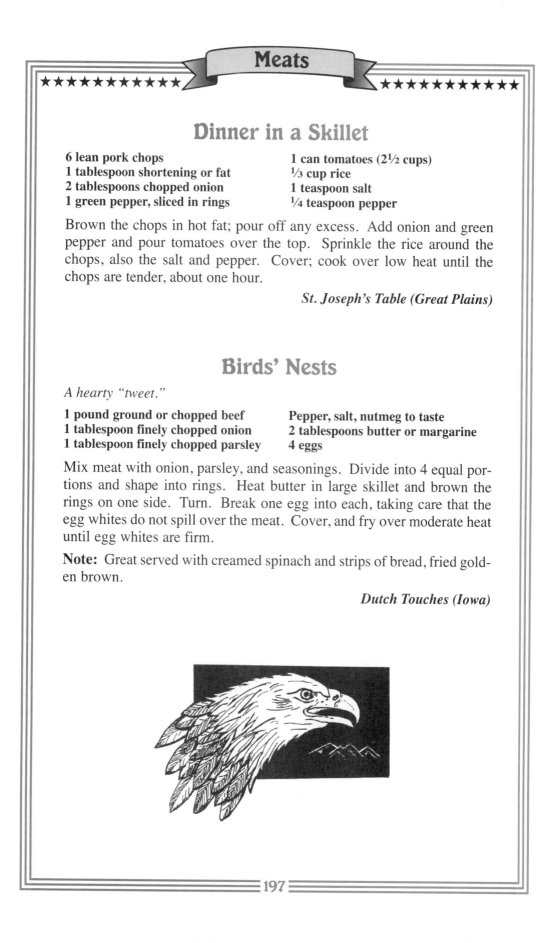

★★★★★★★★★★★★   ★★★★★★★★★★★★

Italian Pork Chops

4 pork chops
Garlic powder, oregano, celery salt
** and pepper to taste**

1 (8-ounce) can tomato sauce
4 slices mozzarella cheese

Sprinkle pork chops on both sides with seasonings. Place in 8x8-inch baking dish. Cover with tomato sauce. Bake at 350° for one hour. Top with cheese. Bake for 5 minutes longer or until cheese is melted. Yields 4 servings.

Per Serving: Cal 326; T Fat 15g; 43% Cal from Fat; Prot 40g; Carbo 5g; Fiber 1g; Chol 113mg; Sod 570mg.

Pioneer Pantry (Illinois)

Pineapple Chops

6 lean pork chops
1 (20-ounce) can pineapple slices
** (in own juice)**

⅓ cup honey
2 tablespoons soy sauce
¼ teaspoon ground ginger

Broil chops 5 inches from heat, 7–8 minutes. Turn chops and broil another 6 minutes.

Meanwhile, drain pineapple, reserving 3 tablespoons juice. Combine juice with the honey, soy sauce, and ginger. Place one pineapple slice atop each pork chop and broil 6–7 minutes, basting frequently with honey-juice mixture. Spoon remaining juice over chops before serving.

Calories 313; Fat 9g.

Good Cooking, Good Curling (Wisconsin)

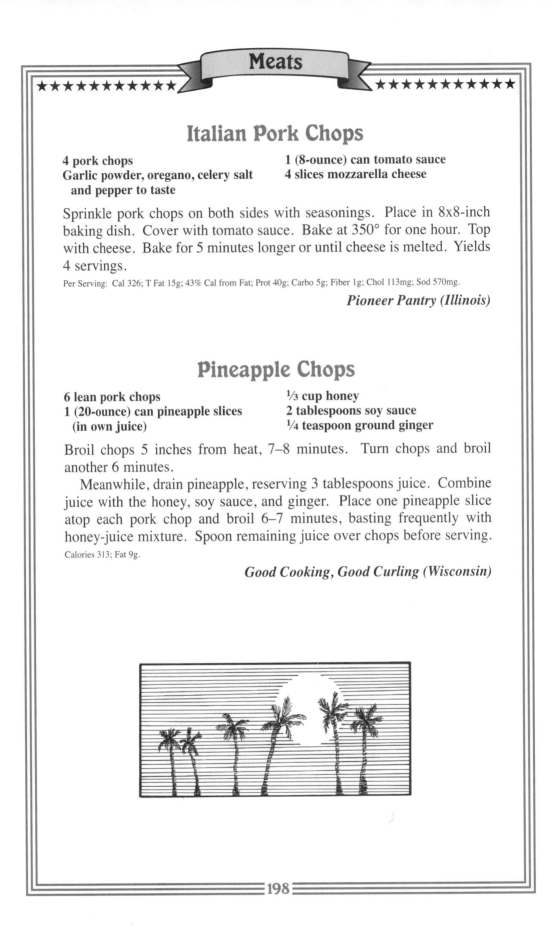

Mushroom-Onion Pork Chops

5 or 6 chops
Salt and pepper
1 package dry onion soup mix

1 can cream of mushroom soup
¼ soup can milk

Brown pork chops. Put in a 9x13-inch pan. Sprinkle with salt and pepper to taste. Mix onion soup mix and cream of mushroom soup. Thin with milk. Pour over chops. Bake in 350° oven for one hour. Soup sauce makes good gravy.

Note: May use recipe in crockpot.

Recipes from the Flock (Minnesota)

Orange Pork Chops

4–6 pork chops
½ cup orange juice
1 teaspoon salt

¼ cup brown sugar
¼ teaspoon pepper
½ teaspoon dry mustard

Put pork chops in a 7x11-inch pan. Mix remaining ingredients and pour over chops. Bake covered at 350° for 45 minutes; uncover and bake 15 minutes more, basting with juice in bottom of pan.

A Taste of Tampa (Florida)

★ **Even Easier**: I used thin pork chops and cut the baking time to 30 minutes. Add a teaspoon of cornstarch if you want it thicker!

Pork Chops with Mandarin Oranges

6 pork chops
3 tablespoons brown sugar
½ teaspoon ground cloves
½ teaspoon cinnamon

1 teaspoon prepared mustard
¼ cup catsup
1 tablespoon vinegar
1 (12-ounce) can mandarin oranges

Brown pork chops. Mix together other ingredients, except oranges, and pour over chops. Cook, covered, until tender (about 30–40 minutes). Remove excess fat. Watch carefully so sauce doesn't evaporate. Add water, if needed. Add mandarin oranges, including juice. Serve with rice or noodles.

Unbearably Good! Sharing Our Best (Wisconsin)

★★★★★★★★★★★ ★★★★★★★★★★★

Rosemary Pork Chops

1½ cups soy sauce
¾ cup water
¼ cup brown sugar

1 tablespoon dried rosemary,
  crushed
4 thick pork chops

Mix soy sauce with water, brown sugar, and rosemary. Marinate pork chops 3–4 hours. Bake uncovered at 350° up to one hour, depending upon thickness. May be grilled. Easy.

If It Tastes Good, Who Cares? II (Great Plains)

Pennsylvania Dutch Chops and Stuffing

4 (½-inch thick) boneless pork
  chops

1 (22-inch) can pie filling (apple or
  fruit of choice)

BREAD STUFFING:
2 cups dry bread crumbs
2 tablespoons chopped onion
⅛ teaspoon pepper
¼ cup butter, melted

½ cup chopped celery
1 egg, beaten
Milk to moisten

Grill chops till brown on both sides. Put chops into 10-inch square pan. Salt and pepper to taste. Pour pie filling evenly over chops. Mix and divide stuffing into 4 equal portions. Place one portion on each chop. Bake at 350° for one hour.

Susie's Cook Book (Pennsylvania)

Pork Medallions in Tarragon Sauce

1¼ pounds pork tenderloin, cut
  into 1-inch slices
Dijon mustard
2 tablespoons butter

½ cup beef broth
½ teaspoon dried tarragon
½ cup half-and-half
Pepper to taste

Cover pork slices with Dijon mustard. Brown pork in the butter and reduce heat; cook until no longer pink (5 minutes). Remove to heated platter. Add beef broth and tarragon to drippings, stirring to scrape brown bits loose. Simmer until ½ has evaporated. Add half-and-half and pepper, and simmer and stir until slightly thick. Pour sauce over pork.

Serve with buttered spinach noodles. May also use lamb chops.

Jubilee (Illinois)

Apple-Glazed Pork Kebabs

1 pound boneless pork loin, cut into
  1-inch cubes

2 tablespoons lemon juice
Salt to taste

APPLE GLAZE:
1 cup apple jelly
2 tablespoons lemon juice

1 teaspoon cinnamon
2 tablespoons butter

Sprinkle lemon juice and salt evenly over pork cubes. In small sauce-pan, make glaze by mixing together the jelly, lemon juice, cinnamon, and butter. Simmer until well blended (makes 1¼ cups).

Thread pork onto skewers and spoon glaze over all. Grill over hot coals, 10–12 minutes, turning frequently. Baste frequently. Serves 4.

Cook Book: Favorite Recipes from Our Best Cooks (Illinois)

★ **Editor's Extra:** This can be done with most any flavor of jelly or preserves. Children could help here, threading the pork cubes while a parent makes the glaze.

The International Apple Festival is held each summer in Medina, Texas, featuring every imaginable apple creation from pies to pizzas. You'll know you're in Medina when you see the big apple—a 20-foot high stone sculpture of an apple in the city park.

Chow Mein

As good as it gets. . . .

½ cup butter
1½ cups diced pork steak
1 cup chopped onions
1 cup diced celery

1 teaspoon salt
⅛ teaspoon pepper
1 cup hot water
1 can drained bean sprouts

THICKENING INGREDIENTS:

⅓ cup cold water
2 tablespoons cornstarch

2 teaspoons soy sauce
1 teaspoon sugar

Melt butter in skillet; add meat and sear. Add onions and fry 5 minutes. Add celery, salt, pepper, and hot water. Cook 5 minutes. Add bean sprouts and mix thoroughly. Heat to boiling point. Mix and add thickening ingredients. Serve over rice or chow mein noodles. Serves 6.

North Dakota...Where Food is Love (Great Plains)

Cakes

★★★★ ★★★★

The Land of Lincoln in Springfield, Illinois, is steeped in history.
Here at Lincoln's Tomb at Oak Ridge Cemetery, we found that
Lincoln is so genuinely revered and loved by his countrymen—
his nose is shiny from people rubbing it.

Special Lemon Cake

1 package yellow cake mix
4 eggs
1½ teaspoons lemon extract
¾ cup Wesson oil
1 package lemon Jell-O, dissolved
   in 1 cup hot water

Mix well. Bake in greased and floured 9x13-inch pan in a moderate 350° oven for 30–35 minutes. When done, prick with fork.

TOPPING:
1½ cups powdered sugar
2 tablespoons lemon juice

Mix well and put on top of the warm cake. It will sink through the pricked holes.

Lehigh Public Library Cookbook (Iowa)

★ **Editor's Extra:** Use lemon zest in cake if you don't have any extract.

Apricot Rum Cake

4 eggs
¾ cup vegetable oil
¾ cup apricot nectar
1 box yellow cake mix
5 ounces margarine
¾ cup sugar
½ cup rum
Confectioners' sugar

In a large bowl, beat eggs lightly and combine with oil, apricot nectar, and cake mix. Beat at medium speed for 4 or 5 minutes until smooth. Pour into large greased and floured Bundt pan or angel food cake pan. Bake at 350° for 50 minutes. Melt margarine and sugar in pan over low heat and stir in rum. As soon as cake is done, place pan on cooling rack and pour rum mixture over cake, allowing it to soak in well. Cool for one hour before removing from pan. Sift confectioners' sugar over top. Yields 12–16 servings.

Friendly Feasts Act II (Florida)

★ **Editor's Extra:** This looks pretty with stenciled-on powdered sugar. Use a doilie or make a cut-out of seasonal shapes—stars, bells, hearts, bunnies, pumpkins, etc.

Ambrosia Cake

1 Duncan Hines Yellow Cake Mix
  with pudding
1 cup orange juice, divided

1 can condensed milk
1 (12-ounce) container Cool Whip
Fresh coconut

Cook by instructions for sheet cake (9x13), but substitute ½ cup orange juice for ½ cup liquid. While warm from oven, punch holes in cake and pour condensed milk over cake. Then pour ½ cup orange juice over cake. Let cool and frost with large container of Cool Whip. Top with fresh coconut.

Cookin' Along the Cotton Belt (Arkansas)

Sunken Treasure Cake

1 package Pillsbury Plus German
  Chocolate Cake Mix
1 cup water

⅓ cup oil
3 eggs
4–6 Heath bars, crushed

Preheat oven to 350°. Grease 9x13-inch pan. In large bowl, mix all cake ingredients, except candy bars, at low speed until moistened; beat 2 minutes at highest speed. Pour into prepared pan. Sprinkle batter with crushed Heath bars. Bake at 350° for 30–40 minutes. Cool completely.

GLAZE:
1 cup powdered sugar
5 teaspoons water

1 teaspoon vanilla

In small bowl, blend Glaze ingredients. Drizzle over cooled cake.

Seasoned with Light (South Carolina)

★ **Even Easier**: Use a bag of Heath Bites. These hard-coated candies, found in the candy section, are going to make crunchier "treasures" than Heath Bits (found in baking section), but all give the same taste.

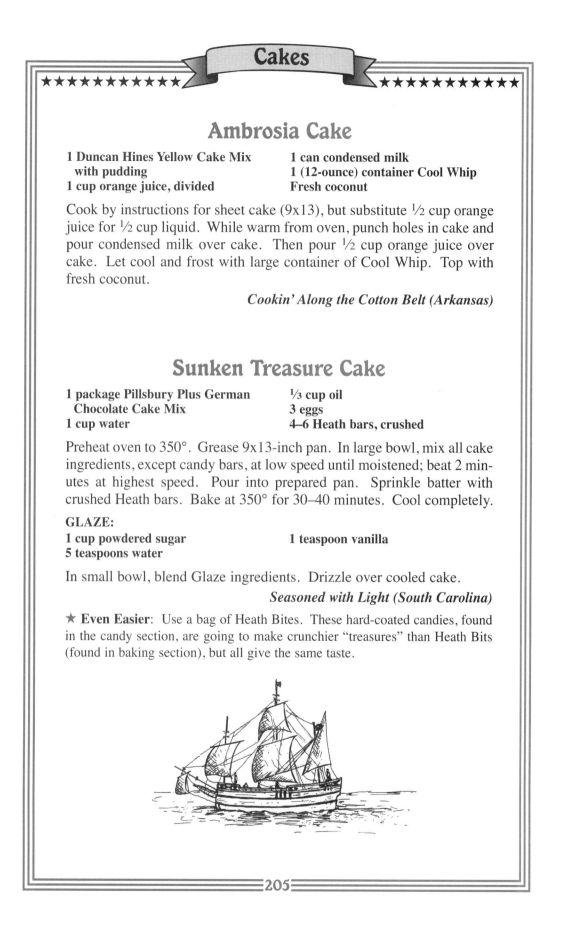

Upside Down German Chocolate Cake

1 box German chocolate cake mix
1 cup coconut
1 cup chopped pecans
1 stick margarine
1 (8-ounce) package cream cheese
3½–4 cups powdered sugar

Mix German chocolate cake mix as directed on box. Sprinkle coconut and pecans on bottom of a greased 9x13-inch pan. Pour batter over coconut and pecans. In saucepan, melt margarine and cream cheese. Then add powdered sugar. Mix. Spread this mixture or drizzle over top of cake. Bake at 350° for 40–50 minutes or until done.

Doc's Delights (Colorado)

Patron's Party Chocolate Cake

Too rich for frosting. Highly successful.

1 package devil's food cake mix
1 (3-ounce) package chocolate or
  fudge instant pudding
¾ cup water
¾ cup oil
4 large eggs
1 tablespoon instant coffee
1 cup sour cream
6 ounces semisweet chocolate chips

Combine all ingredients except chips in a large bowl. Beat slowly at first, then at high speed for 2 minutes. Fold in chips. Bake at 350° for one hour in greased and floured 10-inch tube or Bundt pan or in 10x15x1-inch pan (30 minutes) until done. May be cut in squares, like brownies. Cool completely before removing from pan. Serves 12–16.

The Prima Diner (Florida)

Pistachio Cake

1 white cake mix
1 cup oil
1 cup 7-UP or Sprite
3 eggs
1 package instant pistachio pudding
1 teaspoon almond extract

Mix all ingredients together well. Grease and flour a Bundt pan or a 9x13-inch pan. Bake at 350° for 30–35 minutes for sheet cake; 40–50 minutes for Bundt pan.

The Great Iowa Home Cooking Expedition (Iowa)

★★★★★★★★★★★ ★★★★★★★★★★★

Gooey Chocolate-Toffee Cake

1 box German chocolate cake mix
1 (16-ounce) jar butterscotch
  topping
1 can sweetened condensed milk
8 ounces whipping cream, whipped
4 Skor candy bars, crushed

Prepare cake mix as directed on package for 9x13-inch pan. Let cool 10–15 minutes. Poke holes evenly over entire cake with the end of a wooden spoon. Combine butterscotch topping with sweetened condensed milk. Pour evenly over top of warm cake. Refrigerate at this point to completely cool cake. Finish by icing the top of the cake with whipped cream. Sprinkle crushed candy bars over top. Serves 10–12.

A Taste of Fishers (Indiana)

Kahlua Cake

1 package chocolate cake mix
1 (3-ounce) box instant vanilla
  pudding
1 pint sour cream
4 eggs
¾ cup oil (Wesson or Crisco)
⅓ cup Kahlua
6 ounces chocolate chips

Combine all ingredients and pour into a greased, floured Bundt pan. Bake at 350° for 45–60 minutes or until cake springs back at touch. Sprinkle with powdered sugar when cool. Makes 8 servings.

Kingman Welcome Wagon Club Cookbook (Arizona)

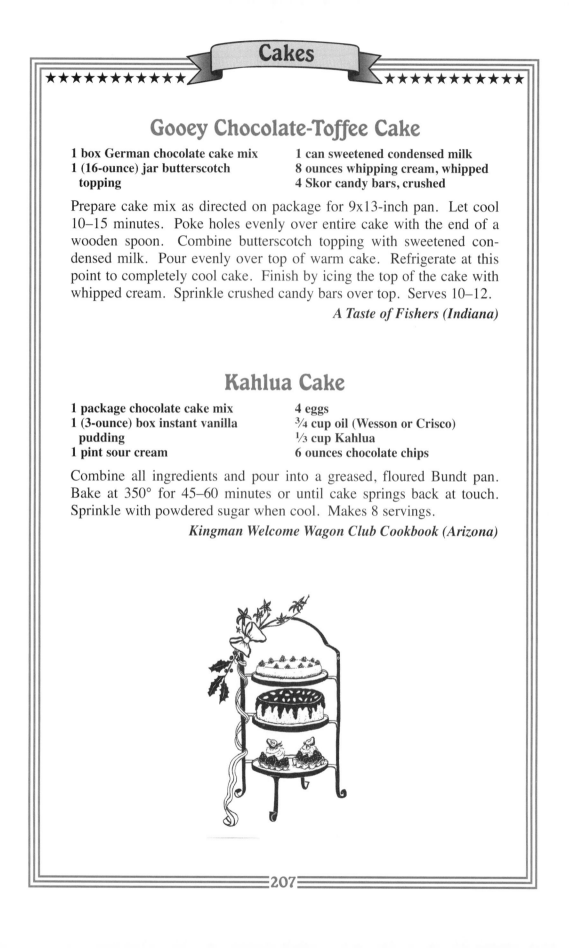

Dump Cake

The only place you'll want to dump this is in your mouth!

1 box butter cake mix
¾ cup melted margarine
1 large can crushed pineapple

1 can cherry pie filling
1 cup chopped nuts

Combine cake mix and butter until crumbly. Stir in pineapple and pie filling. Pour into greased oblong pan. Bake in 350° oven for 35 minutes. Sprinkle with nuts; bake 15 minutes longer.

Treasured Tastes (Alabama)

★ **Editor's Extra:** Some ovens bake "hotter" than others, so "top test" cake with your finger—should leave just the slightest indention. Another "done" clue is a slight browning around the edges with the cake slightly leaving the sides of the pan. And the toothpick "straw" test comes out of a cake middle with no "clumps" of cake on it. I'm more partial to under than overdone—dry cakes are no-no's! Moist is marvelous! I like to check cakes a few minutes earlier than the specified time.

Mandarin Orange Cake

1 package butter cake mix
4 eggs
1 cup cooking oil

1 (11-ounce) can mandarin orange
    sections, cut up and undrained

Mix all ingredients. (Do not use mixer.) Spoon into three (8-inch) greased and floured cake pans. Bake at 350° for 15 minutes.

ICING:

1 (9-ounce) carton whipped topping
1 (3-ounce) instant vanilla pudding
   mix

1 (20-ounce) can crushed pineapple,
   drained

Mix ingredients well. Ice cake. Keep cake in refrigerator.

Tasteful Traditions (Texas)

Dreamy Coconut Cake

Tastes as if it were made from scratch!

1 (18½-ounce) box white cake mix
1 can condensed milk
1 (9-ounce) carton non-dairy
  whipped topping

1 (8½-ounce) can cream of coconut
1 (6-ounce) package frozen
  coconut, thawed

Grease a 9x13-inch baking pan. Bake cake according to package directions. While cake is still hot, punch holes in the top with a fork or straw and pour milk over entire top; cool. Mix whipped topping and cream of coconut together by hand and spread over cake. Top with coconut. Refrigerate leftover cake.

Out of This World (Tennessee)

Apple Kuchen

½ cup butter
1 (18½-ounce) box yellow cake mix
1 (21-ounce) can apple pie filling

½ cup sugar
1 teaspoon cinnamon

Cut the butter into the cake mix (evenly). Spread into a greased 9x13-inch pan, pressing it with a clenched fist so that it goes up the sides of the pan by one inch. This will serve as a crust. Bake at 350° for 10 minutes. Remove from oven and spread apple pie filling all over crust. Mix sugar and cinnamon and sprinkle all over apples. Bake an additional 20 minutes at 350°.

Czech-Out Cajun Cooking (Louisiana II)

★ **Editor's Extra:** You can cut the butter into the cake with a fork or pastry blender, but more evenly and quickly in a food processor.

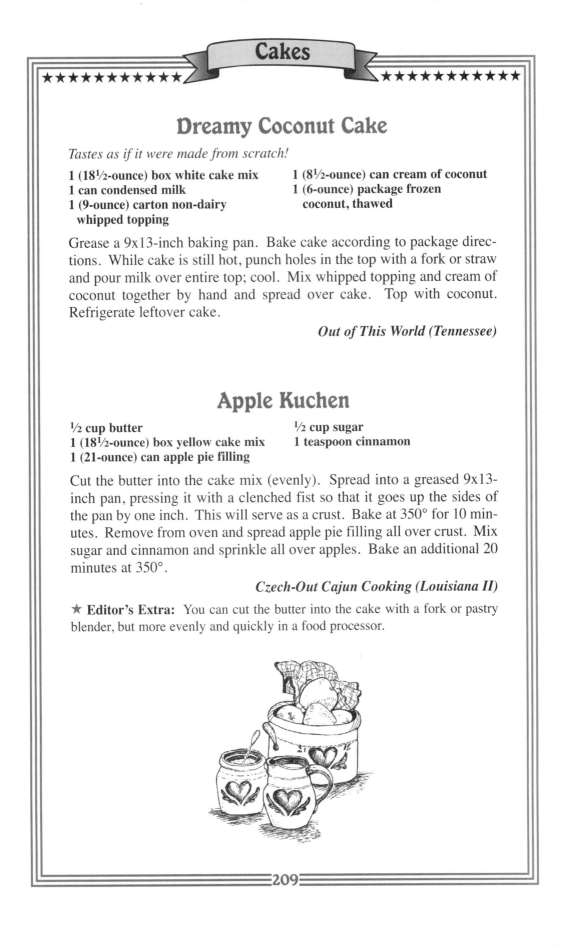

Self-Filled Cupcakes

A taste surprise inside.

1 chocolate cake mix	1 egg
1 (8-ounce) package cream cheese, softened	Dash salt
⅓ cup sugar	1 (6-ounce) package semisweet chocolate pieces (1 cup)

Mix cake according to package directions. Fill paper baking cups in muffin pans ⅔ full. Cream the cheese with sugar. Beat in egg and salt. Stir in chocolate pieces. Drop one rounded teaspoon cheese mixture into each cupcake. Bake as package directs for cup cakes (15 minutes at 350°). Makes 30 cup cakes. Not necessary to frost.

Dishes from the Deep (Arizona)

Cherry Chocolate Cake

First Place Best of Show Mid-South Fair 1989. So simple...so pretty.

1 package Duncan Hines Devil's Food Cake Mix	1 can Duncan Hines Chocolate Frosting
2 cups Cool Whip, thawed	
½ cup maraschino cherries, chopped	

Heat oven to 350°. Grease and flour 2 (9-inch) layer pans. Prepare batter as directed on package. Divide batter evenly between pans. Bake and cool as directed on package. Fold cherries into Cool Whip. Spread between cake layers. Frost with frosting. Store in refrigerator.

Cooking For Good Measure (Arkansas)

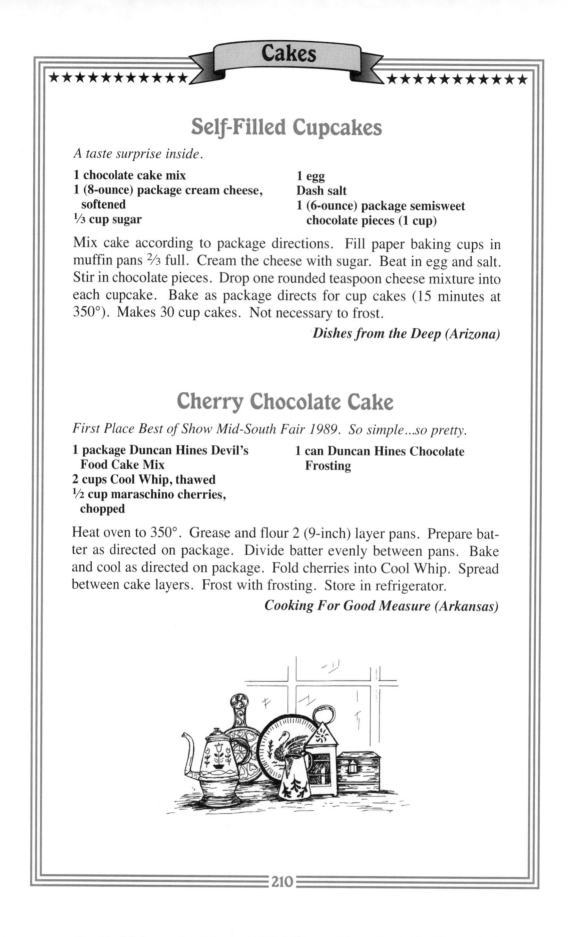

Cherry-Pineapple Cake

This is so yummy, more like a cobbler than a cake.

1 large can cherry pie filling
1 large can crushed pineapple and
  juice

¾ box yellow cake mix
1 stick margarine, chipped
Chopped walnuts, if desired

Layer ingredients as listed in a well-greased 9x13-inch pan. Sprinkle walnuts on top and bake for 50-60 minutes at 350°.

Amistad Community Recipes (New Mexico)

Chocolate Cherry Bars

This tastes like the Black Forest Cake.

1 chocolate cake mix
1 can cherry pie filling

1 teaspoon almond extract
2 eggs, beaten

Grease and flour jellyroll (10x15-inch) pan. In large bowl, combine all ingredients. Stir by hand until well mixed. Pour into prepared pan. Bake at 350° for 25–30 minutes, or until cake tester comes out clean. Frost with chocolate frosting.

Or put mixture into greased and floured 9x13-inch pan; bake for about 35 minutes. Frost with sweetened whipped cream and chocolate curls, if desired.

Our Best Home Cooking (Illinois)

Rhubarb Cake Quicky

1 box yellow or vanilla cake mix
3 cups thinly sliced rhubarb
½ cup chopped nuts

1 cup sugar
1 pint whipping cream, NOT
  whipped

Mix cake as directed and pour into greased and floured 9x13-inch pan. Sprinkle rhubarb and nuts over cake batter. Sprinkle sugar over rhubarb and nuts. Pour unwhipped cream over top. Bake in 350° oven for 40 minutes.

Ritzy Rhubarb Secrets Cookbook (Great Plains)

★★★★★★★★★★★ ★★★★★★★★★★★★

Mandarin Orange Cake

A scratch one-layer cake that is easy, moist and delicious!

1 cup sugar
1 cup flour
1 egg
1 can mandarin oranges, drained

1 teaspoon baking soda
½ teaspoon salt
1 teaspoon vanilla

Combine all ingredients in bowl; beat 2½–3 minutes. Bake 30–35 minutes in 350° oven in an 8-inch buttered pan.

TOPPING:
1 cup brown sugar
4 tablespoons butter

4 tablespoons milk

Bring topping mixture to a boil; pour over cake. Serve warm.

Colesburg Area Cookbook (Iowa)

Stir-in-the-Pan Cake

¼ cup Crisco oil
1 box Swiss chocolate cake mix
2 eggs
1¼ cups water

1 (6-ounce) package chocolate
  instant pudding
1 (6-ounce) package chocolate chips
½ cup chopped pecans

Preheat oven to 350°. Pour oil into 9x13-inch pan. Tilt pan until bottom is covered with oil. Pour cake mix, eggs, water, and pudding into pan. Stir with fork or spoon until blended. Scrape sides and spread batter evenly in pan. Sprinkle on chocolate chips and nuts. Bake at 350° for 35–45 minutes, until toothpick inserted in center comes out clean. Cut and serve directly from pan. Serves 16–20.

Delicious Reading (Missouri)

★ **Editor's Extra:** My favorite part of this recipe is that there is no clean-up till after the cake is gone! Well, okay, the measuring cup and the fork. But it's worth it!

★ ★

Little Dixie Pound Cake

6 tablespoons sugar	1 pinch baking soda
3 tablespoons soft butter	6 tablespoons flour
1 egg	¼ teaspoon vanilla
2½ tablespoons buttermilk	¼ teaspoon orange extract

Beat sugar and butter with mixer until light and fluffy. Beat in egg. Add half the buttermilk and drop the small pinch of baking soda into the buttermilk. Beat vigorously. Blend in half the flour. Stir in remaining buttermilk and beat again. Beat in remainder of flour. Add vanilla (and orange extract, if desired) and blend well. Pour into a well-greased and flour-dusted 1½-pint baking dish and bake at 350° for 30 minutes. Dust with powdered sugar, if desired. Serves 1–3.

Quickies for Singles (Louisiana)

★ **Editor's Extra:** Always get your cake into the oven as soon as you have finished mixing it. Baking soda and baking powder start working at once, so don't let the cake sit on the counter—it needs to get in the oven quickly. And know, too, that baking powder loses its strength after about 6 months, so it's a good idea to test it. Stir a teaspoonful into a half cup of hot water, and if it does not bubble up, it's time to replace it.

Pound Cake with Cherry Topping

Purchase pound cake. Place 2 slices on each dessert plate. Dip warm cherry topping over the cake at serving time.

CHERRY TOPPING:

8 ounces cherries (frozen, pitted, unsweetened)	1 tablespoon cornstarch
	¼ cup sugar
4 tablespoons water, divided	1 tablespoon lemon juice

Place cherries and 2 tablespoons water into a small saucepan. Bring to boil; cook 1 minute.

In a cup, combine cornstarch, 2 tablespoons water, sugar, and lemon juice. Stir to dissolve the cornstarch and sugar in the liquid. Add to the warm cherries. Stir and cook on low heat to form a sauce (approximately 1–2 minutes). Serves 2.

More Home Cooking in a Hurry (Tennessee)

Busy Day Lemon Cheesecake

Light and refreshing.

1 (8-ounce) package cream cheese,
  softened
2 cups milk, divided
1 (3-ounce) package instant lemon
  pudding mix

1 (8-inch) graham cracker pie crust
Graham cracker crumbs

Blend cream cheese with ½ cup milk. Add remaining milk and the pudding mix. Beat slowly with egg beater (or whisk) just until well mixed, about 1 minute (do not overbeat). Pour at once into graham cracker crust. Sprinkle graham cracker crumbs lightly over top. Chill about one hour. Serves 8.

Society of Farm Women of Pennsylvania (Pennsylvania)

Cream Cheese Pound Cake

1 Duncan Hines Butter Cake Mix
½ cup warm water
½ cup sugar
½ cup oil
4 eggs

1 (8-ounce) package cream cheese,
  softened
2 tablespoons margarine or butter,
  softened

Mix cake mix with water and sugar. Add oil and eggs. Add cream cheese and margarine or butter. Mix well. Bake at 350° in greased and floured angel food cake pan for 45–55 minutes or 2 loaf pans for about 35–50 minutes until done.

A Bouquet of Recipes (Louisiana II)

★ **Editor's Extra:** One stick of butter or margarine will soften in about one minute in microwave at 20% power. An 8-ounce package of cream cheese takes about 2 minutes; the low-fat and no-fat varieties are softer and probably need little if any softening.

Cream cheese was never made in Philadelphia! It was invented in 1872 in Chester, New York, by a man named Lawrence. He named it Philadelphia® after the city known for superb foods at that time. And Kraft has been producing Philadelphia® Brand all these years. Easy to keep on hand, an unopened package of cream cheese is good for one month past the "Best When Purchased By" date on the carton. Once opened, it should be used within 10 days.

★★★★★★★★★★★   ★★★★★★★★★★★

Plum Cake

2 cups sugar
3 eggs, beaten
1 cup Wesson oil
1 teaspoon ground cloves
1 teaspoon cinnamon
2 cups self-rising flour
2 small jars baby food plums
1 cup chopped nuts

Mix in order given (not beating). Bake about one hour at 350° in greased, floured Bundt pan (45–50 minutes) or 2 loaf pans (35–40 minutes). Delicious!

Atlanta Natives' Favorite Recipes (Georgia)

★ **Editor's Extra:** Be sure to save a few slices to toast for breakfast. Spread on a pat of butter and bring on the coffee.

Fruit Cocktail Cake

This recipe is fast and simple to make, takes no eggs or shortening.

1 (16-ounce) can fruit cocktail
1 cup flour, sifted
1 cup and 2 tablespoons sugar
¼ teaspoon salt
1 teaspoon soda
1 teaspoon vanilla
½ cup brown sugar
½ cup pecans

Put first 6 ingredients together in pan or mixing bowl and stir with a spoon; do not beat. Pour into greased 8x8-inch pan. Top with brown sugar and pecans. Bake at 350° for 35–40 minutes.

More Heart of the Home Recipes (Great Plains)

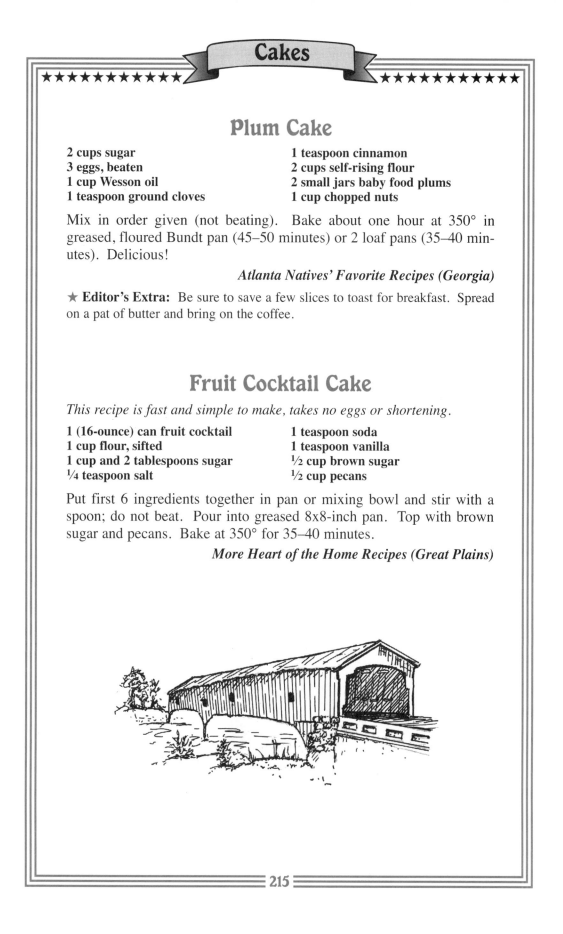

Quick Frosting

The secret to this fast frosting is using a blender to mix it!

**1 (8-ounce) package fat-free cream
  cheese**

**1 cup powdered sugar
1 teaspoon vanilla**

Place all ingredients in a blender or food processor. Blend until smooth and creamy. Completely frost cooled cake. Keep refrigerated. Frosts one 1-layer cake.

Nutrition Analysis Per Serving: Cal 36; Fat 0g; Cal from fat 0%; Chol 0mg; Sod 56mg.

The Heart of Cooking (Indiana)

Never Fail Chocolate Frosting

**1½ cups sugar
6 tablespoons milk
6 tablespoons butter or margarine**

**½ cup chocolate chips
1 teaspoon vanilla**

Just bring to a boil, sugar, milk, and butter or margarine. Then boil one minute. Add chocolate chips and vanilla. Beat until right consistency for frosting. Will frost a 9x13-inch cake.

Fontanelle Good Samaritan Center Commemorative Cookbook (Iowa)

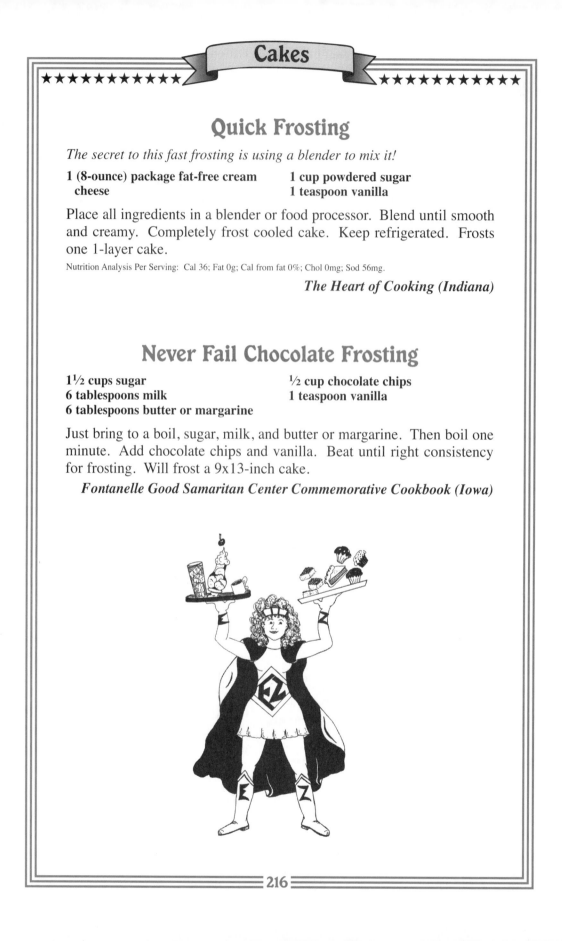

★★★★★★★★★★★★ ★★★★★★★★★★★★

Chocolate Chipper Frosting

Use this frosting any time you need a delicious chocolate frosting. It works well drizzled on Bundt cakes, too.

FOR 9x13-INCH CAKE OR BARS:
1½ cups sugar   ⅓ cup milk
⅓ cup butter or margarine   1 cup chocolate chips

In a 1-quart microwave bowl, combine sugar, butter, and milk. Microwave for 2–3 minutes at HIGH (100%) until mixture boils. Stir in chocolate chips until smooth. (Halve recipe for 8x8-inch cake.) Frost cake or brownies immediately.

Easy Livin' Microwave Cooking (Great Plains)

Quick and Easy Frosting

1 package instant pudding   1 cup cold milk
¼ cup powdered sugar   1 (8-ounce) container Cool Whip

Combine pudding mix, sugar, and milk in a small bowl. Beat slowly with beater at low speed for one minute. Fold in Cool Whip. Keep in the refrigerator.

Cookin' with Farmers Union Friends (Great Plains)

Ice Cream Cake

2 cups Captain Crunch Cereal,   ½ cup brown sugar
  crushed   ½ cup melted margarine
½ cup flaked coconut   ½ gallon ice cream, softened
½ cup chopped nuts

Mix together first 5 ingredients and put ½ in bottom of 9x13-inch pan. Then spread with soft ice cream. Put rest of mixture on top and freeze.

Franklin County Homemakers Extension Cookbook (Illinois)

★ **Editor's Extra:** A food processor does the mixing for you quickly and uniformly.

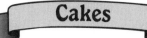

★★★★★★★★★★★ ★★★★★★★★★★★

Worster House Hot Fudge Sunday Cake

Here's one for you gals who need a quick dessert for a last-minute party.

First preheat oven to 350°. Use a 9x9-inch pan and do NOT grease pan.

1 cup flour　　　　　　　　**2 teaspoons baking powder**
¾ cup sugar　　　　　　　　**¼ teaspoon salt**
2 tablespoons cocoa

Combine all ingredients and stir with a fork in the baking pan.

½ cup milk　　　　　　　　**1 teaspoon vanilla**
2 tablespoons oil　　　　　　**1 cup chopped nuts**

Mix in separate bowl; then spread evenly on top of the flour and sugar mixture.

1 cup brown sugar　　　　　　**¼ cup cocoa**

Combine. Sprinkle over everything evenly.

1⅓ cups very hot water

Pour over the entire cake (do not stir). Bake for 35–40 minutes. Serve hot from the oven on top of your best vanilla ice cream.

A Taste of Hallowell (New England)

Cookies
& Candies

★★★★ ★★★★

Unlike here in town, the Amish farmlands all around southeastern Pennsylvania, have no electric wires to mar their beautiful landscape. The whole scene has a calming effect. The Amish bring their delicious pies, meats and goodies to the markets that we delighted in sampling.

Cheesecake Cookies

Absolutely fabulous!

1 cup real butter, softened	2 cups sugar
2 (3-ounce) packages cream cheese, softened	2 cups flour
	1 cup chopped pecans

Preheat oven to 350°. Cream together butter and cream cheese; add sugar, beating until light and fluffy. Add flour and beat well. Stir in pecans. Drop by teaspoonfuls onto ungreased cookie sheet and bake for 12 minutes. Yields 4 dozen.

Cafe Oklahoma (Oklahoma)

Ten Minute Sugar Cookies

These won't stay in the cookie jar very long.

1 cup white sugar	2 cups flour
½ cup softened butter	½ teaspoon soda
1 egg	½ teaspoon salt
2 tablespoons lemon juice	

Mix all ingredients. Roll into small balls. Flatten on greased cookie sheet with the bottom of a glass dipped in sugar. Bake at 375° for 10 minutes.

From the Recipe File of Agnes Gaffaney (Minnesota)

★ **Even Easier**: I don't bother to form perfect balls . . . just spoon on in little dollops. My grandkids don't expect cookies to be perfect circles—those are bought cookies!

Potato Chip Cookies

2 cups margarine, softened
1 cup sugar
3½ cups flour

1 teaspoon vanilla extract
1 cup crushed potato chips
¼ cup confectioners' sugar

Cream margarine and sugar in mixer bowl until light and fluffy. Add flour and vanilla; mix well. Add crushed potato chips gradually, mixing well after each addition. Drop by teaspoonfuls onto ungreased cookie sheet. Bake at 350° for 15 minutes or until golden brown. Cool on wire rack. Sprinkle with confectioners' sugar. Yields 36 servings.

Approx. Per Serving: Cal 168; T Fat 11g; Cal from Fat 57%; Prot 1g; Carbo 16g; Fiber <1g; Chol 0mg; Sod 127mg.

The Pioneer Chef (Oklahoma)

Brown Edge Cookies

You can't make enough!

1 cup butter, softened
⅔ cup sugar
2 eggs

1 teaspoon vanilla
1½ cups flour (sifted)
¼ teaspoon salt

Cream butter and sugar. Add eggs, beating well. Add vanilla. Mix in flour and salt. Drop by teaspoonfuls on greased cookie sheet. Bake in preheated 350° oven for 10 minutes. Makes about 60 cookies.

Note: Allow space between dropped dough, because cookies spread.

The Cook Book (Missouri)

Mexican Wedding Cookies

1 cup soft butter
½ cup powdered sugar
2 cups flour

1 teaspoon vanilla
½ cup pecans, chopped

Whip butter; add sugar, then add flour, vanilla, and nuts. Roll in balls about the size of a walnut. Put on cookie sheet and bake 10–15 minutes at 350°. Cool and roll in powdered sugar.

Cooking with the Warriors (Indiana)

★★★★★★★★★★★ ★★★★★★★★★★★

Chewy Noels

These are good and easy to make.

2 tablespoons margarine
2 eggs
1 cup brown sugar (packed)
5 tablespoons flour

⅛ teaspoon baking soda
1 cup chopped nuts
1 teaspoon vanilla
Powdered sugar

Heat oven to 350°. Melt margarine in a 9-inch square pan over low heat, then remove from heat. Beat eggs slightly. Combine sugar, flour, soda, and nuts and stir into beaten eggs. Add vanilla. Pour over melted margarine; don't stir, but spread evenly. Bake 20 minutes. Turn out onto rack, sprinkle bottom with powdered sugar, then cut in oblongs. Serves 18.

Treasured Recipes Book I (Missouri)

Butterscotch Crunchies

1 (12-ounce) package butterscotch
  morsels
6 ounces (2 cups) chow mein noodles

1 cup pecans, chopped

Melt butterscotch morsels in a heavy pan over low flame. Stir gently to blend. Stir in noodles and nuts until just blended and coated. Spoon mixture by teaspoonfuls onto waxed paper. Cool completely.

Old and New (Oklahoma)

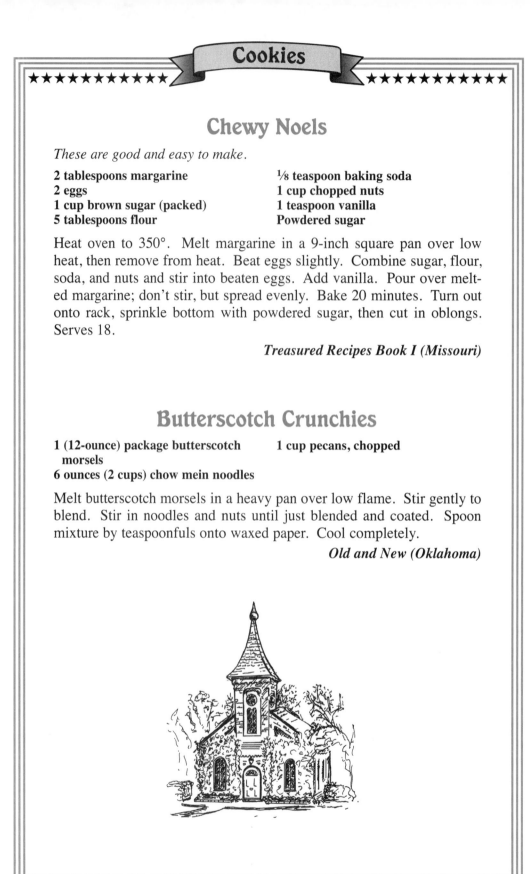

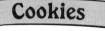

★★★★★★★★★★★   ★★★★★★★★★★★

Cornflake Cookies

These are disappearably delicious!

1 (6-ounce) package butterscotch   ½ cup peanut butter
  chips   3–3½ cups cornflakes

Melt chips, then add peanut butter. When mixed, add cornflakes. Drop
by teaspoonfuls onto waxed paper.

Kitchen Keepsakes (Minnesota)

★ **Even Easier**: Easy to put chips and peanut butter in 4-cup glass measure
and micro on HIGH 1½ minutes.

Horney Toads

½ cup sugar   Pinch of salt
½ cup brown sugar   1 cup peanut butter
1 cup white corn syrup   3 cups cornflakes

Blend sugars, syrup, and salt. Let come to a boil. Reduce heat to warm
and add peanut butter. Blend well. Blend in cornflakes and drop by teaspoonfuls onto waxed paper.

Note: Good using crunchy or creamy peanut butter.

Asbury United Methodist Church Cook Book (Arkansas)

No Bake Cookies

2 cups sugar   3 cups oatmeal
1 cup milk   1 teaspoon vanilla
½ cup butter or Crisco   Pinch of salt
½ cup cocoa

Boil sugar, milk, butter, and cocoa to a full boil. Remove from stove and
add oatmeal, vanilla, and salt. Drop onto waxed paper by teaspoonfuls
and chill. Makes 4–5 dozen.

The Hagen Family Cookbook (Great Plains)

★ **Editor's Extra:** Throw in some coconut and/or chopped nuts for variety.

Skillet Cookies

Great to make on a hot day.

½ cup margarine
2 eggs (slightly beaten)
1 (8-ounce) package chopped dates
1 cup sugar

1 cup chopped nuts
2 cups Rice Krispies
Coconut

Melt margarine in heavy skillet. Add eggs, dates, and sugar. Stir vigorously for 10 minutes, or until mixture is thick and brown. Turn off heat. Add nuts and Rice Krispies. Drop by teaspoonfuls into a small bowl containing coconut. Roll into balls.

Cookies and Bars (Michigan)

Spanish Gold Bricks

So easy and just delicious!

1 package graham crackers (20–24)
½ cup finely chopped pecans
½ cup butter

½ cup margarine
½ cup sugar

Separate sections of graham crackers and line on ungreased jelly roll pan so that the sides of the graham crackers are touching. Sprinkle pecans over graham crackers. In a saucepan, melt together butter, margarine and sugar. Boil and stir for 2 minutes. Pour slowly and evenly over the top of the graham crackers and nuts until all are covered. Bake at 325° for 8–10 minutes. Cool in the pan for about 10 minutes. Separate with a knife. Store in an upright container. These can be frozen.

Gourmet by the Bay (Virginia)

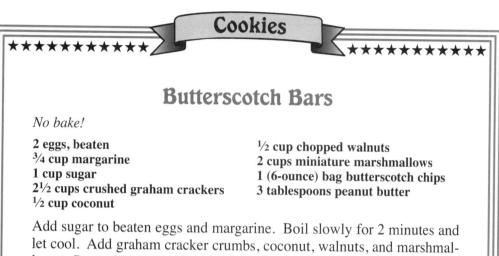

Butterscotch Bars

No bake!

2 eggs, beaten
¾ cup margarine
1 cup sugar
2½ cups crushed graham crackers
½ cup coconut

½ cup chopped walnuts
2 cups miniature marshmallows
1 (6-ounce) bag butterscotch chips
3 tablespoons peanut butter

Add sugar to beaten eggs and margarine. Boil slowly for 2 minutes and let cool. Add graham cracker crumbs, coconut, walnuts, and marshmallows. Press this into a 9x13-inch pan and top with butterscotch chips melted with peanut butter.

Kelvin Homemakers 50th Anniversary Cookbook (Great Plains)

Cheese Cake Bars

A hit with everyone!

⅓ cup butter, softened
⅓ cup brown sugar

1 cup flour
½ cup chopped nuts

Cream butter with brown sugar in small mixing bowl; add flour and nuts. Mix to make a crumb mixture. Reserve one cup for topping. Press remainder into bottom of 8-inch square pan.

FILLING:
1 (8-ounce) package cream cheese,
   softened
¼ cup sugar
1 egg

½ teaspoon vanilla
2 tablespoons milk
1 tablespoon lemon juice

Mix well and beat until creamy. Pour over crumb mixture. Sprinkle remaining crumbs over filling. Bake at 350° for 12–15 minutes.

Mountain Potpourri (North Carolina)

★ **Editor's Extra:** Though nothing beats the taste of real lemon juice, the bottled kind subs quite well, and the frozen variety is almost as good as fresh.

★★★★★★★★★★★★ ★★★★★★★★★★★★

Audrey's Cheese Bars

2 (8-ounce) cans crescent rolls
1½ cups sugar, divided
2 (8-ounce) packages cream cheese,
  softened
1 egg, separated
1 teaspoon vanilla
½ cup nuts
½ teaspoon cinnamon

Press one package of crescent rolls on bottom of 9x13-inch pan. Mix one cup sugar, cream cheese, egg yolk, and vanilla; spread on top of crescent rolls. Put other package of rolls on top and spread beaten egg white on top. Sprinkle with ½ cup sugar, nuts and cinnamon. Bake at 350° for 30 minutes. When cool, cut into 48 (2x1-inch) bars.

Favorite Recipes of Pommern Cooks (Wisconsin)

Chewy Pecan Pie Bars

¼ cup butter or margarine, melted
2 cups packed brown sugar
⅔ cup all-purpose flour
4 eggs
2 teaspoons vanilla
¼ teaspoon baking soda
¼ teaspoon salt
2 cups chopped pecans
Confectioners' sugar

Pour butter into 9x13x2-inch baking pan; set aside. In mixing bowl, combine brown sugar, flour, eggs, vanilla, baking soda, and salt; mix well. Stir in pecans. Spread over butter. Bake at 350° for 30–35 minutes. Remove from oven, and immediately dust with confectioners' sugar. Cool before cutting. Makes 2 dozen.

Par Excellence (Arizona)

★ **Editor's Extra:** The trick of softening brown sugar in the microwave really works great. Simply put the open box alongside a cup of hot water and microwave on HIGH for 2 minutes or so.

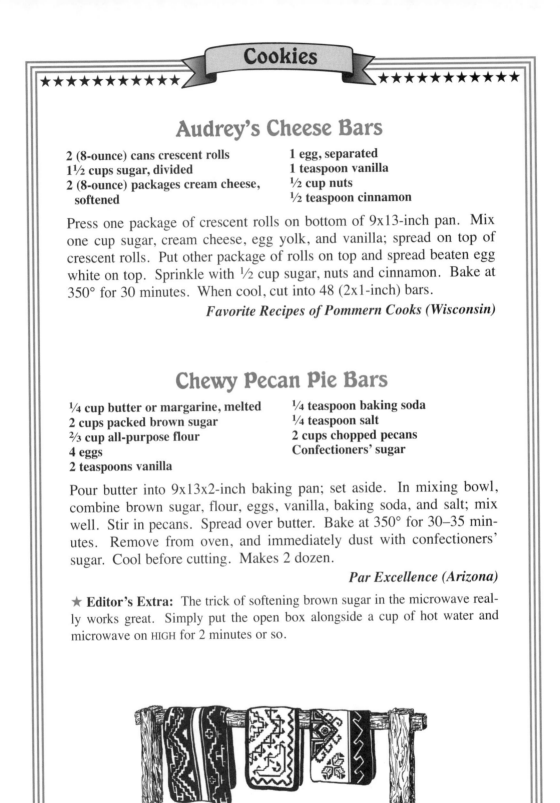

Lemon Squares

Shortbread-y super!

2 cups flour
½ cup powdered sugar
½ pound melted butter
4 eggs, beaten
2 cups sugar

4 tablespoons flour
1 teaspoon baking powder
½ teaspoon salt
4 tablespoons lemon juice

Mix first 3 ingredients and press in a large 12x18-inch pan or cookie sheet with rim. Bake at 325° for 20 minutes.

Mix beaten eggs with remaining ingredients. Spread over crust and bake for 30 minutes at 325°. Cut in squares and dust with powdered sugar.

Home Cooking (Indiana)

★ **Editor's Extra:** This is a "while" recipe . . . while the crust is baking, you throw the filling ingredients together. Though not lightning quick, it's big on easy, and even bigger on taste.

Cookies and Cream Wedges

CRUST:
2 cups finely crushed Oreos
  (24 cookies)

⅓ cup melted butter

FILLING:
2 (8-ounce) packages cream
  cheese
⅔ cup sugar
1 tablespoon vanilla

1 cup cream, whipped (okay to use
  Cool Whip)
2 ounces semisweet chocolate,
  grated (or mini-chocolate chips)

Press Oreo crumbs mixed with butter into bottom of springform pan. Beat cream cheese until fluffy. Add sugar and vanilla. Fold in whipped cream and grated chocolate or mini-chips. Pour over crust. Freeze 2 hours. Serves 8.

Recipe from Leadville Country Inn, Leadville
Pure Gold—Colorado Treasures (Colorado)

Chocolate Chip Cream Squares

**2 (16-ounce) rolls chocolate chip
 cookie dough**
**1 (16-ounce) package cream
 cheese, softened**

2 eggs
½ cup sugar
½ teaspoon vanilla

Pat one roll of dough in bottom of greased 9x13-inch pan. Cream together cream cheese, eggs, sugar, and vanilla. Spread mixture on top of
dough in pan. Crumble the second roll of dough on top of cream mixture. Bake about 30 minutes at 350°. Cookie will be soft in center.
Yields 2 dozen.

Chockful O' Chips (Missouri)

Chocolate Toffee Crunch Bars

Soooo yummy!

COOKIE BASE:
**2 cups (about 26) finely crushed
 vanilla wafers**

¼ cup packed brown sugar
⅓ cup butter, melted

Preheat oven to 350°. In bowl, combine wafer crumbs and brown sugar.
Stir in butter. Press in 9x13-inch pan. Bake for 8 minutes.

½ cup butter
½ cup packed brown sugar

1 (6-ounce) package chocolate chips
½ cup finely chopped nuts

Heat butter and brown sugar in pan over medium heat until boiling. Boil
1 minute. Pour immediately over cookie base and spread to edges. Bake
at 350° for 10 minutes. Let stand 2 minutes. Sprinkle with chocolate
chips (mini-chips work best). Let stand for 2–3 minutes. Then spread
chips. Sprinkle with chopped nuts.

25th Anniversary Cookbook (Ohio)

★ **Editor's Extra:** Once I forgot to bake these before I sprinkled on the chips,
so it was ruined, right? Wrong! It all got eaten and raved over! But the right
way is even better.

Did you know that chocolate morsels are made from only four ingredients? They are: chocolate liquor, sugar, cocoa butter, and vanilla. Morsels keep best when stored in a cool, dry
place. When exposed to temperature changes, the surface of the morsels can develop a
whitish film, called the "bloom," which is actually just fine traces of melted cocoa butter that
have hardened again—it won't affect the flavor or performance of the chocolate.

Peanut Butter Squares

No baking required. Good "kid" recipe.

1 cup peanut butter
1 cup confectioners' sugar

2 sticks (1 cup) margarine, softened
3 cups graham cracker crumbs

Mix above ingredients in a bowl. Pat into a 9x13-inch pan. Top with the following ingredients, melted together.

1 can condensed milk (not
  evaporated milk)

1 (12-ounce) package chocolate chips

The milk and chips can be put into microwave oven in microwave-safe bowl for 1½ minutes at FULL POWER. Whip quickly and spread over squares quickly. Refrigerate for about one hour; then cut into squares.

Note: The milk and chips can also be put into a saucepan on the stove to melt.

Berkshire Seasonings (New England)

Rocky Road Squares

This is incredible . . . and incredibly easy.

1 (12-ounce) package semisweet
  chocolate morsels
1 (14-ounce) can condensed milk
2 tablespoons butter or margarine

2 cups dry roasted peanuts
1 (10½-ounce) package miniature
  white marshmallows

In top of double boiler, melt chocolate morsels with condensed milk and butter. Remove from heat. In large bowl, combine nuts and marshmallows. Fold in chocolate mixture. Spread in waxed-paper-lined 9x13-inch pan. Chill 2 hours or until firm. Remove from pan. Peel off waxed paper and cut into squares. Cover and store at room temperature. Makes about 40 squares. (Pictured on cover.)

Amish Country Cookbook II (Indiana)

★ **Even Easier**: I melt the chocolate, milk, and butter in the microwave for 2 minutes on HIGH.

Favorite Decadence Layer Bars

"What takes minutes to make, combines my guests' favorite cookie ingredients and disappears in seconds? Why, Decadence Layer Bars, of course," comments innkeeper Julie Cahalane.

½ cup butter
2 cups graham cracker crumbs
1 cup (7 ounces) coconut
1 (12-ounce) package semisweet
  chocolate chips

2 cups chopped pecans
1 (14-ounce) can sweetened
  condensed milk

Preheat oven to 350°. While the oven preheats, melt the butter in a 9x13-inch pan. One layer at a time, sprinkle the graham cracker crumbs, coconut, chocolate chips, and pecans over the melted butter. Pour sweetened condensed milk over all. Bake for 30 minutes. Cool and cut into squares. Makes 18 large bars.

Inn on the Rio's Favorite Recipes (New Mexico)

Mixed Nut Bars

1½ cups flour
½ cup butter, softened
¾ cup brown sugar
1 (6-ounce) package butterscotch
  chips

⅓ cup light corn syrup
2 tablespoons butter
1 (11-ounce) can mixed salted nuts

Mix flour, ½ cup butter and sugar together. Pat into greased 9x13-inch pan. Bake 10 minutes at 350° and cool. Heat over low heat the butterscotch chips, corn syrup, and 2 tablespoons butter. Cover bottom of crust with nuts. Pour melted mixture over nuts. Bake for 10 minutes.

What's on the Agenda? (Wisconsin)

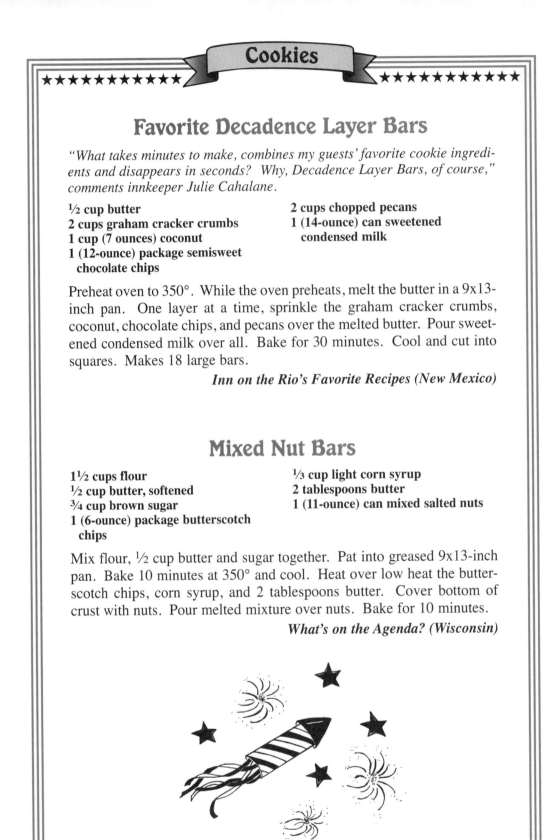

Tiger Stripes

1 pound white chocolate
1 (12-ounce) jar chunky peanut
  butter

2 (8-ounce) packages semisweet
  chocolate, melted

Combine white chocolate and peanut butter in top of double boiler above water heated to boiling. Reduce heat and stir constantly until mixture is melted and well blended. Spread mixture onto a waxed-paper-lined 10x15-inch jelly roll pan. Pour semisweet chocolate over first layer and swirl through with a knife. Chill until firm. Cut into small squares. Store in refrigerator. Yields 6 dozen squares.

Note: Chocolate and peanut butter may be melted in a microwave oven.

Heart of the Mountains (North Carolina)

Choc-Marshmallow Bars

½ cup soft butter or margarine
¾ cup flour
2 eggs
2 tablespoons cocoa

¾ cup white sugar
1 teaspoon vanilla
½ bag mini-marshmallows

Combine all but mini-marshmallows and mix well. Spread in 9x13-inch pan and bake at 350° for 15 minutes. Remove from oven and spread with mini-marshmallows. Return to oven for 3 minutes. Cool and prepare topping. Spread topping over marshmallows.

TOPPING:
1 cup chocolate chips
1 cup crunchy peanut butter

2 cups Rice Krispies

Melt chips and peanut butter together, then stir in Rice Krispies.

First United Methodist Church Cookbook (Minnesota)

Margarine was first made in the U.S. in 1873. So that it would not be confused with butter, it was not allowed to be colored yellow. Thirty-two states and 80% of the U.S. population lived under margarine color bans. While the Supreme Court upheld such bans, it did strike down forced coloration (pink) which had begun in an effort to get around the ban on yellow coloring. During this period, coloring in the home began, with purveyors providing capsules of food coloring to be kneaded into the margarine. This practice continued through World War II. It was not until 1996 that a legislative bill signaled an end to the last piece of legislation that adversely affected the sale of margarine.

Easy Brownies

These cut so pretty—a great make-with-the-kids recipe.

18 graham cracker squares (about
  2 cups)
1 can condensed milk

1 (6-ounce) package chocolate bits
Dash of salt

Roll graham crackers until fine, then mix with remaining ingredients. Pour into 8-inch square pan that has been greased and floured, and bake 30 minutes in 350° oven. Cut in squares while still warm and remove from pan. Yields 20–25 squares.

Note: Nuts may be added, if desired.

The Memphis Cookbook (Tennessee)

★ **Even Easier**: Use 1½ cups of already crumbed graham crackers and any flavor bits—butterscotch, peanut butter, milk chocolate—all yummy!

Quickest Brownies Ever

Moist type.

1 (4-ounce) square bitter chocolate
1 cup butter or margarine
2 cups sugar
4 eggs, unbeaten

1 cup flour
1 cup nuts (optional)
1 teaspoon vanilla

Melt chocolate and butter in large saucepan. Turn off the heat. Add remaining ingredients in order. (Mixes well with a wooden spoon.) Pour into greased 9x13x2-inch pan. Bake at 350° for 30 minutes. Cool and frost with chocolate icing or sprinkle with sifted powdered sugar. Yields approximately 24 squares.

The Guild Cookbook I (Indiana)

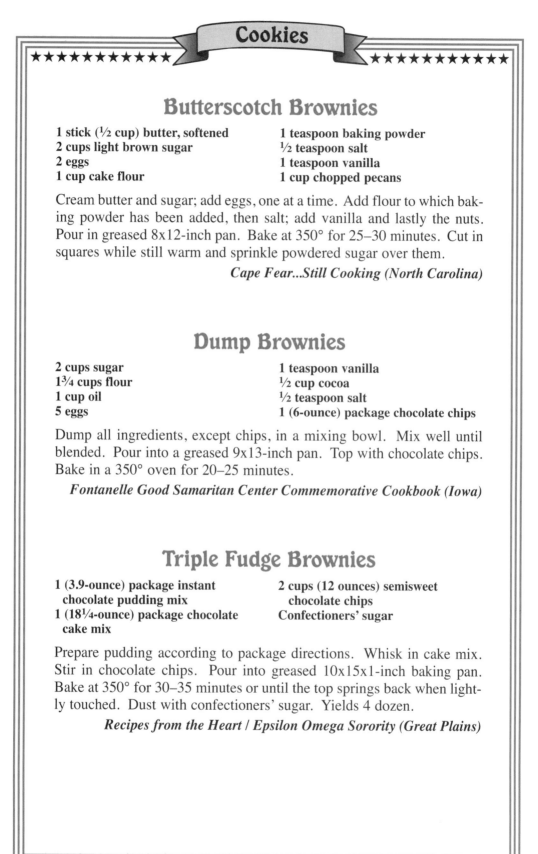

Butterscotch Brownies

1 stick (½ cup) butter, softened
2 cups light brown sugar
2 eggs
1 cup cake flour

1 teaspoon baking powder
½ teaspoon salt
1 teaspoon vanilla
1 cup chopped pecans

Cream butter and sugar; add eggs, one at a time. Add flour to which baking powder has been added, then salt; add vanilla and lastly the nuts. Pour in greased 8x12-inch pan. Bake at 350° for 25–30 minutes. Cut in squares while still warm and sprinkle powdered sugar over them.

Cape Fear...Still Cooking (North Carolina)

Dump Brownies

2 cups sugar
1¾ cups flour
1 cup oil
5 eggs

1 teaspoon vanilla
½ cup cocoa
½ teaspoon salt
1 (6-ounce) package chocolate chips

Dump all ingredients, except chips, in a mixing bowl. Mix well until blended. Pour into a greased 9x13-inch pan. Top with chocolate chips. Bake in a 350° oven for 20–25 minutes.

Fontanelle Good Samaritan Center Commemorative Cookbook (Iowa)

Triple Fudge Brownies

1 (3.9-ounce) package instant
  chocolate pudding mix
1 (18¼-ounce) package chocolate
  cake mix

2 cups (12 ounces) semisweet
  chocolate chips
Confectioners' sugar

Prepare pudding according to package directions. Whisk in cake mix. Stir in chocolate chips. Pour into greased 10x15x1-inch baking pan. Bake at 350° for 30–35 minutes or until the top springs back when lightly touched. Dust with confectioners' sugar. Yields 4 dozen.

Recipes from the Heart / Epsilon Omega Sorority (Great Plains)

Church Windows

For an easy, quick cookie, this is especially pretty for the holidays. Something special means making Church Windows.

1 (12-ounce) package semisweet
  chocolate chips
1 stick (½ cup) margarine
1 cup chopped walnuts or pecans

1 (10-ounce) package miniature
  colored marshmallows
Powdered sugar or coconut

Melt together chocolate chips and margarine. Cool (about 15 minutes). Add chopped walnuts or pecans and marshmallows. Divide mixture in half and form 2 large logs. Roll each log in powdered sugar or in coconut. Wrap tightly in aluminum foil and chill for 24 hours. Slice into ⅓-inch cookies. Makes approximately 3 dozen.

Sharing Our Best (Indiana)

★ **Even Easier**: I make 4 logs—they're easier to cut when smaller, and we like easy!

Crème de Menthe Cookies

No bake!

1 cup vanilla wafer crumbs
1 cup powdered sugar
2 tablespoons corn syrup

¼ cup crème de menthe
¾ cup chopped nuts
Confectioners' sugar to coat

Combine all ingredients. Roll into small balls and roll balls in confectioners' sugar. Store in air-tight containers.

The Dog-Gone Delicious Cookbook (Arizona)

Puppy Chow

1 (12-ounce) bag chocolate chips
1 stick margarine
1 cup creamy peanut butter

1 (12.3-ounce) box Crispix cereal
3 cups powdered sugar

Melt chips, margarine, and peanut butter in microwave for 1½ minutes. Remove and stir. Mix with cereal until cereal is well coated. Put powdered sugar in large brown bag. Add mixture and shake until coated.

Wisconsin's Best (Wisconsin)

Apricot Nut Snowballs

No-bake and oh, so easy.

6 ounces dried apricots
¼ cup apricot jam
1 tablespoon sugar

1 cup chopped nuts
1 cup sweetened coconut
Confectioners' sugar

Put all ingredients in food processor, except confectioners' sugar, and pulse until a mass is formed. Form balls using a rounded teaspoon and roll in confectioners' sugar. Chill, covered loosely, in refrigerator.

The Island Cookbook (New England)

Carnival Popcorn

2 quarts popped popcorn
2 cups brown sugar, packed
½ cup white corn syrup

1 cup margarine or butter
6 ounces roasted, salted peanuts

Set aside popped corn in large bowl or bag. In 4-quart microwave-safe container, combine brown sugar, corn syrup, and margarine. Microwave on HIGH (100%) for 10 minutes. Remove container from oven. Add peanuts and popped corn. Mix well to coat surfaces of corn. Spread onto greased flat tray. Cool. Store in covered container. Yields 2 quarts.

The Texas Microwave Cookbook (Texas)

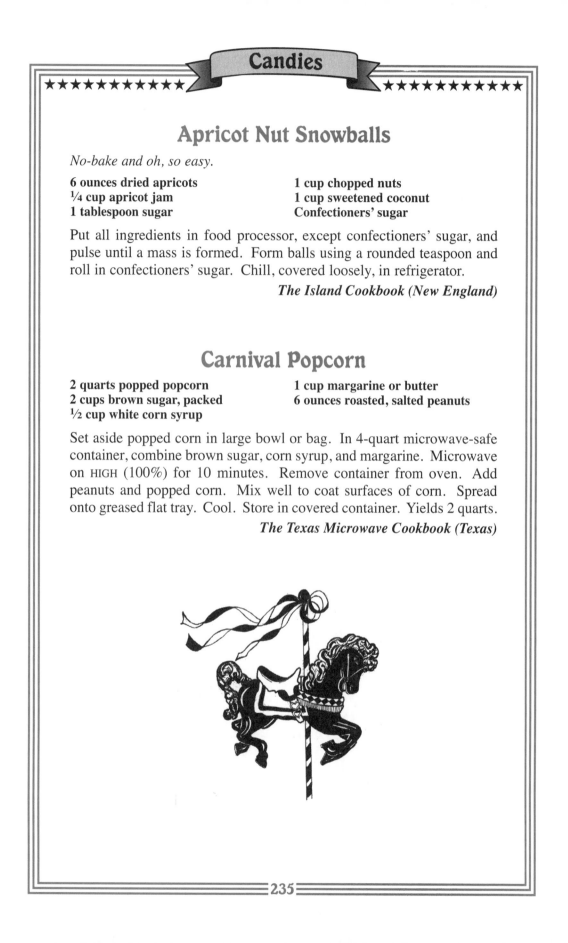

Chocolate Bark

Excellent and different.

40 saltine crackers
1 cup butter (not margarine)
1 cup brown sugar

12 ounces chocolate chips
½ cup finely chopped almonds

Cover bottom and sides of cookie sheet with aluminum foil. Place 40 crackers side-by-side. Melt butter; add sugar. Bring to a rolling boil. Boil exactly 3 minutes. Stir often. Remove from heat and immediately pour gently over saltines. Bake 5–7 minutes (till bubbly brown) at 400°. Sprinkle chocolate chips over crackers and spread as they melt. Sprinkle on nuts. Refrigerate 2 hours. Break into pieces.

Chefs and Artists (Pennsylvania)

Chinese Chews

½ cup butter or margarine,
  softened
2 tablespoons white sugar
1 cup flour
2 eggs

¼ cup coconut
¾ cup chopped nuts
1½ cups brown sugar
2 tablespoons flour
1 teaspoon vanilla

Mix together butter, white sugar, and flour and press into a greased 9x9-inch pan. Bake at 350° for 15 minutes.

Mix eggs, coconut, nuts, brown sugar, flour, and vanilla, and place over the baked part. Bake again at 350° for 25 minutes.

Amish Country Cookbook I (Indiana)

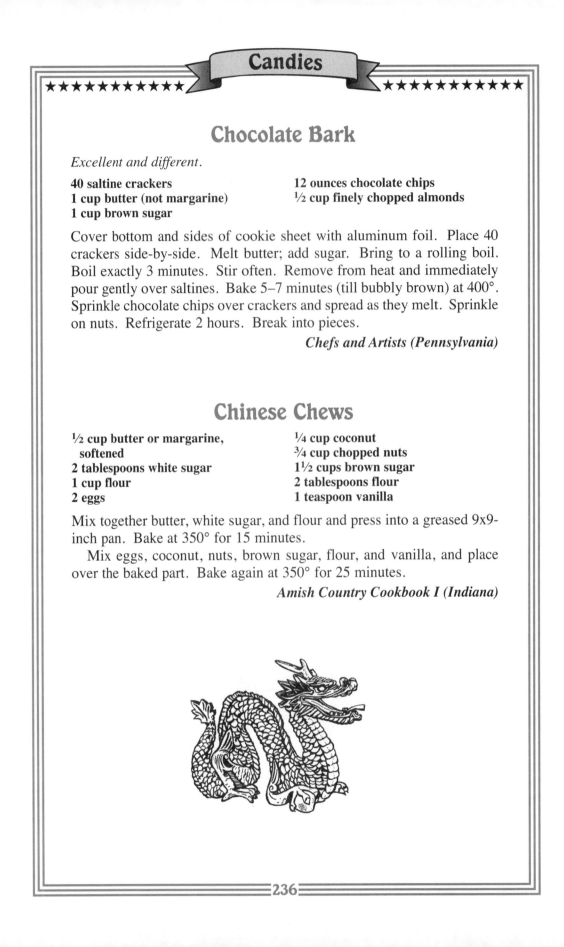

Orange Balls

1 (12-ounce) package vanilla wafers,
  crushed
1 cup confectioners' sugar
¼ cup butter, softened to room
  temperature

½ cup frozen orange juice
  concentrate, thawed
½ teaspoon vanilla
1 cup chopped pecans

Combine crumbs and sugar; blend in butter. Stir in orange concentrate; add vanilla and nuts. Shape mixture into bite-sized balls; shake in plastic bag with additional confectioners' sugar. Arrange orange balls in single layer on tray; store uncovered overnight in refrigerator. Yields 36–40 balls. Roll in coconut, if desired.

Bell's Best (Mississippi)

★ **Editor's Extra:** This is one of my mother's favorite finger food desserts for weddings, teas and showers.

★ **Even Easier:** Frozen orange juice can be thawed right in its container with the top metal lid removed. A 6-ounce container takes 30 seconds on high; a 12-ounce container takes 45 seconds.

Cranberry Surprise

Wow! A different taste experience! Ready in minutes!

1 (1-pound) package almond
  bark

1 (12-ounce) package fresh
  cranberries

Melt almond bark in microwave or in double boiler. Drop dry, fresh cranberries into melted bark a few at a time. Remove each one to wax paper, individually, and let harden. Delicious as hors d'oeuvres, candy or a snack. (Pictured on cover.)

Stir Ups (Oklahoma)

★ **Editor's Extra:** Be sure to do these one at a time. Good with chocolate almond bark, too!

The cranberry is one of only three fruits native to America, the others being the Concord grape and the blueberry.

Rum Balls

1½ cups vanilla wafer crumbs
¼ cup rum
¼ cup honey

2 cups ground walnuts
Confectioners' sugar

Use prepared vanilla wafer crumbs or crush vanilla wafers very fine. (The food processor does this well.) In medium bowl combine all ingredients, except sugar. Mix well. Shape into 1-inch balls. Roll in confectioners' sugar. Store in tightly covered container until ready to use. Can store in refrigerator. Yields 2½ dozen.

In the Pink (Louisiana II)

Chocolate Almond Bark Crunch

10–12 ounces chocolate almond bark
2 tablespoons peanut butter
1 cup nuts

1 cup marshmallows
1½ cups Rice Krispies

Melt almond bark and peanut butter together in a large bowl (microwave on HIGH 90 seconds; stir; microwave more, if necessary). Add nuts, marshmallows, and Rice Krispies. Stir and drop by spoonfuls onto buttered foil.

Country Cooking (Oklahoma)

Pecan Log Roll

1 (6-ounce) package butterscotch
  morsels
⅓ cup condensed milk
½ teaspoon vanilla

½ cup chopped pecans
1 egg white, slightly beaten
Additional chopped pecans

Melt morsels over hot (not boiling) water. Remove from heat. Stir in condensed milk, vanilla and pecans. Chill until firm enough to handle. Roll tightly on waxed paper (sprayed lightly with vegetable cooking spray) to form a 12-inch roll. Brush with egg white, then roll in additional chopped pecans. Chill and slice.

Boarding House Reach (Georgia)

Marshmallow Fudge

4 cups sugar
1 (14½-ounce) can evaporated milk
1 cup butter
1 pint marshmallow cream
1 (12-ounce) package chocolate chips
1 teaspoon vanilla
1 cup chopped nuts

Bring sugar, milk, and butter to a boil. Cook to medium-soft stage (236°), stirring. Remove from heat. Add marshmallow cream, chips, vanilla, and nuts. Stir. Pour into pan, at least 9x9-inches. Cut into squares when cool. Makes 3 pounds.

The Stuffed Griffin (Georgia)

★ **Editor's Extra:** If you don't have a candy thermometer, drop several droplets from a spoon into some tap water in a cup. It will form a ball rather quickly at the medium-soft stage.

Cream Cheese Fudge

A soft, creamy, no-cook sweet treat.

1 (3-ounce) package cream cheese
2 squares unsweetened chocolate
1 tablespoon milk
2 cups confectioners' sugar
1 teaspoon vanilla
⅛ teaspon salt
½ cup chopped nuts

Soften cream cheese at room temperature. Melt chocolate. Combine cream cheese and milk and beat until smooth. Gradually add sugar and chocolate. Blend. Stir in vanilla, salt, and nuts. Spread evenly in pan and cut into squares.

Dinner Bell (Pennsylvania)

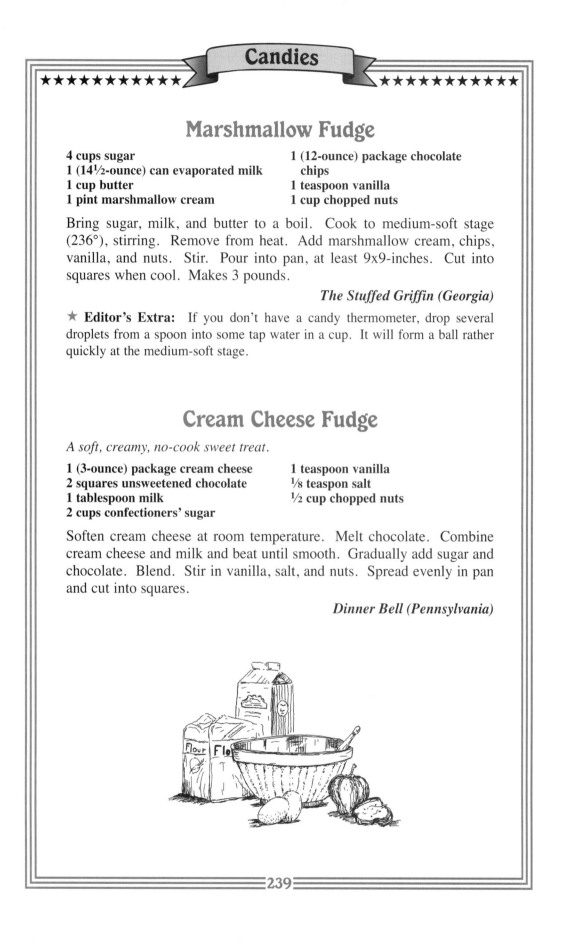

★★★★★★★★★★★ ★★★★★★★★★★★

Grandma's Microwave Fudge

Wonderfully delicious—remarkably easy!

1 box powdered sugar	**1 stick butter**
½ cup cocoa	**1 teaspoon vanilla**
¼ cup milk	**Chopped nuts**

Blend together sugar and cocoa in a glass bowl; add milk. Place butter on top of mixture and microwave 2 minutes. Stir; add vanilla and nuts and mix well. Spread onto foil or waxed-paper-lined pan (for easier removal from pan) and refrigerate for one hour. Cut into squares, remove from pan and serve.

Ramblin' Chefs from Georgia Tech (Georgia)

Easy Candy

2 cups sugar	**1 stick margarine**
1 small can evaporated milk	**6 ounces chocolate chips**
12 marshmallows	**1 cup chopped nuts**

Combine sugar, milk, and marshmallows in heavy saucepan and boil hard for 6 minutes. Remove from heat and stir in margarine, chocolate chips, and nuts. Continue to stir until chocolate chips have melted. Pour quickly onto greased platter and allow to cool before cutting into squares.

Have Fun Cooking with Me (North Carolina)

★ **Even Easier**: Miniature marshmallows melt quicker. Believe it or not, it takes about 10 to make one big puffy marshmallow! (It may take you more time to count than to melt the big ones!)

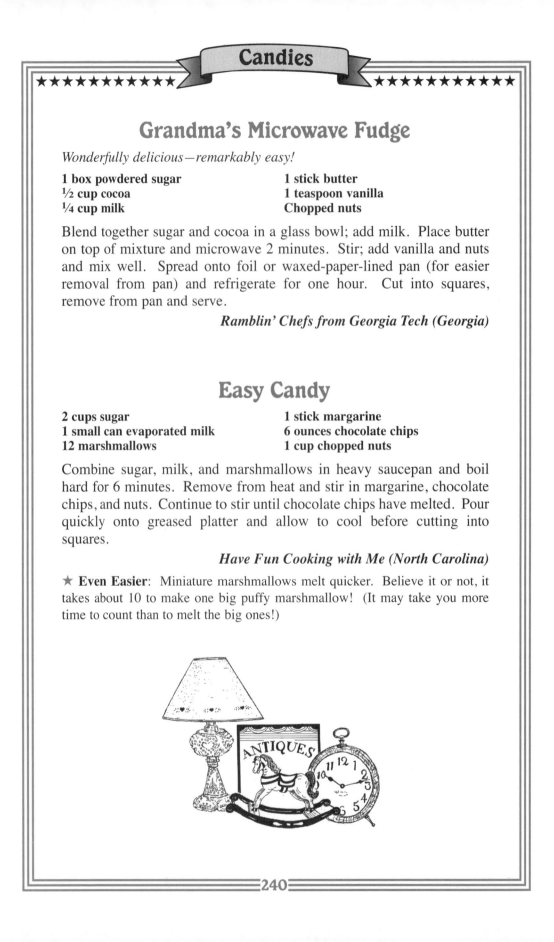

240

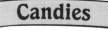

Peanut Butter Sighs

1 (8-ounce) jar natural peanut
  butter, no salt
1 cup margarine

1 pound confectioners' sugar
1 (12-ounce) package semisweet
  chocolate chips

Place peanut butter and margarine in a microwave-safe baking dish. Cover with wax paper and microwave on HIGH (100%) 2 minutes, until margarine and peanut butter melt. Blend together. Add powdered sugar, stirring to mix. Press smoothly into bottom of (8x8-inch) dish.

Place chocolate chips in a flat dish to melt on HIGH (100%) 1½ minutes. Spread over top. Cool in refrigerator and cut into squares. Makes 45 squares.

Tout de Suite á la Microwave II (Louisiana)

★ **Even Easier**: This works with regular or crunchy peanut butter, too.

Peanut Brittle

Easy and delicious!

1 cup sugar
1 cup white corn syrup

1 cup raw peanuts
1 teaspoon baking soda

Heat sugar and syrup until clear. Add raw peanuts and boil until it is amber in color (about like a penny). Remove from heat and add soda. Stir well (will be frothy). Pour into a well-buttered cookie sheet. Cool and break into pieces. Can add large flaked coconut, if desired.

Country Cupboard Cookbook (Iowa)

A few facts about peanuts: As evidenced by pottery decorations and shapes, peanuts have been around about 3,500 years. Vessels of peanuts have been found in ancient Inca ruins; they were left with the dead to provide food in the afterlife. George Washington Carver began research into peanuts in 1903 at Tuskegee Institute in Alabama, leading him to discover more than 300 uses for peanuts, including shoe polish and shaving cream. The call, "Hot Roasted Peanuts," was first heard in the late 1800s at P.T. Barnum's circus, and spread as his wagons traveled around the country. Peanuts contribute over four billion dollars to the U.S. economy each year.

Microwave Pralines

These are bronze beauties.

1 box instant butterscotch pie filling
½ cup brown sugar
1 tablespoon butter
1 cup white sugar
½ cup evaporated milk
½ teaspoon vanilla
1½–2 cups chopped pecans

Mix all ingredients except pecans in 8-cup microwave bowl; cook 3 minutes on HIGH; stir and cook 2 more minutes; stir and cook 2 more minutes. Then add your pecans and beat until creamy. Drop on wax paper.

Czech-Out Cajun Cooking (Louisiana II)

★ **Editor's Extra:** If it gets too thick while you're dipping it onto the wax paper, add a few drops of the milk that's leftover in that little 5-ounce can.

Oh' Henry Bars

1 cup brown sugar
1 cup soft margarine
4 cups quick oatmeal
½ cup white Karo syrup
6 ounces chocolate chips
¾ cup peanut butter

Mix first 4 ingredients together like a pie crust (about 20 pulses in food processor). Pat in ungreased 10x15-inch cookie sheet (with sides). Bake 15–17 minutes at 350°, till brown around edges. Meanwhile, melt chocolate chips and peanut butter in microwave on HIGH for 2 minutes. Spread over slightly cooled oatmeal mixture; refrigerate. Makes 50–60 squares.

Decades of Recipes (Illinois)

Pies &
Other Desserts

★★★★ ★★★★

Great skiers we're not, as Gwen attests by her toe-in, slow-down
ski position. We did learn a little about high altitude cooking, however,
and that food tastes fabulous when you come down off the slopes!

Six-Minute Pecan Pie

Six minutes and let 'er bake! Great!

3 eggs (slightly beaten)
1 cup corn syrup
1 cup sugar
2 tablespoons butter or margarine,
  softened

1 teaspoon vanilla
1½ cups pecans
1 unbaked pie shell

In large bowl stir together first 5 ingredients until well blended. Stir in nuts. Pour into pie shell. Bake in 350° oven 50–55 minutes, or until knife inserted halfway between center and edge comes out clean. Cool.

The Oke Family Cookbook (Minnesota)

Ritz Pecan Pie

At Callaway Gardens there are so many good things served to eat . . . it's hard to decide what you like best . . . but one dessert you'll always enjoy is this delicious pie.

⅔ cup egg whites
1 cup sugar
½ teaspoon baking powder

1 cup chopped pecans
16 Ritz Crackers, crumbled
Whipped cream or Cool Whip

Beat the egg whites. Mix sugar and baking powder. Add to egg whites. Beat until stiff peaks form. Fold in nuts and cracker crumbs. Bake in buttered pie pan 45 minutes at 300°. When cooled, top with whipped cream. Garnish with extra cracker crumbs and pecans.

Country Cookin' (Georgia)

★ **Editor's Extra:** The chef at Callaway Gardens says if you sauté the pecans, it will bring out the flavor.

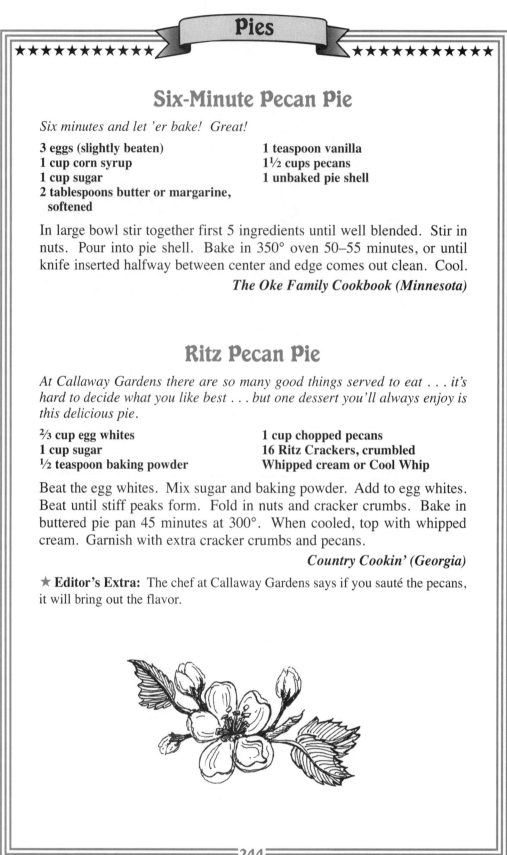

Grandma's House Walnut Pie

3 eggs, beaten
2 cups sugar
1 cup white Karo
1 teaspoon salt

2 teaspoons vanilla
¼ cup melted margarine
2 cups walnuts or pecans
2 unbaked (9-inch) pie shells

Mix eggs, sugar, Karo, salt, and vanilla. Stir in melted margarine and nuts. Pour into unbaked pie shells. Bake at 350° for 45 minutes to 1 hour or until filling is firm. Each pie serves 6–8.

Grandma's House Restaurant & Family Recipes (California)

Impossible Pie

Makes its own crust.

4 eggs
1¾ cups sugar
½ cup flour
1 (7-ounce) can coconut

2 cups milk
1 teaspoon vanilla
½ stick margarine, melted

Butter 2 (9-inch) pie pans. Combine ingredients in order listed. Pour into pie pans and bake at 350° for 30 minutes.

Bay Leaves (Florida)

★ **Editor's Extra:** I sometimes use less sugar, as little as one cup, and it's still yummy!

Chess Pie

1 cup sugar
⅔ stick butter, softened
3 eggs
Nutmeg

2 tablespoons milk
2 tablespoons cornmeal
2 teaspoons vinegar
1 teaspoon vanilla

Cream sugar and butter; add remaining ingredients. Bake at 400° for 10 minutes, then at 300° for 30 minutes.

Bell's Best 2 (Mississippi)

★★★★★★★★★★★ ★★★★★★★★★★★

Pineapple-Coconut Pie

1½ cups sugar
4 eggs
1 stick butter, melted
1 (8¼-ounce) can crushed pineapple

1 cup shredded coconut
1 tablespoon vanilla
2 (8-inch) unbaked pie shells

Mix sugar and eggs together and blend with butter (cooled). Mix in pineapple, coconut, and vanilla. Pour into pie shells. Bake in 350° oven for 35 minutes or until done.

Huntsville Entertains (Alabama)

Coconut Macaroon Pie

¼ cup chopped pecans
1 (8-inch) unbaked pie shell
½ cup water
¼ cup flour
1 (3½-ounce) can flaked coconut

2 eggs, slightly beaten
1½ cups sugar
¼ teaspoon salt
½ cup melted butter

Sprinkle pecans over bottom of pie shell. Combine remaining ingredients; pour into pie shell. Bake in slow oven (325°) until golden brown and almost set (about 45 minutes). Cool and serve.

Home Cooking (Indiana)

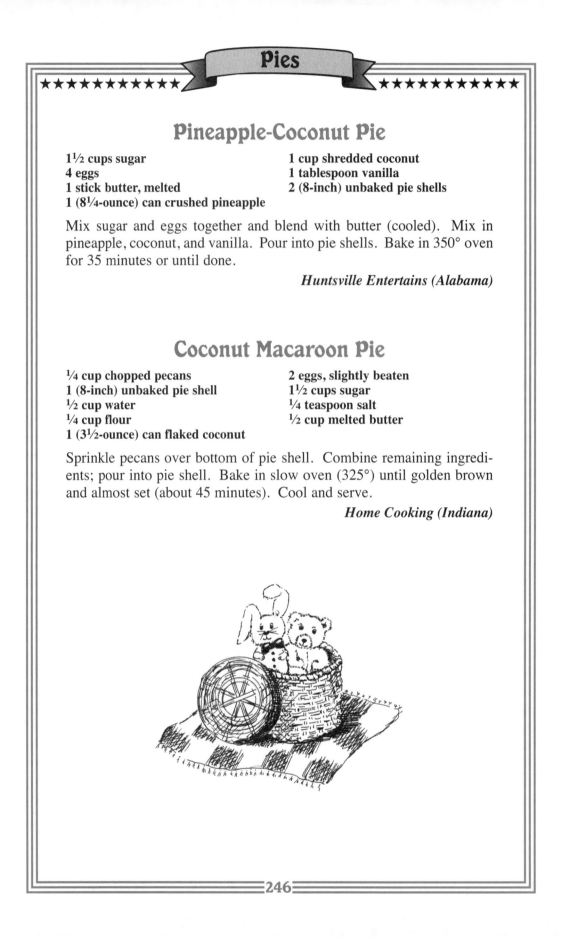

Dixie's Buttermilk Pie

Lemony delicious!

1 (9-inch) unbaked pie shell
1½ cups sugar
3 tablespoons flour
2 eggs, well beaten

½ cup butter, melted
1 cup buttermilk
2 teaspoons vanilla
1 teaspoon lemon extract

Combine sugar and flour; stir in eggs. Add melted butter and buttermilk; mix well. Stir in vanilla and lemon extract. Pour into chilled pie shell and bake at 425° for 10 minutes. Reduce heat to 350° and bake 35 additional minutes. Serves 8.

Kitchen Keepsakes (Colorado)

★ **Even Easier**: Thaw a frozen pie shell while you melt the butter and set the oven; the rest is a snap!

Buttermilk Pie

This is so good, you will want to eat the whole pie!

1 cup sugar
3 tablespoons flour
½ teaspoon salt
3 egg yolks
2 cups buttermilk

4 tablespoons butter, melted
3 stiffly beaten egg whites
1 (9-inch) pie shell, unbaked
Mace or freshly grated nutmeg
   (optional)

Combine sugar, flour, and salt, blending well. Beat the egg yolks slightly and add the buttermilk and cooled melted butter to them. Gradually add buttermilk mixture to the dry ingredients and blend thoroughly. Fold in egg whites. Pour pie filling into pie shell. Sprinkle mace or a grating of nutmeg on top, if desired. Bake at 375° for 45 minutes, or until a silver knife inserted in the center comes out clean.

The Midwestern Country Cookbook (Indiana)

★ **Editor's Extra:** I had a bit too much to fit into my pie shell, so I just put it in a custard cup and baked it alongside the pie. What a treat!

★★★★★★★★★★★ ★★★★★★★★★★★

Crumb Top Apple Pie

This 1939 recipe has no bottom crust.

4 medium-size tart apples
1 tablespoon butter
½ teaspoon nutmeg

3 tablespoons water
½ cup sugar

Peel, core and slice apples in pie dish. Dot with butter chips and sprinkle nutmeg and water and sugar.

CRUST:
1 cup flour
½ cup butter

½ cup brown sugar

Mix flour and butter and brown sugar with fork until crumbly and spread over top. Bake in 400° oven for 20 minutes; then 350° for 15 minutes. Serve warm with whipped cream or ice cream.

Dixie Cook Book V (Arkansas)

Mini Apple Pies

1 (12-ounce) package refrigerator
  biscuits
1 tart apple, peeled and chopped fine
¼ cup raisins

3 tablespoons sugar
1 teaspoon cinnamon
2 tablespoons butter or margarine

Using a rolling pin, flatten each biscuit to a 3- to 4-inch circle. Combine the apple, raisins, sugar, and cinnamon. Place a tablespoonful on each biscuit. Dot with butter. Bring up sides of biscuits to enclose filling and pinch to seal. Place in ungreased muffin cups. Bake at 375° for 11–13 minutes or until golden brown. Serves 10.

A Taste of Kennedy Cook Book (Minnesota)

Everyone has heard the phrase "as American as apple pie." Long before America's discovery, early European "pyes," mostly meat, were baked in narrow pans called "coffins," and their crusts were often inedible. English tradition credits Queen Elizabeth I with making the first cherry pie, but one has to wonder if she spent much time in the kitchen. Apple pie may not have been "invented" in America, but it certainly got perfected here. When the Pennsylvania Dutch put their abundant fruits into edible crusts in shallow round pottery plates, the results were so delicious that the men who fought in the Revolution carried the news of them back across the ocean, establishing pie as "the great American dessert."

★★★★★★★★★★★★   ★★★★★★★★★★★★

Frosty Cranberry Pie

1¼ cups crushed cornflakes
¼ cup butter, melted
1 (8-ounce) package cream cheese,
　softened

1 cup whipped topping
1 (16-ounce) can whole berry
　cranberry sauce
Additional whipped topping

Combine cornflakes and butter. Press mixture into lightly greased 9-inch pie pan. Bake at 350° for 8 minutes. Cool. Beat cream cheese; fold in whipped topping. Mash cranberry sauce. Fold into cream cheese mixture. Spoon mixture into crust. Freeze. Remove from freezer 15–20 minutes before serving. Garnish with whipped topping.

The Holiday Hostess (Georgia)

★ **Editor's Extra:** For a sweeter crust, I like to add ¼ cup sugar to the crushed cornflakes—or use frosted flakes.

Peach Sunburst Pie

Peeled, raw peach halves
1 unbaked crust
½ cup butter, softened

1 cup sugar
2 tablespoons flour
1 egg, slightly beaten

Place peach halves, cut-side-down, in crust. Cream the softened butter with sugar to which flour has been added. Combine with beaten egg. Pour over peaches. Bake at 350° for 55 minutes.

Note: A drop or two of almond extract, a few grains of salt, as well as nutmeg will add to this pie.

Sharing Our Best Volume II (Michigan)

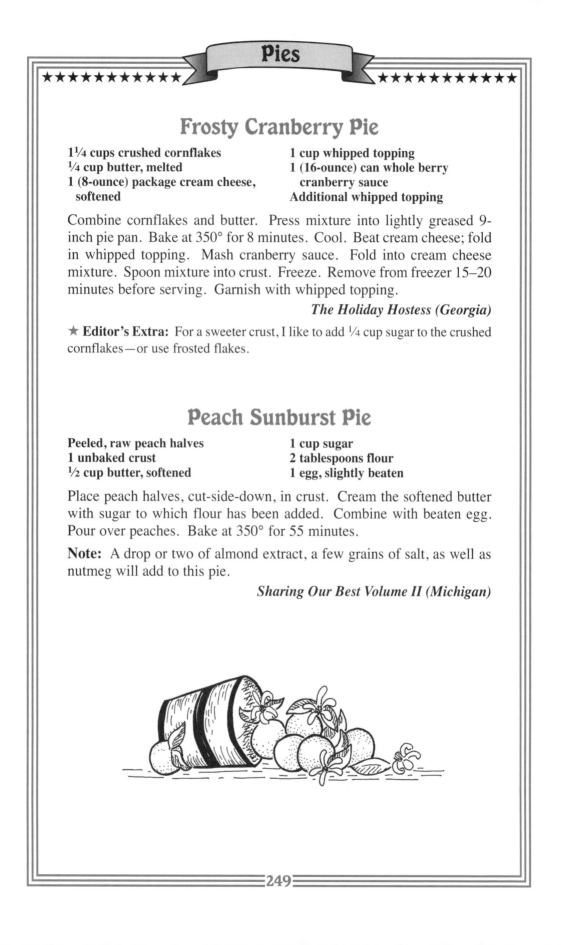

★★★★★★★★★★★ ★★★★★★★★★★★

Springtime Simply Strawberry Pie

As good as it sounds.

1 (3-ounce) box strawberry Jell-O
1 (3-ounce) box vanilla pudding
  (not instant)
2 cups water

2 cups sliced strawberries
Baked or graham cracker pie crust
Whipped cream

Combine Jell-O, pudding, and water. Cook until thickened. Add strawberries and gently blend. Turn into prepared graham cracker crust or regular baked pie crust. Chill 3–4 hours. Garnish with whipped cream for serving. Serves 6–8.

Recipes & Remembrances / Courtland Covenant Church (Great Plains)

Strawberry Pie

1 quart fresh strawberries, stemmed
1 (9-inch) pastry shell (baked)
¾ cup water
1 cup sugar

3 tablespoons cornstarch
1 teaspoon lemon juice
1 cup whipped cream (or Cool
  Whip)

Place all but one cup of berries in the bottom of a baked pastry shell. Spread out well, and set aside. In a saucepan, simmer the other cup of berries in water for 5 minutes. Add sugar and blend well. Add cornstarch. After mixture thickens, add lemon juice. Cook until clear. Pour sauce over berries in shell. Chill in refrigerator, and top with whipped cream.

The Encyclopedia of Cajun and Creole Cuisine (Louisiana)

★ **Editor's Extra:** I like to use small strawberries, or if large, cut them in half.

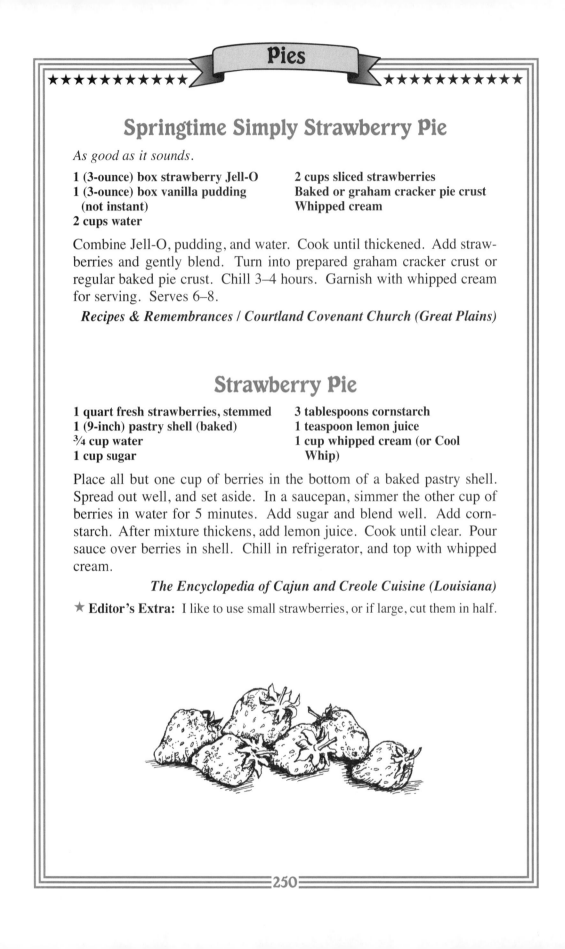

My Father's Lemon Pie

As good as lemon meringue pie—but not so fragile.

4 eggs	**¼ cup melted butter or margarine**
1½ cups sugar	**⅓ cup fresh lemon juice**
1 tablespoon flour	**Rind grated from one lemon**
1 tablespoon white cornmeal	**1 unbaked pie shell**
¼ cup milk	

Beat eggs with sugar in medium bowl. Mix flour and cornmeal; stir into egg mixture. Mix rest of ingredients into the above. Pour into pie shell. Bake at 375° for about 40 minutes. Cool before slicing. Refrigerate leftovers—if any. Pie can be frozen.

Portal's Best Little Cookbook (Arizona)

★ **Even Easier**: There's nothing like fresh lemons, but bottled lemon juice and zest will certainly work. "My Father," however, probably wouldn't approve.

Delicate Raspberry Pie

1 envelope unflavored gelatin	**2 cups mashed raspberries**
¼ cup orange juice	**1 cup cream, whipped**
½ cup sugar	**1 graham cracker crust**

Sprinkle gelatin over orange juice and heat until dissolved. Add sugar to berries (check for personal taste); combine with gelatin mixture. Fold in whipped cream and pour into crust. Swirl top with fork. Chill for 24 hours before serving. (Pictured on cover.)

...and garnish with Memories (Tennessee)

★ **Even Easier**: It's almost always okay to substitute Cool Whip for whipped cream. The texture will be the same; the taste is "like margarine for butter."

Raspberries and blackberries are more fragile than other berries. They should be used as soon as possible after purchasing. If you must wait a day or two, place the berries separated from each other on a tray or cookie sheet, and don't rinse until ready to use. Raspberries are also available frozen and canned.

Leftover berries? Make raspberry vinaigrette. It's great on salads, especially mixed with a little vegetable oil, minced garlic and seasoning. Simply soak a cup of fresh raspberries in ½ cup of vinegar and let sit for a half hour, then strain by pushing the back of a spoon against the strainer.

Impossible Rhubarb Pie

2½ cups cut up rhubarb
1 cup sugar
½ cup Bisquick
1 teaspoon cinnamon

¾ cup milk
2 eggs
2 tablespoons butter, melted
¼ teaspoon nutmeg

STREUSEL:
2 tablespoons firm butter
½ cup Bisquick

¼ cup brown sugar
¼ cup chopped nuts

Arrange rhubarb in a greased 9-inch pie plate. Mix remaining ingredients. Pour over top. Sprinkle evenly with Streusel topping. Bake at 375° for 40 minutes or until knife comes out clean.

Cookin' for Miracles (Iowa)

Sunrise Cherry Pie

A very pretty pie.

1 (8-ounce) can crushed pineapple
 (in heavy syrup), divided
1 (8-ounce) package cream cheese,
 softened
1 teaspoon vanilla

1 can cherry pie filling, divided
¼ cup sugar
1 cup heavy cream
1 graham cracker crust

Drain pineapple and reserve 2 tablespoons juice. Combine cream cheese, vanilla, and juice; mix until well blended. Stir in ¼ cup pineapple and ½ cup pie filling. Gradually add sugar to cream in small mixing bowl, beating until soft peaks form. Fold into cheese mixture. Pour into crust. Top center with remaining pie filling, and circle outer edge of pie with remainder of pineapple. Chill until firm.

Natchez Notebook of Cooking (Mississippi)

Michigan produces about ¾ of the world's tart cherries. Brought over by European settlers, cherry trees only have a productive life of about five years. Traverse City, Michigan, is known as the "Cherry Capital of the World."

Amazing Fruit Cobbler

1 stick margarine, softened
1 cup sugar
1 cup self-rising flour

1 cup milk
1 can pie filling (any fruit)

Mix all ingredients together in a baking dish. Bake at 350° for one hour. Serve hot. Serves 4–6.

Hint: If you have bananas that are ripening too quickly, peel the skin and discard. Wrap banana in Saran Wrap, twist ends and freeze. Cut into chunks while still frozen and enjoy. Tastes like ice cream.

Alone at the Range (Florida)

Cherry Cobbler

Simply wonderful!

1 cup flour
1 cup sugar, divided
3 teaspoons baking powder

½ cup milk
1 tablespoon melted margarine
1 can sour cherries

Combine flour, ½ cup sugar, and baking powder. Mix well. Blend milk and margarine. Stir into flour mixture until moistened. Pour batter into a 9-inch baking pan. Combine cherries, juice, and remaining sugar in a saucepan. Bring to a boil. Pour hot sweetened cherries over batter. Bake at 350° for 30 minutes or until golden. Serves 9.

Heavenly Delights (Missouri)

★ **Editor's Extra:** Having the cherries hot speeds this up, but be sure to use potholders putting it into the oven, or fill at oven.

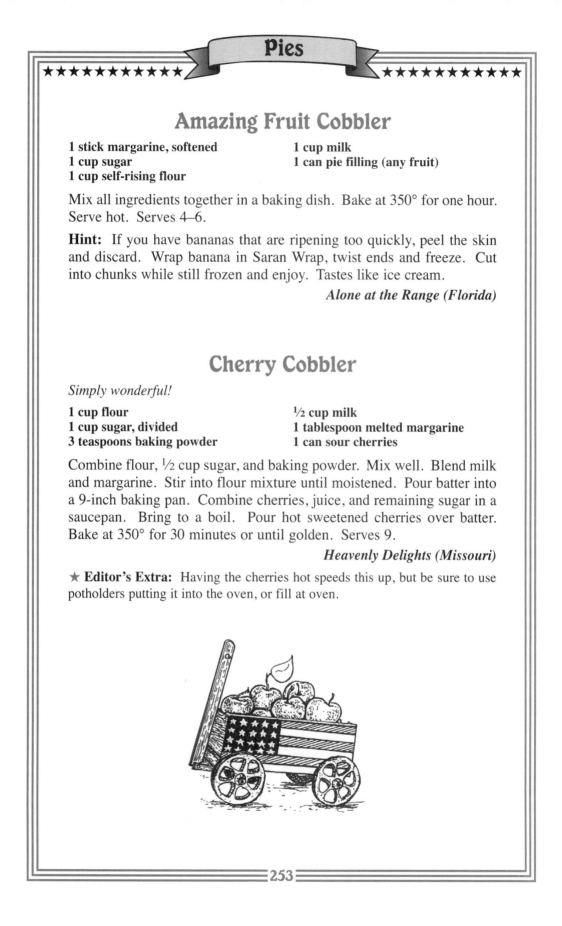

★★★★★★★★★★★ ★★★★★★★★★★★

Chantilly Peanut Pie

Great make-ahead-and-freeze dessert.

1 quart vanilla ice cream, slightly
  softened
¾ cup creamy peanut butter
1 cup chopped unsalted peanuts,
  divided

1 tablespoon vanilla
1 (10-inch) chocolate crumb crust
Whipped cream (sweetened)
Hot fudge sauce

Combine ice cream, peanut butter, ½ cup peanuts, and vanilla in bowl.
Mix well. Pour into prepared crust. Sprinkle with remaining nuts.
Freeze. Remove from freezer about 10 minutes before serving. Garnish
with whipped cream and serve hot fudge sauce drizzled over each slice.

Educated Taste (Georgia)

★ **Editor's Extra:** To soften ice cream, put it on the counter while you gather
and measure the rest of the ingredients. Faster, scoop out one quart in a big
bowl. Fastest, but riskiest, you can put it in the microwave and soften one quart
for one minute on #3 (defrost) power, more if needed.

Peanut Butter Cream Cheese Pie

A hands-down favorite.

6 ounces cream cheese, softened
¾ cup sifted powdered sugar
½ cup peanut butter

2 tablespoons milk
2 cups Cool Whip
1 (8-inch) graham cracker pie crust

Beat cream cheese and sugar till light and fluffy. Add peanut butter and
milk. Beat till smooth and creamy. Fold in Cool Whip and turn into
crust. Chill 5–6 hours or overnight.

Maple Hill Cookbook (Minnesota)

★ **Editor's Extra:** You can freeze it, too. Try using a chocolate crumb crust.
And maybe slice a banana into it before you pour the filling in.

Peanut sauces have been around many centuries in Africa and China, but peanut
butter as we know it was introduced at the 1904 World's Fair in St. Louis. It was
packed in tin cans until World War I when the demand for metal forced manufac-
turers to switch to glass, which has obviously become the container of choice.

★★★★★★★★★★★ ★★★★★★★★★★★

Hot Fudge Pie

No crust!

½ cup (1 stick) butter
2 squares semisweet chocolate
2 eggs, beaten
1 cup sugar
¼ cup all-purpose flour

⅛ teaspoon salt
1 teaspoon vanilla extract
1 cup chopped nuts
Whipped cream or ice cream

Preheat oven to 350°. Melt butter and chocolate together in small saucepan over low heat. Combine remaining ingredients (except cream) and blend with chocolate mixture. Spray 9-inch pie pan with nonstick cooking spray. Pour batter into pie pan and bake for 25 minutes. Serve warm with sweetened whipped cream or ice cream. Makes 8 servings.

What's Cooking Inn Arizona (Arizona)

Chocolate Chip Pie

1 cup sugar
½ cup flour
2 eggs, well beaten
1 stick butter, melted

1 teaspoon vanilla
1 cup milk chocolate chips
¾ cup pecans
1 unbaked deep-dish pie shell

Blend sugar, flour, eggs, butter, and vanilla well. Stir in chocolate chips and pecans. Pour into unbaked pie shell and bake at 350° for 30–35 minutes or until firm.

St. Philomena School 125th Anniversary (Louisiana II)

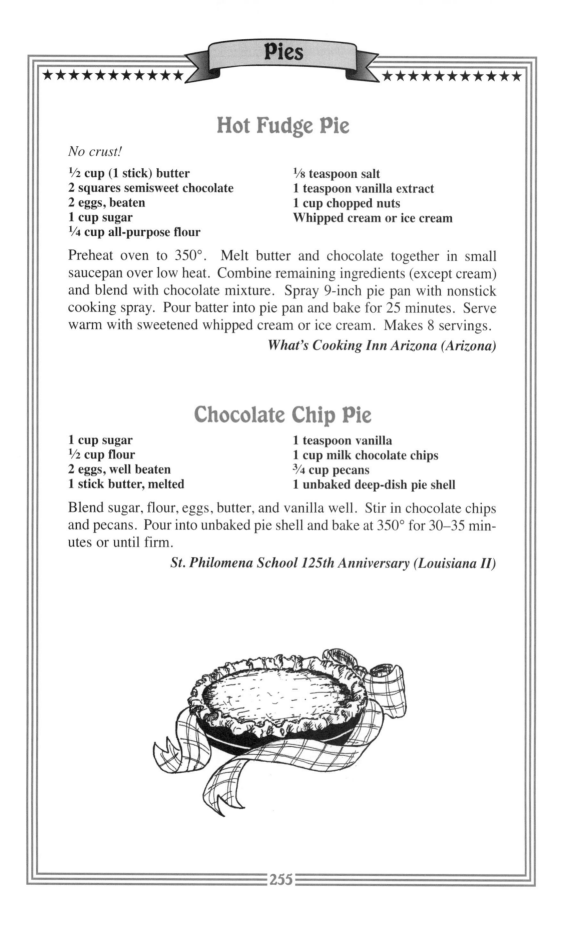

Hershey Bar Pie

Classically delicious.

17 marshmallows
¼ pound (1 stick) butter
6 Hershey bars with or without almonds

½ pint whipping cream, whipped
1 graham cracker crust

Melt marshmallows in top of double boiler with butter. Add Hershey bars. Melt all together and stir well. Cool mixture slightly and add whipped cream. Pour into graham cracker crust and chill before serving.

The Amish Way Cookbook (Ohio)

Easy Pumpkin Cheesecake Pie

1 (16-ounce) can pumpkin
1 (8-ounce) package cream cheese, softened
¼ teaspoon vanilla
3 eggs

¾ cup brown sugar
½ cup Bisquick Baking Mix
1½ teaspoons pumpkin spice
Whipped topping

Place all ingredients in blender, except topping. Blend on high for 2 minutes. Pour into large greased pie plate. Bake for 45 minutes at 350°. Pick-test center, till toothpick comes out dry. Do not overbake. Cool. Spread with whipped topping.

The Best of the Pumpkin Recipes (Pennsylvania)

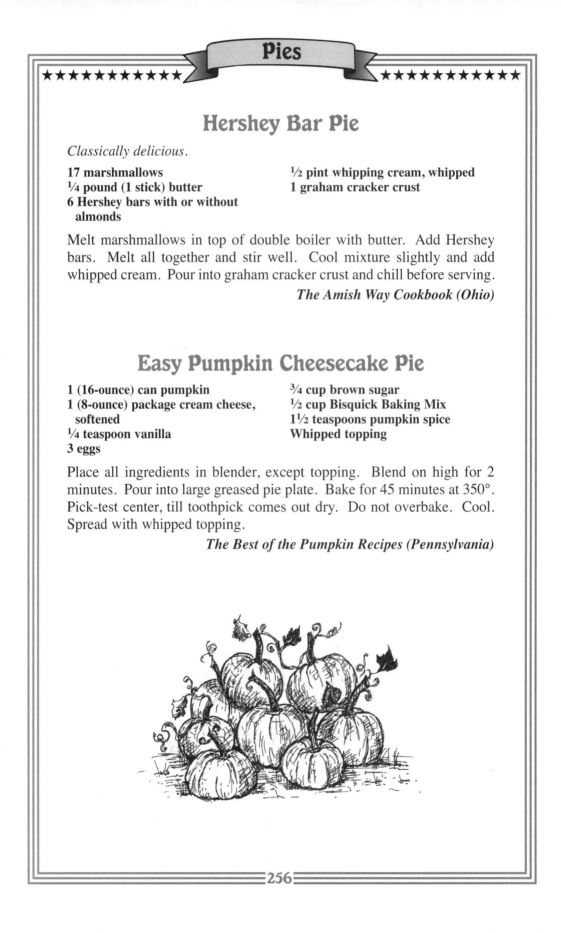

15-Minute Custard Pie

Not too sweet . . . a quick treat. This custard does not get watery and is very tasty.

4 slightly beaten eggs
½ cup sugar
¼ teaspoon salt
1 teaspoon vanilla

2½ cups scalded milk
1 (9-inch) unbaked pie shell
  (⅛-inch thick)
Nutmeg

Preheat oven to 475°. Thoroughly mix eggs, sugar, salt, and vanilla; beat slightly. Slowly stir in hot milk. At once, pour into unbaked pastry shell. (To avoid spills, fill at oven.) Dash top with nutmeg. Bake in very hot oven for 5 minutes. Reduce heat to 425°. Bake 10 minutes longer or until knife inserted halfway between center and edge comes out clean. Cool on rack. Serve cool or chilled. Keep unused portion refrigerated.

175th Anniversary Quilt Cookbook (Ohio)

Miracle Custard Pie

2 cups milk
4 eggs
½ cup sugar
½ cup flour
1 teaspoon vanilla

¼ cup margarine or butter,
  softened
½ teaspoon salt
1 cup flaked coconut

In a blender container, combine milk, eggs, sugar, flour, vanilla, butter or margarine, and salt. Cover; blend about 10 seconds or until well mixed. Stir in coconut. Pour into greased 9-inch pie plate. Bake at 350° for 40 minutes or until a knife inserted comes out clean. Cool and chill.

A Century in His Footsteps (Great Plains)

Apple Custard Pie

1 cup sugar
1½ tablespoons flour
1 teaspoon apple pie spice or
  cinnamon

1 stick butter, melted
2 eggs, slightly beaten
1 unbaked pie crust
2 cups chopped apples

Mix dry ingredients. Mix with melted butter. Add eggs. Pour into unbaked pie shell and add chopped apples. Bake at 375° for 30-45 minutes. Serves 6–8.

An Apple a Day (California)

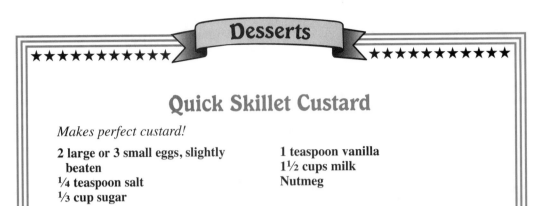

★★★★★★★★★★ ★★★★★★★★★★

Quick Skillet Custard

Makes perfect custard!

2 large or 3 small eggs, slightly
  beaten
¼ teaspoon salt
⅓ cup sugar

1 teaspoon vanilla
1½ cups milk
Nutmeg

Mix all ingredients except nutmeg. Pour into custard cups (5 or 6). Sprinkle with nutmeg. Place cups in a deep skillet. Pour hot tap water in around the cups as high as possible. Bring water to a full boil. Turn off heat. Cover skillet and let stand 10–20 minutes, or until knife inserted into the custard comes out clean. Remove cups from the water and chill.

Country Lady Nibbling and Scribbling (Iowa)

Bread and Butter Pudding

1⅓ cups sugar
¾ cup soft butter
8 slices thick bread
2 cups powdered sugar

5 cups milk
4 eggs
1 teaspoon nutmeg

Cream together sugar and butter; spread on trimmed bread slices. Cut each slice into 4 squares. Place in greased 9x13-inch baking dish. Mix remaining ingredients and pour over bread. Bake in 350° oven for 30–40 minutes. Serve warm with a dab of whipped cream. Serves 8.

Kountry Kooking (Tennessee)

★ **Even Easier**: You don't have to trim the bread, nor cut it into squares. I make half of this because we "pig out." This is so soupy good, you'll want to eat the whole thing.

Glorified Rice

A great way to use up rice from the night before.

1 cup cold rice
½ cup sugar
1½ cups crushed pineapple, drained
½ teaspoon vanilla
1 cup whipping cream, whipped

8 large marshmallows, cut up (or
  1½ cups mini's)
¼ cup chopped maraschino
  cherries

Mix all ingredients and chill thoroughly. Makes 6–8 servings.

Note: Here's an idea you can go wild with. Use any flavor yogurt, fresh or canned fruit, nuts, honey, cinnamon, peanut butter, etc. Use whatever sounds good to you; see how easy it is to be creative.

Mystic Mountain Memories (Colorado)

Pineapple Pudding

8–10 slices white bread
½ cup milk
1 stick margarine, softened
2 cups sugar

3 eggs
1 large can crushed pineapple,
  drained

Trim bread. Cut enough into cubes to measure 4 cups, and soak in milk. Cream together margarine, sugar, and eggs. Add crushed pineapple and bread cubes. Mix well. Pour into greased casserole and bake at 350° until firm, about 30–40 minutes. Cut into squares. Serve with whipped cream or whipped topping or plain.

Note: If desired, a little grated cheese may be added to mixture, or sprinkle a little on top the last 10 minutes of baking.

Olivia's Favorite Menus and Recipes (South Carolina)

★ **Editor's Extra:** When my assistant, Terresa, tested this recipe, she declared it an immediate family favorite. Who could argue?

In 1493, Columbus landed in Guadeloupe and found pineapples, a fruit that had grown in the Carribean for a thousand years. The Spanish thought they looked like pine cones, and tasted like sweet apples, hence the name "pineapple." Captain Cook brought the fruit to the Hawaiian Islands in 1777, where they have grown so abundantly that the pineapple has come to be associated with Hawaii.

Rice Pudding

1 cup cooked rice
1 cup milk
2 well-beaten eggs

⅓ cup sugar
½ teaspoon salt
Dash mace

Mix ingredients. Spread in pan 1-inch deep. Bake at 350° for 30 minutes or until light brown on top. Cut in squares.

A Heritage of Good Tastes (Arkansas)

Peach Crisp

. . . or cherry or apple or apricot . . .

1 (16-ounce) can peach pie filling
1 (7½-ounce) box yellow cake mix
  (1-layer size)

1 stick margarine
½–1 cup chopped pecans

Preheat oven to 350°. Pour can of pie filling into 8x8-inch baking pan. Sprinkle dry cake mix over pie filling. Cut margarine into small slices and lay on top of cake mix. Sprinkle chopped nuts on top. Bake at 350° for 30–35 minutes.

Look Mom, I Can Cook (Georgia)

★ **Editor's Extra:** Great with ice cream or Cool Whip served on top while warm.

Nutty Peach Crisp

1 (29-ounce) can sliced peaches
  with syrup (or frozen peaches)
1 package Betty Crocker Butter
  Pecan Cake Mix

½ cup butter, melted
1 cup flaked coconut
1 cup chopped pecans

Heat oven to 325°. Layer ingredients in order listed in 9x13x2-inch ungreased oblong pan; bake about 45 minutes.

Family Favorites by the Miller's Daughters (Tennessee)

★ **Editor's Extra:** If you can't find butter pecan, just use a butter cake mix. This is yummy!

Cherry Cha-Cha

18 crushed graham crackers
3 tablespoons sugar
⅓ cup melted butter

1 cup whipping cream
4 cups miniature marshmallows
1 can cherry pie filling

Mix first 3 ingredients and pat in bottom of 9x13-inch pan. Bake for 10 minutes at 325°. Cool. Whip cream; add marshmallows and cherry pie filling. Pour over crust. Top with a few graham cracker crumbs. Refrigerate.

Kelvin Homemakers 50th Anniversary Cookbook (Great Plains)

Cherry Delight

2½ cups crushed graham crackers
⅔ cup melted margarine or butter
½ cup sugar
12 ounces cream cheese at room temperature

1 (8-ounce) container whipped topping
½ cup chopped walnuts
2 cups powdered sugar
1 can cherry pie filling

Mix graham cracker crumbs, margarine, and sugar. Press into large baking dish to form crust. (Chill, or bake a few minutes in oven to set crust, then cool). Combine cream cheese, whipped topping, walnuts, and powdered sugar. Pour into crumb crust. Chill. Spread pie filling over top.

Note: Six double honey grahams equals one cup crumbs.

More Goodies and Guess-Whats (Colorado)

★ **Even Easier**: Or use 2 ready-made graham cracker crusts. This delightfully refreshing dessert lends itself perfectly to low-fat substitutions. Super either way.

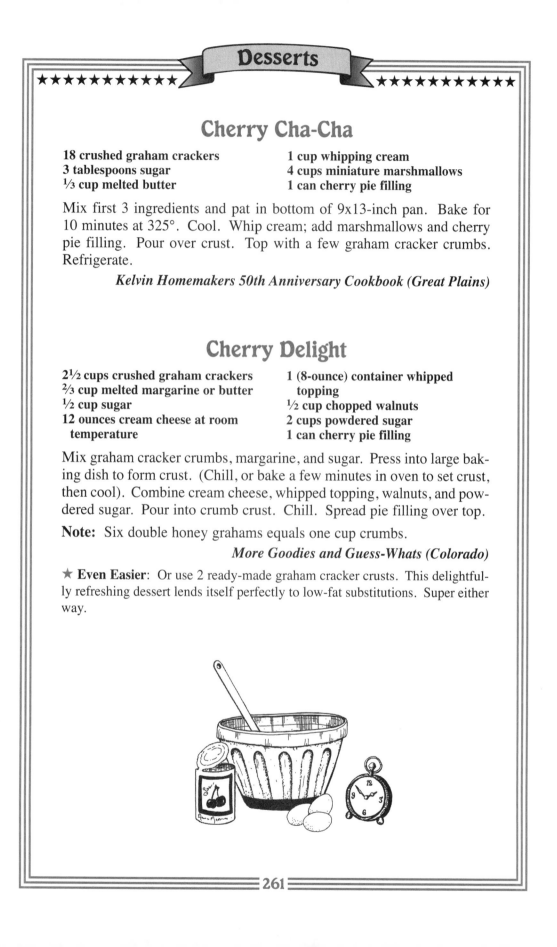

★★★★★★★★★★★★ ★★★★★★★★★★★★

Mrs. Z's Strawberry Delite

CRUST:

3 egg whites
1 cup sugar
1 teaspoon vanilla

18 crushed soda crackers
1 teaspoon baking powder
½ cup chopped pecans or walnuts

Beat egg whites until stiff; gradually add sugar, then the vanilla. Fold in dry ingredients. Spread in 9-inch pie pan. Bake at 350° for 30 minutes.

FILLING:

1 (10-ounce) box frozen strawberries,
   thawed and drained

2 cups Cool Whip

Combine strawberries and Cool Whip. Spread over cooled crust. Refrigerate 4 hours or more before serving.

More Kitchen Keepsakes (Colorado)

★ **Editor's Extra:** Super easy, cool and pretty presentation. Also good without the nuts.

Banana Split Dessert

When you're ready to serve this treat, top it with chopped pecans, cherries, and a drizzle of chocolate syrup!

2 cups graham cracker crumbs
6 tablespoons margarine, melted
2 (3½-ounce) packages instant
   vanilla pudding mix
2 cups milk

3 bananas, sliced
1 (20-ounce) can crushed pineapple,
   drained
1 (12-ounce) container whipped
   topping

In a bowl, combine crumbs and margarine. Press mixture into an oblong baking dish and set aside. In another bowl, prepare pudding mix with milk according to package directions. Spread pudding over crumb mixture. Layer with banana slices, then pineapple, then whipped topping. Chill 3 hours or overnight. Cut into squares to serve. Yields 12 squares.

Tony Chachere's Second Helping (Louisana II)

Bananas were probably the first fruit farmed by man, dating back to Alexander the Great's conquest of India, where he first discovered the fruit in 327 B.C. Spanish explorers brought them to the New World in 1516. Bananas are one of nature's best energy sources, and have no fat, cholesterol or sodium. Gulfport, Mississippi, is the largest banana importing port in the United States.

Million Dollar Dessert

1 box Jiffy Yellow Cake Mix
1 (8-ounce) package cream cheese
2 cups milk, divided

1 package instant vanilla pudding
1 can pie filling (any flavor)
1 container Cool Whip

Mix cake mix as directed. Put into 9x13-inch pan. Bake for 12–15 minutes at 350°. Let cool. Combine cream cheese with ½ cup milk. Mix pudding with remaining 1½ cups milk, then mix together with cream cheese mixture. Spread on cake and let set. Cover with pie filling. Serve topped with Cool Whip. Makes 12–15 servings.

Inn-describably Delicious (Illinois)

Centennial State Celebration Punch Bowl Cake

1 yellow cake mix
1 can cherry pie filling
1 large can crushed pineapple,
   drained
1 large box instant vanilla pudding,
   prepared

1 large container Cool Whip
¼ cup chopped pecans,
¼ cup cherries
¼ cup shredded coconut

Make cake according to directions. Let cool. Into a large punch bowl, layer ½ each: crumbled cake, cherry pie filling, crushed pineapple, pudding (prepared as directed), and Cool Whip. Repeat. Garnish top with pecans, cherries, and coconut. Cover with plastic wrap and chill. Serve with large spoon. Serves a crowd.

Colorado Foods and More... (Colorado)

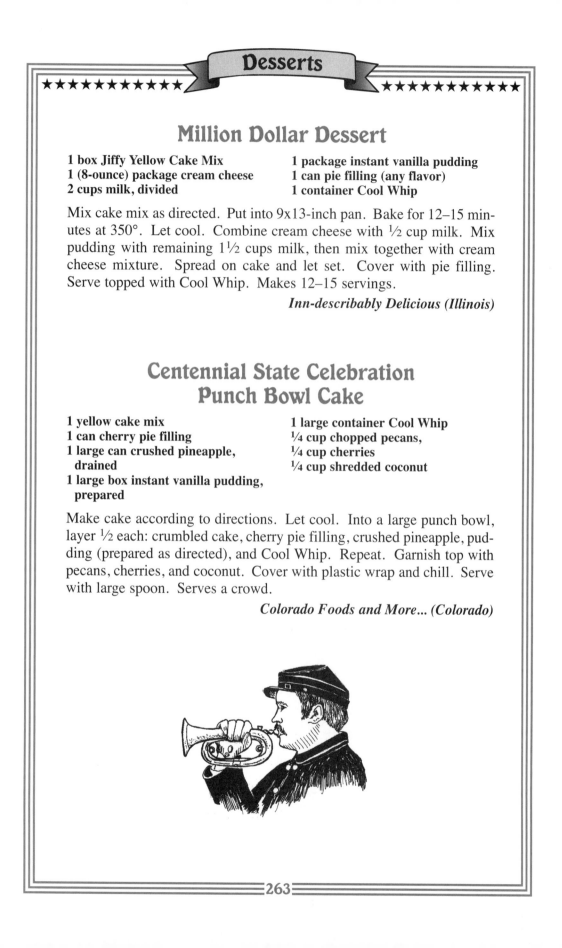

Swiss Chocolate Trifle

1 Duncan Hines Brownie Mix or
  chocolate cake mix
3 bananas, sliced
2 large instant mousse or chocolate
  pudding mixes, prepared

2 (8-ounce) containers Cool Whip
Chopped nuts
Cherries

Prepare brownies or cake according to package directions; cool and cut into cubes. In 9x13-inch pan, layer ½ of cake or brownie cubes, then top with ½ of bananas, ½ of pudding, and ½ of Cool Whip. Sprinkle nuts on top. Repeat layers and top with cherries.

Crystal Clear Cooking (Michigan)

Chocolate Trifle

1 (18½-ounce) package chocolate
  fudge cake mix
1 (6-ounce) package instant
  chocolate pudding mix
½ cup strong coffee

1 (12-ounce) carton frozen whipped
  topping, thawed
6 (1.4-ounce) chocolate covered
  toffee bars, crushed

Bake cake according to package directions. Cool. Prepare pudding according to package directions and set aside. Crumble cake, reserving ½ cup. Place half the remaining cake crumbs in the bottom of a 4½- or 5-quart trifle bowl. Layer with half the coffee, half the pudding, half the whipped topping and half the crushed candy bars. Repeat the layers of cake, coffee, pudding and whipped topping. Combine remaining cake crumbs and crushed candy bars. Sprinkle over top and refrigerate 4–5 hours before serving. Makes 8–10 servings.

The L.O.V.E. Chocolate Cookbook (Iowa)

★ **Editor's Extra:** Frozen whipped topping can be thawed in the microwave, but do it gradually. Try an 8-ounce container at 30% power for 1 minute, and large containers at additional 15-second intervals till there is still a frozen ball in the center, but able to be stirred soft. This takes watching, so do it gradually or you'll end up with sweet soup.

Kahlua Angel Food

Great way to liven up a bought cake.

1 bought angel food cake
2 tablespoons plus ¼ cup Kahlua,
  divided

¼ cup cream
1 (12-ounce) tub Cool Whip

Poke holes all over top of cake with thin knife or skewer. Combine 2 tablespoons Kahlua and ¼ cup cream and pour half of it into holes. Place cake in refrigerator for 2 hours. Pour the rest of Kahlua and cream mixture into holes and refrigerate 2 more hours. Combine Cool Whip and ¼ cup Kahlua and spread on top and side of cake—now it's ready to serve.

A Taste of the Holidays (Georgia)

★ **Even Easier:** A light dessert that's sure to please. I have done this all at once without waiting for refrigerator time, and it works fine.

Butterscotch Toffee Heavenly Delight

1½ cups whipping cream
5½ ounces butterscotch syrup
½ teaspoon vanilla

1 angel food cake
1 pound English toffee (Heath or
  Skor bars), crushed

Whip cream until it starts to thicken. Add butterscotch syrup and vanilla slowly. Continue beating until thick. Cut cake into 3 layers. Spread whipped cream mixture on layers. Sprinkle each layer generously with toffee. Stack layers on top of each other. Frost sides and sprinkle with toffee. Chill cake for a minimum of 6 hours.

Tostitos Fiesta Bowl Cookbook (Arizona)

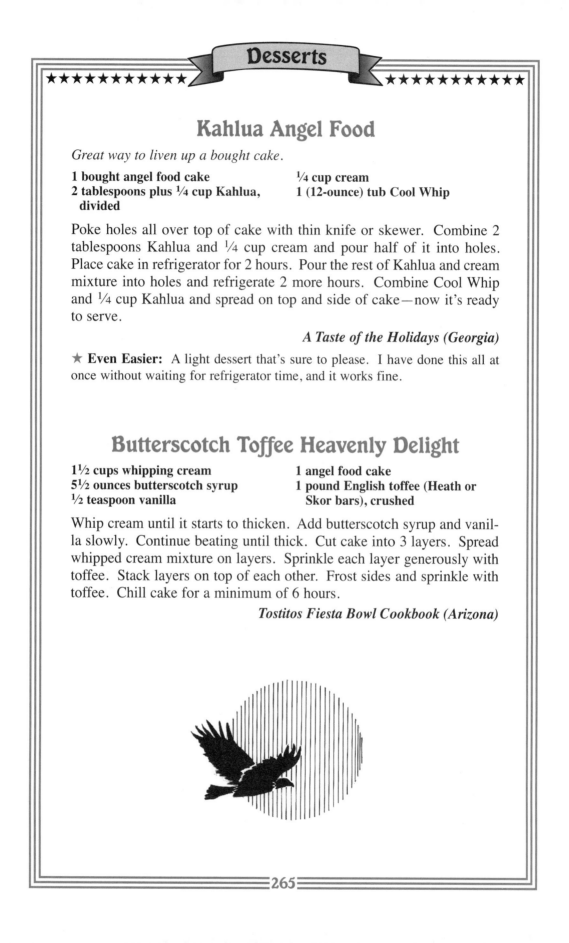

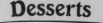

Coffee Mallow

A light, elegant, easy dessert. Few people can guess the secret ingredient—marshmallows!

16 marshmallows
½ cup hot double-strength coffee

1 cup heavy cream
½ teaspoon vanilla

With wet scissors, cut marshmallows into quarters. Put in the top of a double boiler with coffee. When melted, take from heat and cool until it begins to thicken.

Beat cream until thick; fold together with marshmallow mixture and vanilla. Chill in pretty dishes until set.

Jubilee (Illinois)

★ **Editor's Extra:** Use about 3 cups of miniature marshmallows to cut-out the cutting-up!

Blueberry Snow

Pretty in a trifle bowl.

1 (8-ounce) package cream cheese
½ cup milk
¼ cup sugar

Cool Whip
Angel food cake
1 can blueberry pie filling

Cream first 3 ingredients. Fold in Cool Whip. Break up angel food cake in 9x13-inch pan. Spread part of mixture on cake cubes, then spread blueberries, then mixture again. Refrigerate. Serve cold. Serves 8–10.

Heart of the Home (Louisiana II)

★ **Editor's Extra:** I used a small angel food cake, but works with any size.

No egg yolks and no shortening make angel food cakes a fabulous no-fat sweet. Angel food cake, and its chiffon and sponge cake cousins, depend mostly on beaten egg whites for lightness. Angel food cakes have no added leavening (such as baking powder), shortening, or egg yolks, and have a high proportion of beaten egg whites to flour. Chiffon cakes are a cross between an angel food cake and a butter cake. They're made with leavening, vegetable oil, and egg yolks, as well as beaten whites. Sponge cakes use both egg whites and yolks and sometimes a little leavening, but like angel food cakes, they don't contain shortening.

Snicker Buns

8 small Snicker candy bars
1 package refrigerator crescent rolls
½ stick melted butter or margarine

½ cup powdered sugar
1 tablespoon milk
¼ teaspoon almond extract

Wrap one candy bar in each triangle of dough; roll it in the melted margarine and place in a muffin pan. (Fill remaining 4 holes in pan halfway with water, for even heat distribution.) Bake at 375° for 10 minutes. Make glaze with remaining ingredients; cover while hot.

Optional: For smaller buns, use 16 Snicker snackers and cut each crescent triangle in half. Use the mini-muffin pans instead.

A Taste of Fishers (Indiana)

Fudge Striped Cookie Salad

Dessert or salad—delicious any time.

2 small packages instant vanilla or
   coconut cream pudding
1½ cups half-and-half
1 (12-ounce) carton whipped
   topping

1 (11-ounce) can mandarin
   oranges, drained
1 (8-ounce) can pineapple tidbits,
   drained
1 package fudge-striped cookies

Beat pudding and half-and-half in large bowl. Fold in whipped topping. Add wel-drained fruit. Break cookies into small pieces. Fold half of the cookies into the mixture. Put the rest on top. Cool for 4 hours. Serves 10–12.

Grade A Recipes (Colorado)

★ **Editor's Extra:** This dish is can't-wait-to-dive-into attractive in a trifle bowl.

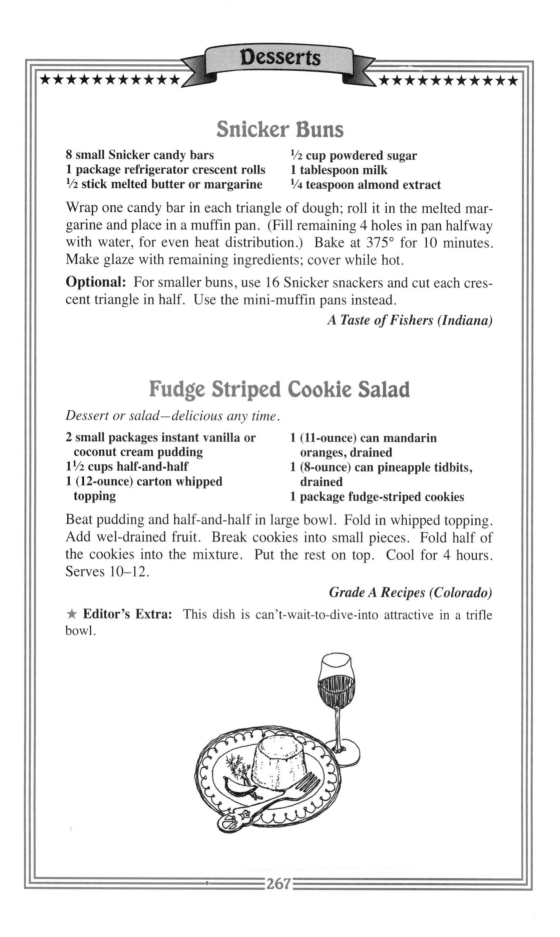

Dirt Cups

1 (16-ounce) package chocolate
  sandwich cookies
2 cups cold milk
1 (4-serving) package chocolate
  instant pudding

1 (8-ounce) tub Cool Whip
8–10 (7-ounce) paper or plastic cups
Decorations (gummy worms and
  frogs, candy flowers, chopped
  peanuts or granola)

Crush cookies in zipper-style plastic bag with rolling pin or in food processor. Pour milk into large bowl; add pudding mix. Beat with wire whisk 2 minutes; let stand 5 minutes. Stir in Cool Whip and ½ of the crushed cookies.

Place about 1 tablespoon crushed cookies in each cup. Fill cups about ¾-full with pudding mixture. Top with remaining crushed cookies. Refrigerate one hour or until ready to serve. Decorate as desired.

Thank Heaven for Home Made Cooks (Illinois)

★ **Editor's Extra:** An easier version of the traditional "dirt" cake. Fun to put tiny artificial stemmed flowers or mini-marshmallows, sprinkles, M&Ms, etc. Kids love 'em!

Creamy Caramel Apples

1 bag caramels
1 can condensed milk
1 (8-ounce) carton Cool Whip

Sliced apples
Chopped nuts

In fondue pot, melt peeled caramels and condensed milk. Then add container of Cool Whip and stir mixture. Slice apples in bowl, pour some caramel mixture over them and sprinkle nuts on top.

Good Cookin' Cookbook (Illinois)

Cherry Fluff

1 can cherry pie filling
1 large can crushed pineapple
1 can sweetened condensed milk

1 (8-ounce) container Cool Whip
½ cup chopped nuts (optional)

Mix all ingredients and refrigerate overnight.

Taste & See (Wisconsin)

★ **Editor's Extra:** A versatile delight, it can be served in a parfait glass with a stemmed cherry on top, as well as scooped on a lettuce leaf for a sweet salad.

Strawberry Fluff

1 medium-size angel food cake
2 small packages strawberry
 Jell-O
1½ cups hot water

2 (10-ounce) packages frozen
 strawberries
1 cup cold water
½ pint whipping cream, whipped

Arrange bite-size pieces of cake in a 9x13-inch pan. Make Jell-O with hot water; add frozen berries and cold water. Let stand until slightly congealed. Add the whipped cream; mix well. Pour over cake and stir a little to be sure all of cake pieces are covered. Put in refrigerator and let set. Serves 15.

Cookin' for Miracles (Iowa)

★ **Even Easier**: Use Cool Whip in place of whipped cream. There are 3 cups of Cool Whip in an 8-ounce tub, 4½ cups in a 12-ounce tub, and 6 cups in a 16-ounce tub. Generally, an 8-ounce tub subs for ½ pint of whipping cream, whipped.

Oops! Forgot Dessert

2 (1-pound) pound cakes
2 cans cherry pie filling
2 (12-ounce) containers Cool Whip,
  thawed, divided

Fresh fruit (such as kiwi,
  strawberries, raspberries,
  blueberries, blackberries, etc.)

Slice pound cake into ¼-inch slices. Layer the entire bottom of a 11x15-inch pan with slices of pound cake. Spread pie filling over cake. Spread a layer of Cool Whip, then layer more pound cake over Cool Whip. Layer more Cool Whip over cake; decorate top of cake with sliced fresh fruit. Serve now or chill. Serves 12–16.

Lion's Club of Globe Cookbook (Arizona)

Bourbon Peaches

Just enough zing.

1 (16-ounce) can peach halves
6 macaroons, crumbled
4 tablespoons butter or margarine,
  melted

1 (1¾-ounce) package pecan halves
1 tablespoon brown sugar
2 tablespoons bourbon
Salt

Place peach halves in muffin tins to help keep their shape. Fill cavities with a mixture of the remaining ingredients and bake in 300° oven for 15 minutes. Yields 6 servings.

Encore! Nashville (Tennessee)

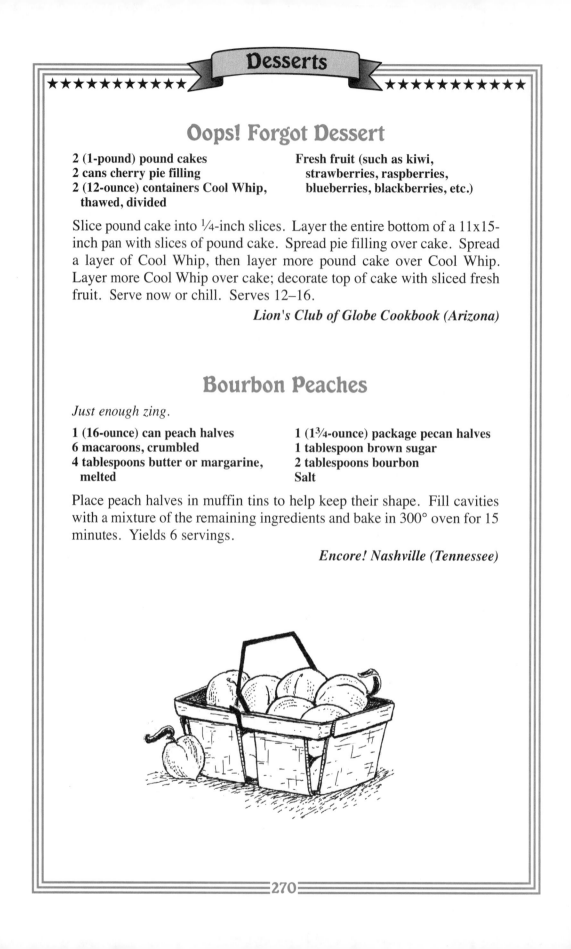

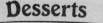

Apricot Whip

1 cup whipping cream
1–2 tablespoons sugar

1 (7¾-ounce) jar junior food,
  apricots with tapioca

Whip cream; fold in sugar and apricots. Turn into sherbet glasses. Keep refrigerated until serving time.

Home Cooking in a Hurry (Tennessee)

★ **Editor's Extra:** Talk about impressive! Put a mint sprig on top, serve them on a silver tray, and act like this "whip-up" took you all day to do.

Sensational Strawberries

Sensational says it all.

¾ cup sugar
½ cup heavy cream
¼ cup light corn syrup
2 tablespoons butter
½ cup Heath Toffee candy bars,
  chopped

1 quart fresh strawberries, washed
  and hulled
Sour cream

Combine sugar, cream, corn syrup, and butter in a saucepan. Bring to a boil and cook for 3 minutes. Stir occasionally. Remove from heat and add candy. Stir until most of the candy is dissolved. Cool. Serve strawberries topped with a dollop of sour cream and drizzle with sauce. Serves 6.

Sugar Beach (Florida)

Baked Bananas

6 bananas, peeled
⅓ cup butter, melted
3 tablespoons lemon juice
⅓ cup brown sugar

1 teaspoon cinnamon
1 cup coconut, grated
1 cup walnuts, chopped

Place bananas in large baking dish. Combine butter, lemon juice, sugar, cinnamon, coconut, and walnuts. Distribute evenly over the bananas, turning them to thoroughly coat each banana. Bake in 375° oven for 20 minutes, turning once after 10 minutes. Serve warm. Serves 6.

Sedona Cook Book (Arizona)

Banana Boats

12 bananas
4 (1½-ounce) Hershey bars, cut in
  thirds

2 cups miniature marshmallows
½ cup pecan pieces

Peel back narrow strip in inside curve of bananas. Scoop out a small amount of banana. Add chocolate, marshmallows, and pecans. Cover with banana skin. Wrap in foil. Place in coals. Cook until banana is hot. Yields 12 servings.

Approximately Per Serving: Cal 233; Prot 3.0g; T Fat 8.3g; Chol 2.9mg; Carbo 41.4g; Sod 17.5mg; Potas 524.8mg.

River Valley Recipes (Illinois)

★ **Even Easier**: Chocolate chips to the rescue! The peel gets darkened by the heat, but once it gets tasted, nobody cares what the peel looks like! Great to put in the campfire.

Warm Bananas Kahlua

1 ounce light brown sugar
1 ounce table sugar
6 large bananas

4 ounces Kahlua liqueur
2 ounces butter

Caramelize sugars in a hot, dry sauté pan, being careful not to burn the sugar. Add sliced bananas, Kahlua, and butter. Remove pan from burner (butter and Kahlua should not cook). This is excellent served directly, or over ice cream.

Recipe from The Chatham Squire, Chatham, Massachusetts
Cape Cod's Night at the Chef's Table (New England)

★ **Editor's Extra:** An ounce is ⅛ cup or 1½ tablespoons. Dry sugar will liquify and turn brown—carmelize—when heated quickly in a skillet.

Bananas do not grow on trees! They grow on tropical plants that have no trunk. Bananas are really gigantic herbs that spring from underground stems. What looks like a trunk is a false stem formed by tightly wrapped leaf sheaths. Their stalks grow to 25 feet in height making them the largest plant on earth without a woody stem.

Pralines & Cream Dream

1 cup light brown sugar
¼ cup light corn syrup
½ cup half-and-half
2 tablespoons butter

1 cup coarsely chopped pecans
½ teaspoon vanilla
Vanilla ice cream

In a small saucepan, combine brown sugar, corn syrup, and cream. Place over medium heat and cook for 7–8 minutes. Stir in butter, pecans, and vanilla. Remove and cool completely. To serve, spoon alternate layers of ice cream and praline sauce in a wine glass or parfait glass. Serves 6. (Pictured on cover.)

Kay Ewing's Cooking School Cookbook (Louisiana II)

Praline Parfait Sauce

⅓ cup boiling water
⅓ cup brown sugar

1 cup white corn syrup
1 cup chopped pecans

Bring water to a boil. Add sugar, then add corn sryup. Cook slowly until the mixture comes to a boil. Add the pecans. When cool, pour into a jar or similar container and refrigerate. Mixture will thicken when cool. Pour over ice cream.

Recipes and Reminiscences of New Orleans I (Louisiana)

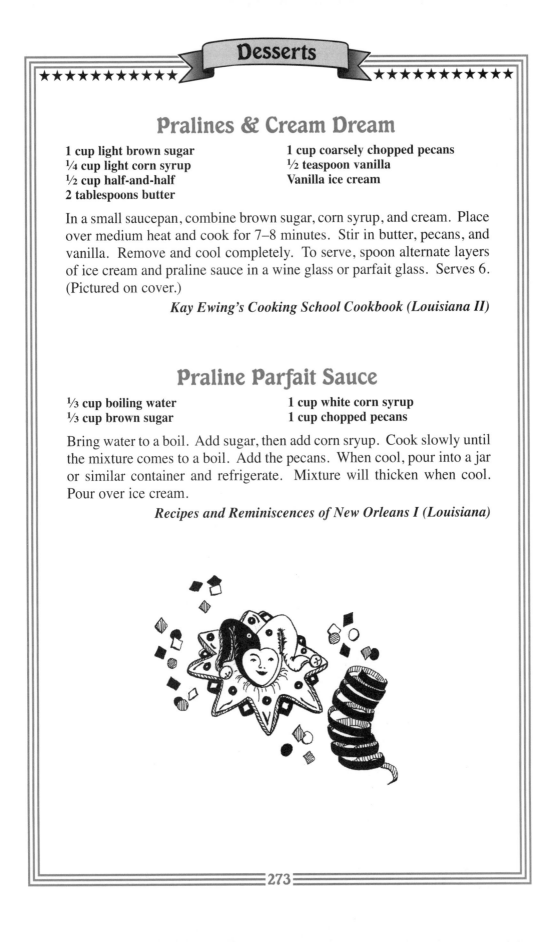

Quick Strawberry Ice Cream

It doesn't need an ice-cream freezer! I didn't expect much from this recipe when I tried it, but the ice cream is surprisingly good, definitely superior to packaged ice cream, and embarrassingly easy. You need a blender or food processor to make it.

3 cups whole frozen strawberries　　**⅓ cup granulated sugar**
½ cup whipping cream　　**2 teaspoons lemon juice**
2 eggs　　**½ teaspoon vanilla**

Soften the berries a few minutes before beginning. Mix the cream, eggs, and sugar in the blender or food processor. Turn the machine on and off quickly, processing just enough to mix the ingredients.

With the motor running, feed in the frozen strawberries one at a time. Blend or process until the mixture is smooth, stopping to stir with a spatula, if necessary. Add the lemon juice and vanilla in the last few seconds of processing.

Serve at once or store in your freezer. If you store the ice cream in the freezer, remove about 15 minutes before serving to soften it slightly. Makes about 4 servings. (To double the recipe, prepare in 2 batches.)

Enjoying the Art of Southern Hospitality (Arkansas)

★ **Editor's Extra:** I like this sherbet-like ice cream even without the lemon juice. So easy to make, so good with cake or coffee, so elegant in parfait glasses. A one-pound bag of strawberries equals about 3 cups.

When a recipe calls for raw eggs, it is a simple process to "home pasteurize" them by coddling them for a few seconds in hot water. Place the whole egg on a spoon and dip it into boiling water for 40 seconds, then immediately put it into cold water to stop the cooking process.

List of Contributors

Barbara is dwarfed by the impressive Iwo Jima Memorial in Arlington, Virginia. It literally brings tears to your eyes to gaze up into the strengths and emotions of these life-like figures who represent all the men who have fought for our country . . . so moving.

Listed below are the cookbooks that have contributed recipes to the *Recipe Hall of Fame Quick & Easy Cookbook,* along with copyright, author, publisher, city and state. The information in parentheses indicates the BEST OF THE BEST cookbook in which the recipe originally appeared.

Alone at the Range ©1985 Team Cookbooks, by Mary Lou Freeman, Fernandina Beach, FL (Florida)

Amish Country Cookbook I ©2001 Evangel Publishing House, Nappanee, IN (Indiana)

Amish Country Cookbook II ©2001 Evangel Publishing House, Nappanee, IN (Indiana)

Amish Country Cookbook III ©2001 Evangel Publishing House, Nappanee, IN (Indiana)

The Amish Way Cookbook ©1994 Adrienne Lund, Jupiter Press, Chagrin Falls, OH (Ohio)

Amistad Community Recipes, Amistad Community Members, Amistad, NM (New Mexico)

...and garnish with Memories ©1985/1998 (Third Edition) The Overmountain Press, by Patty Smithdeal Fulton, Johnson City, TN (Tennessee)

An Apple a Day ©1996 Rea Douglas, San Diego, CA (California)

Anoka County 4H Cook Book, Anoka County 4-H Youth Development Program, Andover, MN (Minnesota)

Apalachicola Cookbook ©1984 The Philaco Woman's Club, Eastpoint, FL (Florida)

Applause Applause, Old Opera House, Coggon, IA (Iowa)

Apples Etc. Cookbook ©1998 Santa Cruz, CA Chapter of Hadassah, Aptos, CA (California)

Appletizers, Johnny Appleseed Metro Park District, Lima, OH (Ohio)

Arizona Highways Heritage Cookbook ©1988 Department of Transportation, State of Arizona, Phoenix, AZ (Arizona)

Arizona Small Game and Fish Recipes ©1992 Golden West Publishers, by Evelyn Bates, Golden West Publishers, Phoenix, AZ (Arizona)

Asbury United Methodist Church Cook Book ©1990 Asbury United Methodist Church, Magnolia, AR (Arkansas)

Atlanta Natives' Favorite Recipes ©1975 Ladair, Inc., Atlanta, GA (Georgia)

Atlanta's Pet Recipes ©1976 Atlanta Humane Society Auxiliary, Inc., Atlanta, GA (Georgia)

Bay Leaves ©1975 The Junior Service League of Panama City, Inc., Panama City, FL (Florida)

Bell's Best ©1981 Telephone Pioneers of America-Mississippi Chapter #36, Jackson, MS (Mississippi)

Bell's Best 2 ©1982 Telephone Pioneers of America-Mississippi Chapter #36, Jackson, MS (Mississippi)

Berkshire Seasonings, Junior League of Berkshire County, Pittsfield, MA (New England)

The Best from New Mexico Kitchens ©1978 New Mexico Magazine, by Sheila MacNiven Cameron, New Mexico Magazine, Sante Fe, NM (New Mexico)

Best of Bayou Cuisine ©1970 St. Stephens Episcopal Church, Indianola, MS (Mississippi)

Best of the Historic West ©2000 David and Savana Richardson, Greenwood Village, CO (Colorado)

The Best of the Pumpkin Recipes ©1992 E.B. Dandar, Sterling Specialties Cookbooks, Penndel, PA (Pennsylvania)

The Best of Zucchini Recipes ©1992 E.B. Dandar, Sterling Specialties Cookbooks, Penndel, PA (Pennsylvania)

Big Mama's Old Black Pot ©1987 Stoke Gabriel Enterprises, Inc., Alexandria, LA (Louisiana II)

Blew Centennial Bon-Appetit, Blew Family, Phillipsburg, KS (Great Plains)

The Bloomin' Cookbook, DuBoistown Garden Club, South Williamsport, PA (Pennsylvania)

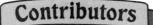
Boarding House Reach ©1981 Dot Gibson Publications, Waycross, GA (Georgia)

The Bonneville House Presents ©1990 The Bonneville House Association, Fort Smith, AR (Arkansas)

Bouquet Garni ©1983 Pascagoula-Moss Point Mississippi Junior Auxiliary, Pascagoula, MS (Mississippi)

A Bouquet of Recipes, Homer Flower and Garden Club, Homer, LA (Louisiana II)

Bravo ©1984 The Greensboro Symphony Guild, Greensboro, NC (North Carolina)

Breakfasts Ozark Style ©1986 Kay Cameron, Katydid Publications, Point Lookout, MO (Missouri)

Bringing Grand Tastes to Grand Traverse ©1994 Newcomers Club of Grand Traverse, Traverse City, MI (Michigan)

Brunch Basket ©1984 Junior League of Rockford, Inc., Rockford, IL (Illinois)

C.D.A. Angelic Treats, Louisiana State Catholic Daughters, Franklin, LA (Louisiana II)

C-U in the Kitchen, Champaign-Urbana Hadassah, Champaign, IL (Illinois)

Café Oklahoma ©1994 Junior Service League, Midwest City, Midwest City, OK (Oklahoma)

Cajun Cooking, Acadian House Publishing, Lafayette, LA (Louisiana II)

Cajun Cuisine: Authentic Cajun Recipes from Louisiana's Bayou Country ©1985 Beau Bayou Publishing Co., Acadian House Publishing, Lafayette, LA (Louisiana II)

Canopy Roads ©1979 Tallahassee Junior Woman's Club, Tallahassee, FL (Florida)

Cape Cod's Night at the Chef's Table ©1993 Shank Painter Publishing Co., Provincetown, MA (New England)

Cape Fear...Still Cooking, The Ministering Circle, Wilmington, NC (North Carolina)

Caring is Sharing, Nurses of Highland Park Hospital, Highland Park, IL (Illinois)

Carolina Cuisine Encore! ©1981 The Junior League of Anderson, SC, Inc., Anderson, SC (South Carolina)

CEASRA of Slippery Rock Cookbook, Citizens Environmental Association of the Slippery Rock Area Inc., Slippery Rock, PA (Pennsylvania)

Celebrating California ©1995 Children's Home Society of California, Oakland, CA (California)

Celebrating Iowa, First United Methodist Church UMW, Iowa City, IA (Iowa)

Centennial Cookbook ©1997 San Carlos School, Monterey, CA (California)

Centennial Cookbook, St. Peter's Lutheran Church, New York Mills, MN (Minnesota)

Centennial Cookbook, First Christian Church CWF, Seiling, OK (Oklahoma)

The Centennial Society Cookbook, Centennial Society Union Congregational Church, Elk River, MN (Minnesota)

Centerville Community Centennial Cookbook, Centerville Community Church, Centerville, KS (Great Plains)

A Century in His Footsteps, by Judy Ridenour, Mullen United Methodist Church, Mullen, NE (Great Plains)

CHAMPIONS: Favorite Foods of Indy Car Racing ©1993 by C.A.R.A., Championship Auto Racing Auxiliary, Indianapolis, IN (Indiana)

Charleston Receipts ©1950 The Junior League of Charleston, Inc., Charleston, SC (South Carolina)

Charleston Receipts Repeats ©1989 The Junior League of Charleston, Inc., Charleston, SC (South Carolina)

Chefs and Artists, Black Mountain Memorial Library, Dallas, PA (Pennsylvania)

Children's Party Book ©1984 The Junior League of Hampton Roads, Inc., Newport News, VA (Virginia)

Chockful O' Chips, ©1990 Peggy Seemann, L. E. B. Products, Livonia, MI (Missouri)

A Cleveland Collection ©1992 The Junior League of Cleveland, Inc., Cleveland, OH (Ohio)

Colesburg Area Cookbook, Sesquicentennial Committee, Colesburg, IA (Iowa)

Collectibles II ©1983 Mary Pittman, Van Alstyne, TX (Texas)

A Collection of Recipes From St. Matthew Lutheran Church, Galena, IL (Illinois)

College Avenue Presbyterian Church Cookbook, Presbyterian Women of College Avenue Church, Aledo, IL (Illinois)

The College Cookbook FOR Students BY Students ©1993 NJL Interests, Houston, TX (Texas II)

College Survival Cookbook ©1992 Nadine Z. Ujevich, by Nadine Z. Ujevich, Aliquippa, PA (Pennsylvania)

Colorado Foods and More... ©1990 Judy Barbour, Bay City, TX (Colorado)

Come Grow With US, United Methodist Women, Sayre, OK (Oklahoma)

Company Fare I, Presbyterian Women First Presbyterian Church, Bartlesville, OK (Oklahoma)

Company's Coming ©1988 The Cookbook Collection, Junior League of Kansas City, MO (Missouri)

Connecticut Cooks III ©1982 American Cancer Society, Connecticut Division, Wallingford, CT (New England)

Cook and Deal ©1982 D.J. Cook, Wimmer Companies, Memphis, TN (Florida)

Cook Book, Mary Martha Society of Redeemer Lutheran Church, Chico, CA (California)

The Cook Book ©1979 National Council of Jewish Women, Shawnee Mission, KS (Missouri)

Cook Book: Favorite Recipes from Our Best Cooks, Central Illinois Tourism Council, Brighton, IL (Illinois)

Cook of the Week Cookbook, Humboldt Independent Newspaper, Humboldt, IA (Iowa)

Cook'em Horns: The Quickbook ©1981 Ex-Students' Association of the University of Texas, Austin, TX (Texas II)

A Cook's Tour of Shreveport, Junior League of Shreveport, Shreveport, LA (Louisiana II)

A Cook's Tour of the Azalea Coast ©1982 The Auxiliary to the Medical Society of New Hanover, Pender and Brunswick Counties, Wilmington, NC (North Carolina)

Cookbook 25 Years ©1981 Madison County Farm Bureau Women's Committee, Edwardsville, IL (Illinois)

Cookies and Bars ©1986 Dorothy Zehnder, Frankenmuth, MI (Michigan)

Cookin' Along the Cotton Belt, Stephens Chamber of Commerce, Stephens, AR (Arkansas)

Cookin' for Miracles, 310 Community Credit Union, Des Moines, IA (Iowa)

Cookin' in the Spa, Hot Springs Junior Auxiliary, Hot Springs, AR (Arkansas)

Cookin' with Farmers Union Friends, North Dakota Farmers Union Youth Group, Center, ND (Great Plains)

Cooking For Good Measure, Hughes High School Junior Auxiliary, Hot Springs, AR (Arkansas)

Cooking on the Fault Line—Corralitos Style, Corralitos Valley Research and Educational Association, Corralitos, CA (California)

Cooking with Class ©1990 Union Baptist Church, Ruth Bible Class, Chincoteague, VA (Virginia)

Cooking with Cops, Kingman Police Department, Kingman, AZ (Arizona)

Cooking with Daisy's Descendants, by Elaine Gilbert Davis, Fairmount, IL (Illinois)

Cooking With Grace, St. Bernard Parish, Wauwatosa, WI (Wisconsin)

Cooking with Mr. "G" and Friends, by Kevin Grevemberg, Anacoco, LA (Louisiana II)

Cooking with the Warriors, Whiteland Community High School, Whiteland, IN (Indiana)

Cooking with Tradition ©1984 The Woodward Academy Parents Club, Fairburn, GA (Georgia)

Country Cookin': Recipes From Callaway Gardens ©1980 Garden Services, Inc., The Gardens Country Store, Pine Mountain, GA (Georgia)

Country Cooking, Port Country Cousins, Sentinel, OK (Oklahoma)

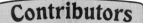

★★★★★★★★★★★★ ★★★★★★★★★★★★

Country Cupboard Cookbook, Panora Church of the Brethren Women, Panora, IA (Iowa)

Country Cupboard Cookbook ©1985 Central High School Athletic Boosters Club, Thomasville, GA (Georgia)

The Country Gourmet ©1982 Mississippi Animal Rescue League, Jackson, MS (Mississippi)

Country Lady Nibbling and Scribbling ©1994 Alice Howard, Elgin, IA (Iowa)

Covered Bridge Neighbors Cookbook, Covered Bridge Neighbors, St. Peters, MO (Missouri)

Crystal Clear Cooking ©1995 Judy Brouwer, Beulah, MI (Michigan)

Cuisine a la Mode, Les Dames Richelieu du Rhode Island, Woonsocket, RI (New England)

Culinary Classics ©1981 Young Matron's Circle for Tallulah Falls School, Roswell, GA (Georgia)

Czech-Out Cajun Cooking ©1989 Katherine Guillot and Ina Potmesil, Bossier City, LA (Louisiana II)

Dan River Family Cookbook ©1982 Dan River, Inc., Dan River Outlet, Danville, VA (Virginia)

A Dash of Down East ©1986 The Junior Guild of Rocky Mount, Inc., Rocky Mount, NC (North Carolina)

Decades of Recipes, Fairmount Jamaica Historical Society, Fairmount, IL (Illinois)

Deep in the Heart ©1986 Dallas Junior Forum, Inc., Richardson, TX (Texas II)

Delicious Reading, Friends of the St Charles City Library, St Peters, MO (Missouri)

Dinner Bell, Lancaster County Society of Farm Women #22, Millersville, PA (Pennsylvania)

Dishes from the Deep, Arizona Perch Base Submarine Veterans, Sun City West, AZ (Arizona)

Diversity is Delta's Main Dish, Delta Sigma Theta Sorority, Inc., Long Beach, CA (California)

Dixie Cook Book V ©1972 Women of the Church First Presbyterian Church, Fort Smith, AR (Arkansas)

Doc's Delights, Keefe Memorial Hospital, Cheyenne Wells, CO (Colorado)

The Dog-Gone Delicious Cookbook, Humane Society of the White Mountains, Pinetop, AZ (Arizona)

Down Home Cookin' Without the Down Home Fat ©1996 Dawn Hall, Logan, OH (Ohio)

Down-Home Texas Cooking, Taylor Wilson Company, Austin, TX (Texas II)

Duck Creek Collection, Junior League of Garland, Garland, TX (Texas II)

Duluth Woman's Club 70th Anniversary Cookbook, Duluth Woman's Club, Duluth, MN (Minnesota)

Durham's Favorite Recipes, Durham Woman's Club, Durham, CA (California)

Dutch Touches ©1996 Penfield Press, Iowa City, IA (Iowa)

Easy Does It Cookbook, Woman Time Management, TX (Texas)

Easy Livin' Microwave Cooking ©1989 Karen Kangas Dwyer, Omaha, NE (Great Plains)

Eat To Your Heart's Content, by Woody and Betty Armour, Hot Springs, AR (Arkansas)

Educated Taste, LeGrange College Alumni Association, LeGrange, GA (Georgia)

Elsah Landing Heartland Cooking, by Helen Crafton and Dorothy Lindgren, Grafton, IL (Illinois)

Encore! Nashville ©1977 The Junior League of Nashville, Inc., Nashville, TN (Tennessee)

The Encyclopedia of Cajun and Creole Cuisine ©1983 The Encyclopedia of Cajun and Creole Cuisine, by John D. Folse, Baton Rouge, LA (Louisiana)

Enjoying the Art of Southern Hospitality ©1990 Sara Pitzer, August House Publishers, Little Rock, AR (Arkansas)

Fabulous Favorites, Los Altos United Methodist Women, Los Altos, CA (California)

Families Cooking Together ©1998 Georgia O'Keeffe Friends of the Library, Albuquerque, NM (New Mexico)

Family Favorites by the Miller's Daughters, by Harva U. Thomas & Christine U. Kyte, Kodak, TN (Tennessee)

Family Secrets ©1986 Denise Wilson, Greenville, MS (Mississippi)

The Farmer's Daughters ©1987 S-M-L, Inc., by Flora Sisemore, Martha Merritt and Mary Mayfield, DeWitt, AR (Arkansas)

Favorite Recipes, St. Nicholas Orthodox Church, Barton, OH (Ohio)

Favorite Recipes, Exline Committee, Exline, IA (Iowa)

Favorite Recipes of Collinsville Junior Service Club, Collinsville Junior Service Club, Collinsville, IL (Illinois)

Favorite Recipes of Pommern Cooks, Pommerscher Verein Freistadt, Germantown, WI (Wisconsin)

Favorites for All Seasons, Desert Foothills Library, Cave Creek, AZ (Arizona)

Feeding the Flock, Maple Grove Evangelical Free Church, Maple Grove, MN (Minnesota)

Fessin' Up with Bon Appetit ©1992 Sue W. Fess, Shreveport, LA (Louisiana II)

Fiesta Mexicana ©1982 T & E Enterprises, by Toby Arias and Elaine Frassanito, Albuquerque, NM (New Mexico)

15 Minute, Storage Meals ©1996 Jayne Benkendorf, Ludwig Publishing, Edmond, OK (Oklahoma)

Fiftieth Anniversary Cookbook, Northeast Louisiana Telephone Co., Inc., Collinston, LA (Louisiana II)

First Christian Church Centennial Cookbook, Christian Women's Fellowship, Mason City, IA (Iowa)

First United Methodist Church Cookbook, United Methodist Women, Worthington, MN (Minnesota)

The Fishlady's Cookbook ©1998 Patricia Kendall, Springfield, IL (Illinois)

500 Favorite Recipes, The Ladies of Whispering Pines Mennonite Church, Honea Path, SC (South Carolina)

Flaunting Our Finest ©1982 Franklin Junior Auxiliary, Nashville, TN (Tennessee)

The Flavor of Waverly ©1986 Waverly Community House, Inc., Waverly, PA (Pennsylvania)

Flavored With Tradition ©1979 Flavored With Tradition, Inc., Charleston, SC (South Carolina)

Florence Cook Book, Trinity Episcopal Churchwomen, Florence, AL (Alabama)

Fontanelle Good Samaritan Center Commemorative Cookbook, Fontanelle Good Samaritan Center, Fontanelle, IA (Iowa)

For Crying Out Loud...Let's Eat ©1988 The Service League of Hammond, Inc., Hammond, IN (Indiana)

Franklin County Homemakers Extension Cookbook, Franklin County Homemakers Extension, Benton, IL (Illinois)

The French-Icarian Persimmon Tree Cookbook ©1992 Louise Lum, Pollard Press, by Louise Lum, Icarian Living History Museum, Nauvoo, IL (Illinois)

Friendly Feasts Act II, Friends of Riverside Theatre, Vero Beach, FL (Florida)

From A Louisiana Kitchen ©1996 Holly B. Clegg, Inc., Baton Rouge, LA (Louisiana)

From My Apron Pocket, by Suzanne Collins, Dallas, TX (Texas)

From the Recipe File of Agnes Gaffaney, by Cindy Stamness, Mora, MN (Minnesota)

Gardener's Delight, The Ohio Association of Garden Clubs, Inc., Green Springs, OH (Ohio)

Gardeners' Gourmet II ©1985 Garden Clubs of Mississippi, Inc., Yazoo City, MS (Mississippi)

Gatlinburg Recipe Collection, by Nancy Blanche Cooper, Gatlinburg, TN (Tennessee)

Gazebo I Christmas Cookbook ©1982 Rex Barrington, Auburn, AL (Alabama)

Generations ©1994 Junior League of Rockford, Inc., Rockford, IL (Illinois)

The Give Mom a Rest (She's on Vacation) Cookbook ©1998 Rita Hewson, Larned, KS (Great Plains)

Good Cookin' Cookbook, First Baptist Church, New Life Class, Benton, IL (Illinois)

Good Cooking, Good Curling, Alpine Curling Club, Monroe, WI (Wisconsin)

Gourmet By The Bay ©1989 Dolphin Circle of the King's Daughters and Sons, Virginia Beach, VA (Virginia)

Gourmet: The Quick and Easy Way, by Diana Allen, Enid, OK (Oklahoma)

Grade A Recipes, Idalia Playground and Park Committee, Idalia, CO (Colorado)

Grand Detour Holiday Sampler, by Karen Stransky, Dixon, IL (Illinois)

Grandma's Home Kitchen ©1994 Wanda Peterson Mango, Amherst Press, Minocqua, WI (Wisconsin)

Grandma's House Restaurant & Family Recipes, Flo Barnes, Yreka, CA (California)

Great Grandmother's Goodies, Pennsylvania's State Federation of Negro Women's Clubs, Inc., Erie, PA (Pennsylvania)

The Great Iowa Home Cooking Expedition, Lighthouse Revival Center, Brooklyn, IA (Iowa)

Green Chile Bible ©1996-99 Clear Light Publishers, Sante Fe, NM (New Mexico)

The Guild Cookbook I ©1972 Valparaiso University Guild, Valparaiso, IN (Indiana)

The Guild Cookbook II ©1978 Valparaiso University Guild, Valparaiso, IN (Indiana)

Gulfshore Delights ©1984 The Junior Welfare League of Fort Myers, Fort Myers, FL (Florida)

Guten Appetit, German-American Klub, Indianapolis, IN (Indiana)

The Hagen Family Cookbook, by Marilee Nelson, Noonan, ND (Great Plains)

Have Fun Cooking with Me, by Lela J. Clarke, Statesville, NC (North Carolina)

The Heart of Cooking II ©1992 The Heart Center of Fort Wayne, Fort Wayne, IN (Indiana)

Heart of the Home, East Baton Rouge Extension Homemaker's Council, Inc., Baton Rouge, LA (Louisiana II)

Heart of the Mountains ©1987 Buncombe County Extension Homemakers, Asheville, NC (North Carolina)

Heavenly Delights, Mothers and Daughters of Zion, Independence, MO (Missouri)

Heavenly Delights, United Methodist Women, Page, AZ (Arizona)

Heavenly Food II, United Methodist Women/Sunbury United Methodist Church, Sunbury, OH (Ohio)

Heavenly Hostess, St. John's Episcopal Church, Monroeville, AL (Alabama)

Herbal Favorites, Gennessee County Herb Society, Linden, MI (Michigan)

Here's To Your Heart: Cooking Smart, The Heart Care Center, Waukesha, WI (Wisconsin)

A Heritage of Good Tastes, Arkansas Post Museum State Park, Gillett, AR (Arkansas)

A Heritage of Good Tastes ©1980 The Twig, Junior Auxiliary of the Alexandria Hospital, Alexandria, VA (Virginia)

High Cotton Cookin' ©1978 Marvell Academy Mothers' Association, Marvell, AR (Arkansas)

The Holiday Hostess, Valdosta Junior Service League, Valdosta, GA (Georgia)

Home at the Range III, Chapter EX-P. E. O., Oakley, KS (Great Plains)

Home at the Range IV, Chapter EX-P. E. O., Oakley, KS (Great Plains)

Home Cookin', NPS Denver Employees' Association, Denver, CO (Colorado)

Home Cookin': First Congregational United Church of Christ, Morenci, MI (Michigan)

Home Cookin' is a Family Affair, Aldersgate United Methodist Women, Marion, IL (Illinois)

★★★★★★★★★★★★ ★★★★★★★★★★★★

Home Cooking, 49er's Club of Dana, Dana, IN (Indiana)

Home Cooking II, 49er's Club of Dana, Dana, IN (Indiana)

Home Cooking in a Hurry ©1985 Broadman Press, by Sarah Howell, Broadman Press, Nashville, TN (Tennessee)

Honest to Goodness ©1990 The Junior League of Springfield, Inc., Springfield, IL (Illinois)

Hopewell's Hoosier Harvest II, Hopewell Prebytery Church Circle of the Covenant, Franklin, IN (Indiana)

Hudson's Cookbook ©1982 Brian and Gloria Carmines, Hudson's Seafood House, Hilton Head Island, SC (South Carolina)

The Hungry Hog ©1995 Phil D. Mayers, Lafayette, LA (Louisiana II)

Huntsville Entertains ©1983 Historic Huntsville Foundation, Huntsville, AL (Alabama)

I Cook—You Clean ©1992 Coldwater Press, Barbara C. Jones, Bonham, TX (Texas II)

If It Tastes Good, Who Cares? I ©1992 Spiritseekers Publishing, by Pam Girard, Bismarck, ND (Great Plains)

In the Kitchen with Kate ©1995 Capper Press, Inc., Ogden Publications, Inc., Topeka, KS (Great Plains)

In The Pink, Beauregard Memorial Hospital Auxiliary, DeRidder, LA (Louisiana II)

Incredible Edibles, Youngstown/Warren Dental Association, Cortland, OH (Ohio)

Indiana's Finest Recipes, Beech Grove Central Elementary PTA, Beech Grove, IN (Indiana)

The Indiana's Kid's Cookbook ©1995 Gallopade Publishing Group, Peachtree City, GA (Indiana)

Inn on the Rio's Favorite Recipes, by Julie Cahalane, Taos, NM (New Mexico)

Inn-describably Delicious ©1992 Tracy M. Winters and Phyllis Y. Winters, Winters Publishing, Greensburg, IN (Illinois)

International Garlic Festival Cookbook ©1994 Caryl L. Simpson/Garlic Festival®, Gourmet Gold Press, Gilroy, CA (California)

Iola's Gourmet Recipes in Rhapsody, by Iola Egle, McCook, NE (Great Plains)

The Island Cookbook ©1993 Barbara Sherman Stetson, Stetson Laboratories, Inc., North Scituate, RI (New England)

It's About Thyme ©1988 Marge Clarke-Thyme Cookbooks, by Marge Clarke, West Lebanon, IN (Indiana)

Italian Cooking for a Healthy Heart ©1989 Joanne D'Agostino, Frank J. D'Agostino, Easton, PA (Pennsylvania)

Italian Dishes et cetera ©1991 Shirley Michaels, Loveland, CO (Colorado)

Jarrett House Potpourri, The Jarrett House, Dillsboro, NC (North Carolina)

The Joy of Sharing, Scottsbluff Cosmopolitans, Scottsbluff, NE (Great Plains)

Jubilee, Emmanuel Memorial Episcopal Church, Champaign, IL (Illinois)

The Junior League of Grand Rapids Cookbook I ©1976 The Junior League of Grand Rapids, Inc., Grand Rapids, MI (Michigan)

Just For Kids, by Jen Bays Avis, LDN, RD & Kathy F. Ward, LDN, RD, West Monroe, LA (Louisiana II)

Kay Ewing's Cooking School Cookbook ©1994 Kay Ewing, Baton Rouge, LA (Louisiana II)

Kelvin Homemakers 50th Anniversary Cookbook, Kelvin Homemakers, Dunseith, ND (Great Plains)

Kingman Welcome Wagon Club Cookbook, Welcome Wagon Club of Kingman, Kingman, AZ (Arizona)

Kitchen Keepsakes ©1986 Bonnie Welch and Deanna White, Calhan, CO (Colorado)

Kitchen Keepsakes, The Houselog Family, Ellsworth, MN (Minnesota)

Kitchen Prescriptions, American Academy of Family Physicians Foundation, Kansas City, MO (Missouri)

Kompelien Family Cookbook, Kompelien Family, Cottonwood, MN (Minnesota)

Kooking with the Krewe, Twin Cities' Krewe of Janus, Monroe, LA (Louisiana II)

Kountry Kooking ©1974 Phila Hach, Clarksville, TN (Tennessee)

Kum' Ona' Granny's Table, Elizabeth Wright Apartments / Senior Citizen's Retirement Facility, Montgomery, AL (Alabama)

The L.o.V.E. Chocolate Cookbook, by Jean Van Elsen Haney, Waterloo, IA (Iowa)

L'Heritage Du Bayou Lafourche, Lafourche Association for Family & Community Education, Lockport, LA (Louisiana II)

La Bonne Cuisine ©1980, 1981 Episcopal Churchwomen of All Saints', Inc., New Orleans, LA (Louisiana)

Lasting Impressions ©1988 St. Joseph's Hospital of Atlanta Auxiliary, Atlanta, GA (Georgia)

Laurels to the Cook ©1988 Laurels to the Cook, Talus Rock Girl Scout Council, Inc., Johnstown, PA (Pennsylvania)

The Lazy Gourmet ©1987 Valerie Bates, Whittier, CA (California)

Lehigh Public Library Cookbook, Lehigh Public Library, Lehigh, IA (Iowa)

License to Cook New Mexico Style, Penfield Press, Iowa City, IA (New Mexico)

Lion's Club of Globe Cookbook, Lion's Club of Globe, Miami, AZ (Arizona)

A Little Taste of Texas ©1990 Barbara C. Jones, Bonham, TX (Texas II)

Look Mom, I Can Cook ©1987 Dot Gibson Publications, by Dot Gibson, Waycross, GA (Georgia)

Look What's Cooking at C.A.M.D.E.N., C.A.M.D.E.N. Foundation, Milton, WI (Wisconsin)

The Louisiana Crawfish Cookbook ©1984 Louisiana Crawfish Cookbook, Inc., Lettsworth, LA (Louisiana)

Louisiana Largesse ©1983 Capital City Press, Baton Rouge Morning Advocate, Baton Rouge, LA (Louisiana)

Louisiana's Original Creole Seafood Recipes, by Tony Chachere, Creole Foods of Opelousas, Inc., LA (Louisiana)

Love Yourself Cookbook ©1987 Edie Low, Charlotte, NC (North Carolina)

Lowfat, Homestyle Cookbook ©1995 Christina Korenkiewicz, Brook Forest Publishing, Conifer, CO (Colorado)

Maple Hill Cookbook, Maple Hill Senior Citizens and Community Club, Hibbing, MN (Minnesota)

The Marlborough Meetinghouse Cookbook, Congregational Church of Marlborough, Marlborough, CT (New England)

MDA Favorite Recipes, Maple Dale Elementary School, Cincinnati, OH (Ohio)

The Memphis Cookbook ©1952, 1980 The Junior League of Memphis, Inc., Memphis, TN (Tennessee)

Microwave Know-How ©1981, 1985 CiCi Williamson and Ann Steiner, McLean, VA (Texas)

The Microwave Touch ©1984 The Microwave Touch, by Galen N. Hill, Greensboro, NC, (North Carolina)

The Midwestern Country Cookbook ©1993 Marilyn Kluger, Prima Publishing, Rocklin, CA (Indiana)

Miss Daisy Entertains ©1980 Daisy King, Rutledge Hill Press, Nashville, TN (Tennessee)

Mississippi Memories ©1983 American Cancer Society, Mississippi Division, Inc., Jackson, MS (Mississippi)

More Delectable Cookery of Alexandria ©1980 Polly Norment Burke/Anne Mudd Cabaniss, Alexandria, VA (Virginia)

More Fiddling With Food, First Baptist Church of Mobile, Mobile, AL (Alabama)

More Goodies and Guess-Whats ©1981 Helen Christiansen, Walsh, CO (Colorado)

More Heart of the Home Recipes ©1982 Capper Press, Inc., Topeka, KS (Great Plains)

More Home Cooking in a Hurry ©1985 Broadman Press, by Sarah Howell, Broadman Press, Nashville, TN (Tennessee)

More Kitchen Keepsakes ©1986 Bonnie Welch and Deanna White, Kiowa, CO (Colorado)

More of the Four Ingredient Cookbook, by Linda Coffee, Kerrville, TX (Texas II)

Mountain Elegance ©1982 The Junior League of Asheville, Inc., Asheville, NC (North Carolina)

Mountain Potpourri ©1979 The Haywood County Hospital Auxiliary, Clyde, NC (North Carolina)

Mrs. Noah's Survival Guide, New Mexico Christian Children's Home Ladies, Portales, NM (New Mexico)

My Own Cook Book Gladys Taber, Parnassus Imprints, Hyannis, MA (New England)

Mystic Mountain Memories ©1990 Josie and Jerry Minerich, C & G Publishing, Greeley, CO (Colorado)

Natchez Notebook of Cooking ©1986 Trinity Episcopal Day School, Natchez, MS (Mississippi)

New Beginnings Cookbook, First Congregational United Church of Christ, DeWitt, IA (Iowa)

The New Gourmets & Groundhogs, by Elaine K. Light, Easter Seal Society, Punxsutawney, PA (Pennsylvania)

Nibbles Cooks Cajun ©1983 Suzie Stephens, Fayetteville, AR (Arkansas)

North Dakota...Where Food is Love ©1994 Marcella Richman, Tower City, ND (Great Plains)

Nuggets, Nibbles and Nostalgia, Kern County Museum Foundation, Bakersfield, CA (California)

Nun Better ©1996 St. Cecilia School Sacred Heart Parish, Broussard, LA (Louisiana II)

The Oke Family Cookbook ©1994 Bethany House Publishers, Bloomington, MN (Minnesota)

Old and New, Abell F.C.E. Club, Guthrie, OK (Oklahoma)

Old Fashioned Cooking, Raleigh Historical Society, Raleigh, IL (Illinois)

Olivia's Favorite Menus and Recipes, by Olivia H. Adams, Greenville, SC (South Carolina)

On the Road Again Cookbook, Lone Cypress Winnitascans, San Jose, CA (California)

101 Ways to Make Ramen Noodles ©1993 Toni Patrick, C & G Publishing, Greeley, CO (Colorado)

175th Anniversary Quilt Cookbook, Oak Grove Mennonite Church, Smithville, OH (Ohio)

One Magnificent Cookbook ©1988 The Junior League of Chicago, Inc., Chicago, IL (Illinois)

The Original Philadelphia Neighborhood Cookbook ©1988 Camino Books, by Irina Smith & Ann Hazan, Philadelphia, PA (Pennsylvania)

Our Best Home Cooking, by Pearl Luttman, Red Bud, IL (Illinois)

Our Best Home Cooking, Roosevelt County Family and Community Educators, Portales, NM (New Mexico)

Our Daily Bread, Ashland United Methodist Church, Ashland, KS (Great Plains)

Our Favorite Recipes, Saint Mary's Hospital Auxiliary, Rochester, MN (Minnesota)

Our Favorite Recipes, The Women's Guild Zion's United Church of Christ, Hamburg, PA (Pennsylvania)

Our Favorite Recipes, Union County Hospital Auxiliary, Anna, IL (Illinois)

Our Heritage Cookbook, United Reedeemer Lutheran Church, Zumbrota, MN (Minnesota)

Out of This World ©1983 The Oak Hill School Parents' Assn., Nashville, TN (Tennessee)

Palate Pleasers, Forest Hills United Methodist Church, Brentwood, TN (Tennessee)

Palates ©1995 MVA Colorado Springs Fine Arts Center, Members' Volunteer Association, Colorado Springs, CO (Colorado)

Par Excellence, Pinetop Lakes Golf & Country Club, Pinetop, AZ (Arizona)

The Parkview Way to Vegetarian Cooking, Parkview Memorial Hospital Auxiliary, Brunswick, ME (New England)

Pass the Plate ©1984 Pass the Plate, Inc., by Alice G. Underhill and Barbara S. Stewart, New Bern, NC (North Carolina)

The Peach Sampler, by Eliza Mears Horton, West Columbia, SC (South Carolina)

The Peach Tree Tea Room Cookbook ©1990 Peach Tree Gift Gallery and Tea Room, by Cynthia Collins Pedregon, Fredericksburg, TX (Texas II)

People Pleasers, by Goldie Pope Lohse, Fairmont, MN (Minnesota)

Philadelphia Homestyle Cookbook ©1984 Norwood-Fontbonne Home & School Assn., Philadelphia, PA (Pennsylvania)

The Pilgrimage Garden Club Antiques Forum Cookbook ©1986 Pilgrimage Garden Club, Natchez, MS (Mississippi)

A Pinch of Sunshine ©1982 Junior Service League of Brooksville, Brooksville, FL (Florida)

Pineapple Gold ©1983 Joann Hulett Dobbins, Meridian, MS (Mississippi)

The Pioneer Chef ©1991 Telephone Pioneers of America, Oklahoma Chapter 41, Oklahoma Pioneers of America, Bethany, OK (Oklahoma)

Pioneer Family Recipes ©1983 Danielle Stephens, Kingman, AZ (Arizona)

Pioneer Pantry, Telephone Pioneers of America, Lucent Technologies Chapter #135, Lisle, IL (Illinois)

Plantation Country ©1981 The Women's Service League of West Feliciana Parish, St. Francisville, LA (Louisiana)

Please Don't Feed the Alligators ©1985 Hilton Head Elementary PTA, Hilton Head Island, SC (South Carolina)

Portal's Best Little Cookbook, Portal Rescue, Portal, AZ (Arizona)

Prairie Harvest, St. Peter's Episcopal Churchwomen, Hazen, AR (Arkansas)

The Prima Diner ©1981 Sarasota Opera Society, Sarasota, FL (Florida)

Pulaski Heights Baptist Church Cookbook, Members and Friends of the Congregation, Little Rock, AR (Arkansas)

Pure Gold-Colorado Treasures ©1992 Winters Publishing, Greensburg, IN (Colorado)

Putting On The Grits ©1984 The Junior League of Columbia, Inc., Columbia, SC (South Carolina)

Quasquicentennial / St. Olaf of Bode, St. Olaf Lutheran Church, Bode, IA (Iowa)

Quick Breads, Soups and Stews, ©1991 Mary Grubser, Council Oak Books, Tulsa, OK (Oklahoma)

Quickies for Singles ©1980 Quail Ridge Press, Inc., Brandon, MS (Louisiana)

Ramblin' Chefs From Georgia Tech ©1985 Georgia Tech Women's Forum, School of Chemistry, Georgia Institute of Technology, Atlanta, GA (Georgia)

REC Family Cookbook ©1987 North Dakota Association of Rural Electric Cooperatives, North Dakota REC/RTC Magazine, Mandan, ND (Great Plains)

Recipes and Memories, St. Peter Evangelical Lutheran Church, Ceylon, MN (Minnesota)

Recipes & Remembrances, Covenant Women of Courtland Kansas, Courtland, KS (Great Plains)

Recipes & Remembrances, Dotson Family, Lima, OH (Ohio)

Recipes and Reminiscences of New Orleans I, ©1971 Parents Club of Ursuline Academy Inc., Ursuline Convent Cookbook, New Orleans, LA (Louisiana)

Recipes and Reminiscences of New Orleans II ©1971 Parents Club of Ursuline Academy Inc., Metairie, LA (Louisiana)

Recipes From a New England Inn ©1992 Trudy Cutrone, Country Roads Press, Castine, ME (New England)

Recipes: From Arizona with Love ©1985 Ferol Smith Golden and Lisa Golden, Strawberry Point, Inc., Prior Lake, MN (Arizona)

Recipes from Miss Daisy's ©1978 Miss Daisy's Tearoom, Rutledge Hill Press, Nashville, TN (Tennessee)

Recipes from the Flock, Tonseth Lutheran Church, Erhard, MN (Minnesota)

Recipes from the Heart, by Epsilon Omega Sorority, Dalton, NE (Great Plains)

Rehoboth Christian School Cookbook ©1981 Tse Yaaniichii Promoters, Rehoboth, NM (New Mexico)

★★★★★★★★★★★★ ★★★★★★★★★★★★

Ritzy Rhubarb Secrets Cookbook ©1992 Litchville Committee 2000, Community Cookbooks/Jane Winge, Editor, Litchville, ND (Great Plains)

River Valley Recipes, Rock River Valley Council of Girl Scouts, Rockford, IL (Illinois)

Rush Hour Superchef! ©1983 Dianne Stafford Mayes & Dorothy Davenport Stafford, Carthage, MO (Missouri)

Salem Mennonite Cookbook, Salem W.M.S.C., Wooster, OH (Ohio)

San Angelo Junior League Cookbook ©1977 Junior League of San Angelo, Inc., San Angelo, TX (Texas)

San Antonio Cookbook II, The San Antonio Symphony League, San Antonio, TX (Texas)

Savannah Style ©1980 The Junior League of Savannah, GA (Georgia)

Sawgrass and Pines, Perry Garden Club, Perry, FL (Florida)

Seafood Sorcery, Junior League of Wilmington, Wilmington, NC (North Carolina)

Seasoned with Light, First Baptist Church - Baptist Women, Hartsville, SC (South Carolina)

Seasoned With Love, Faith United Methodist Women, Woodward, OK (Oklahoma)

Seasoned with Sunshine ©1982 P.A.C.E. Grace Lutheran School, Winter Haven, FL (Florida)

Sedona Cook Book ©1994 Golden West Publishers, by Susan K. Bollin, Golden West Publisher, Phoenix, AZ (Arizona)

Seems Like I Done It This A-Way II, by Cleo Stiles Bryan, Tahlequah, OK (Oklahoma)

Seems Like I Done It This A-Way III, by Cleo Stiles Bryan, Tahlequah, OK (Oklahoma)

Settings: From Our Past to Your Presentation ©1990 The Junior League of Philadelphia, Inc., Bryn Mawr, PA (Pennsylvania)

Shared Treasures, First Baptist Church, Monroe, LA (Louisiana II)

Sharing God's Bounty, Tri-Parish First Lutheran Church, Clay Center, KS (Great Plains)

Sharing our "Beary" Best II, Teddy Bear Day Care, Groton, SD (Great Plains)

Sharing our Best/Bergen Lutheran Church, Bergen Lutheran Church, Montevideo, MN (Minnesota)

Sharing Our Best, by Eileen Hardway, Martinsville, IL (Indiana)

Sharing Our Best, The Old Homestead, Waukon, IA (Iowa)

Sharing Our Best Volume II, Harietta Area Civic Club, Harrietta, MI (Michigan)

Shattuck Community Cookbook, Shattuck Chamber of Commerce, Shattuck, OK (Oklahoma)

Ship to Shore I ©1986 Ship to Shore, Inc., by Jan Robinson, Charlotte, NC (North Carolina)

Silver Dollar City's Recipes ©1988 Silver Dollar City, Inc., Branson, MO (Missouri)

Simply Scrumptious Microwaving ©1982 Simply Scrumptious, by Mary Ann Robinson, Rosemary Dunn Stancil, & Lorela Nichols Wilkens, Kitchen Classics, Stone Mountain, GA (Georgia)

Simply Simpatico ©1981 The Junior League of Albuquerque, Inc., Albuquerque, NM (New Mexico)

Singing in the Kitchen ©1992 Mavis Punt, Sioux Center, IA (Iowa)

Society of Farm Women of Pennsylvania, Society of Farm Women/Naomi Bupp, Glen Rock, PA (Pennsylvania)

Some Enchanted Eating ©1986 Friends of the Symphony, Muskegon, MI (Michigan)

South Carolina's Historic Restaurants ©1996 Dawn O'Brien and Jean Spaugh, John F. Blair, Publisher, Winston-Salem, NC (South Carolina)

South Dakota Sunrise-A Collection of Breakfast Recipes ©1997 Tracy Winters, Bed & Breakfast Innkeepers of South Dakota, Greensburg, IN (Great Plains)

A Southern Lady's Spirit, Riddicks Folly, Suffolk, Virginia (Virginia)

Southwest Cookin', Southwest Regional Medical Center Auxiliary, Little Rock, AR (Arkansas)

Spindletop International Cooks, Spindletop Oilmen's Golf Charities, Inc., Houston, TX (Texas)

Spotsylvania Favorites ©1985 Spotsylvania County Woman's Club, Spotsylvania, VA (Virginia)

Square House Museum Cookbook ©1973 Carson County Square House Museum, Panhandle, TX (Texas)

★★★★★★★★★★★ ★★★★★★★★★★★★

St. Francis in the Foothills 30th Anniversary Cookbook, St. Francis in the Foothills UMC, Tucson, AZ (Arizona)

St. Joseph's Parish Cookbook, St. Joseph's Altar and Rosary, Greeley, IA (Iowa)

St. Joseph's Table, St. Joseph's Catholic Church, Spearfish, SD (Great Plains)

St. Philomena School 125th Anniversary, St. Philomena Home & School Association, Labadieville, LA (Louisiana II)

Steamboat Entertains ©1991 Steamboat Springs Winter Sports Club, Steamboat Springs, CO (Colorado)

Still Gathering: A Centennial Celebration ©1992 Auxiliary to the American Osteopathic Assn., Chicago, IL (Illinois)

Stir Crazy! ©1986 Junior Welfare League of Florence, Inc., Florence, SC (South Carolina)

Stir Ups ©Junior Welfare League of Enid, Enid, OK (Oklahoma)

Stirling City Hotel Afternoon Tea, by Charlotte Ann Hilgeman, C/L Productions, Stirling City, CA (California)

Strictly For Boys ©1980 Betty L. Waskiewicz, by Betty L. Waskiewicz, Beaufort, SC (South Carolina)

The Stuffed Griffin, The Utility Club of Griffin, Griffin, GA (Georgia)

Sugar Beach ©1984 Junior Service League of Fort Walton Beach, Fort Walton Beach, FL (Florida)

Susie's Cook Book, The Family of John C. and Susie S. Clemens, Hatfield, PA (Pennsylvania)

Talk About Good II ©1972 The Junior League of Lafayette, Lafayette, LA (Louisiana)

Talk About Good III, Forsyth Library Friends, Forsyth, MO (Missouri)

Taste & See, Women Ministries of Sardinia Baptist, Westport, IN (Indiana)

Taste & See, St. Philip Neri Catholic Church, Milwaukee, WI (Wisconsin)

Taste of Coffeyville ©1998 Rita Hewson, Larned, KS (Great Plains)

A Taste of Fishers ©1993 Fishers Tri Kappa, Fishers, IN (Indiana)

A Taste of Hallowell ©1992 Alice Arlen, Hallowell, ME (New England)

A Taste of Kennedy Cook Book, Kennedy Elementary PTSA, Willmar, MN (Minnesota)

A Taste of South Carolina ©1983 The Palmetto Cabinet of South Carolina, Sandlapper Publishing Co., Inc., Orangeburg, SC (South Carolina)

A Taste of Tampa ©1978 The Junior League of Tampa, Inc., Tampa, FL (Florida)

A Taste of the Holidays ©1988 Dot Gibson Publications, Waycross, GA (Georgia)

A Taste of Twin Pines, Twin Pines Alumni, West Lafayette, IN (Indiana)

Tasteful Traditions ©1983 Women for Abilene Christian University, Abilene, TX (Texas)

Tasting Tea Treasures ©1984 Greenville Junior Woman's Club, Greenville, MS (Mississippi)

The Texas Microwave Cookbook ©1981 Carolyn H. White (Texas)

Thank Heaven for Home Made Cooks, C.H.O.S.E.N. Youth Group, South Side Church, Litchfield, IL (Illinois)

Thank Heaven for Home Made Cooks, First Congregational U.C.C., Oconomowoc, WI (Wisconsin)

There Once Was a Cook ©1985 by The Wesley Institue, Pittsburgh, PA (Pennsylvania)

Think Healthy, Fairfax County Department of Extension, Fairfax, VA (Virginia)

Thoroughbred Fare ©1984 Thoroughbred Fare Cookbook, Aiken, SC (South Carolina)

Three Rivers Cookbook I ©1973 Child Health Association of Sewickley, PA (Pennsylvania)

Three Rivers Cookbook II ©1981 Child Health Association of Sewickley, PA (Pennsylvania)

Three Rivers Cookbook III ©1990 Child Health Association of Sewickley, PA (Pennsylvania)

Thyme Waves ©1981 Junior Museum of Bay County, Inc., Panama City, FL (Florida)

Titonka Centennial Cookbook, Titonka Centennial Committee, Titonka, IA (Iowa)

To Tayla with TLC, RCRH Medical Imaging Department, Rapid City, SD (Great Plains)

Tony Chachere's Second Helping ©1995 Tony Chachere's Creole Foods of Opelousas, Inc., Opelousas, LA (Louisiana II)

Tostitos Fiesta Bowl Cookbook ©1995 The Fiesta Bowl, Tempe, AZ (Arizona)

Touches of the Hands & Heart, by Karen A. Maag, Columbus Grove, OH (Ohio)

Tout de Suite a la Microwave II ©1977 Jean K. Durkee, Lafayette, LA (Louisiana)

Traditionally Wesleyan, Wesleyan College Business Club, Macon, GA (Georgia)

Treasured Recipes, St. Joseph of Cupertino Parish and School, Cupertino, CA (California)

Treasured Recipes Book I, Taneyhills Library Club, Branson, MO (Missouri)

Treasured Recipes from Treasured Friends, by Colleen Beal, Faribault, MN (Minnesota)

Treasured Tastes ©1986 Mobile College, Mobile College Auxiliary, Daphne, AL (Alabama)

Trinity Lutheran Church of Norden Anniversary Cookbook, Norden Youth League, Mondovi, WI (Wisconsin)

Tucson Treasures: Recipes and Reflections ©1999 Tucson Medical Center Auxiliary, Tucson, AZ (Arizona)

Turnip Greens in the Bathtub ©1981 Genie Taylor Harrison, Baton Rouge, LA (Louisiana)

The Twelve Days of Christmas Cookbook ©1978 Quail Ridge Press, Inc., Ruth Moorman and Lalla Williams, Brandon, MS (Mississippi)

25th Anniversary Cookbook, Lancaster Montessori School, Lancaster, OH (Ohio)

Unbearably Good! ©1986 Americus Junior Service League, Americus, GA (Georgia)

Unbearably Good! Sharing Our Best, Waushara County Homemakers, Wautoma, WI (Wisconsin)

Upper Crust: A Slice of the South ©1986 The Junior League of Johnson City, Inc., Johnson City, TN (Tennessee)

Uptown Down South ©1986 Greenville Junior League Publications, Greenville, SC (South Carolina)

Vincent Russo's Seafood Cookbook, by Vincent Russo, Savannah, GA (Georgia)

Visions of Home Cook Book, York Hospital, York, ME (New England)

Visitation Parish Cookbook, St. Rita's Circle of Visitation Parish, Stacyville, IA (Iowa)

Vistoso Vittles II, Sun City Vistoso, Tucson, AZ (Arizona)

We Love Country Cookin': Mar-Don's Family Favorites, by Marlene Grager and Donna Young, Sykeston, ND (Great Plains)

The What In The World Are We Going To Have For Dinner Cookbook? ©1987 Sarah E. Drummond, Richmond, VA (Virginia)

What's Cooking at Trinity, Trinity Evangelical Lutheran Church, Wexford, PA (Pennsylvania)

What's Cooking Inn Arizona ©1996 Tracy M. Winters and Phyllis Y. Winters, Winters Publishing, Greensburg, IN (Arizona)

What's on the Agenda?, The Woman's Club, DePere, WI (Wisconsin)

When Friends Cook ©1992 The Friends of the Minneapolis Institute of Arts, Minneapolis, MN (Minnesota)

Wisconsin Pure Maple Syrup Cookbook, Wisconsin Maple Syrup Producers, Holcombe, WI (Wisconsin)

Wisconsin's Best, Women's Auxiliary WAPHCC, Waukesha, WI (Wisconsin)

With Hands & Heart Cookbook ©1990 Bethesda General Hospital Womens Board, Bethesda Hospital, St. Louis, MO (Missouri)

Woman's Exchange Cookbook I ©1964 and 1967 The Woman's Exchange of Memphis, Inc., Memphis, TN (Tennessee)

Woman's Exchange Cookbook II ©1976 The Woman's Exchange of Memphis, Inc., Memphis, TN (Tennessee)

Woodbine Public Library, Woodbine Public Library, Woodbine, IA (Iowa)

Extra Help

★★★★ ★★★★

*Winter, summer, spring, or fall, Central Park is always the needed
breath of fresh air from the concrete and skyscrapers of Manhattan.
New York, New York, a wonderful town . . . there's nothing else like it—
and that certainly includes the food.*

EQUIVALENTS:

Apple: 1 medium = 1 cup chopped

Banana, mashed: 1 medium = $\frac{1}{3}$ cup

Berries: 1 pint = $1\frac{3}{4}$ cup

Bread: 1 slice = $\frac{1}{2}$ cup soft crumbs = $\frac{1}{4}$ cup fine, dry crumbs

Broth, beef or chicken: 1 cup = 1 bouillon cube dissolved in 1 cup boiling water

Butter: 1 stick = $\frac{1}{4}$ pound = $\frac{1}{2}$ cup

Cabbage: 2 pounds = 9 cups shredded or 5 cups cooked

Cheese, grated: 1 pound = 4 cups; 8 ounces = 2 cups

Chicken: 1 large boned breast = 2 cups cooked meat

Crabmeat, fresh: 1 pound = 3 cups

Chocolate, bitter: 1 square or 1 ounce = 2 tablespoons grated

Coconut: $3\frac{1}{2}$-ounce can = $1\frac{1}{3}$ cups

Cool Whip: 8 ounces = 3 cups

Cornmeal: 1 pound = 3 cups

Crackers, saltine: 23 = 1 cup crushed

Crackers, graham: 15 = 1 cup crushed

Cream, heavy: 1 cup = $2-2\frac{1}{2}$ cups whipped

Cream cheese: 3 ounces = $6\frac{2}{3}$ tablespoons

Eggs: 4–5 = 1 cup

Egg whites: 8–10 = 1 cup

Evaporated milk: $5\frac{1}{3}$-ounce can = $\frac{2}{3}$ cup; 13-ounce can = $1\frac{1}{4}$ cups

Flour: 1 pound = $4\frac{1}{2}$ cups

Flour, self-rising : 1 cup = 1 cup all-purpose + $1\frac{1}{2}$ teaspoons baking powder + $\frac{1}{2}$ teaspoon salt

Garlic powder: $\frac{1}{8}$ teaspoon = 1 average clove

Ginger root: 1 teaspoon = $\frac{3}{4}$ teaspoon ground

Grits: 1 cup = 4 cups cooked

Herbs, fresh: 1 tablespoon = 1 teaspoon dried

Lemon: 1 medium = 3 tablespoons juice

Marshmallows: $\frac{1}{4}$ pound = 16 large; 10 mini = 1 large

Mushrooms: $\frac{1}{4}$ pound fresh = 1 cup sliced

Mustard, dry : 1 teaspoon = 1 tablespoon prepared

Noodles: 1 pound = 7 cups cooked

Nuts, chopped: $\frac{1}{4}$ pound = 1 cup

Onion: 1 medium = $\frac{3}{4}-1$ cup chopped = 2 tablespoons dried chopped (flakes)

Orange: 3-4 medium = 1 cup juice

Pecans: 1 pound shelled = 4 cups

Potatoes: 1 pound = 3 medium

Rice: 1 cup = 3 cups cooked

Spaghetti: 1 pound uncooked = 5 cups cooked

Spinach, fresh: 2 cups chopped = 1 (10-ounce) package frozen chopped

Sugar, brown: 1 pound = $2\frac{1}{2}$ cups

Sugar, powdered: 1 pound = $3\frac{1}{2}$ cups

Sugar, white: 1 pound = $2\frac{1}{4}$ cups

Vanilla wafers: 22 = 1 cup fine crumbs

Whole milk: 1 cup = $\frac{1}{2}$ cup evaporated + $\frac{1}{2}$ cup water

SUBSTITUTIONS:

1 slice cooked **bacon** = 1 tablespoon bacon bits

1 cup **buttermilk** = 1 cup plain yogurt; or 1 tablespoon lemon juice or vinegar + plain milk to make 1 cup

1 cup sifted **cake flour** = $7/8$ cup sifted all-purpose flour

1 ounce **unsweetened chocolate** = 3 tablespoons cocoa + 1 tablespoon butter or margarine

1 ounce **semisweet chocolate** = 3 tablespoons cocoa + 1 tablespoon butter or margarine + 3 tablespoons sugar

1 tablespoon **cornstarch** = 2 tablespoons flour (for thickening)

1 cup **heavy cream** (for cooking, not whipping) = $1/3$ cup butter + $3/4$ cup milk

1 cup **sour cream** = $1/3$ cup milk + $1/3$ cup butter; or 1 cup plain yogurt

1 cup **tartar sauce** = 6 tablespoons mayonnaise or salad dressing + 2 tablespoons pickle relish

1 cup **tomato juice** = $1/2$ cup tomato sauce + $1/2$ cup water

1 cup **vegetable oil** = $1/2$ pound (2 sticks) butter

1 cup **whipping cream**, whipped = 6–8 ounces Cool Whip

1 cup **whole milk** = $1/2$ cup evaporated milk + $1/2$ cup water

MEASUREMENTS:

3 teaspoons = 1 tablespoon

1 tablespoon = $1/2$ fluid ounce

2 tablespoons = $1/8$ cup

3 tablespoons = 1 jigger

4 tablespoons = $1/4$ cup

8 tablespoons = $1/2$ cup or 4 ounces

12 tablespoons = $3/4$ cup

16 tablespoons = 1 cup or 8 ounces

3/8 cup = $1/4$ cup + 2 tablespoons

5/8 cup = $1/2$ cup + 2 tablespoons

7/8 cup = $3/4$ cup + 2 tablespoons

1/2 cup = 4 fluid ounces

1 cup = $1/2$ pint or 8 fluid ounces

2 cups = 1 pint or 16 fluid ounces

1 pint, liquid = 2 cups or 16 fluid ounces

1 quart, liquid = 2 pints or 4 cups

1 gallon, liquid = 4 quarts or 8 pints or 16 cups

OVEN-TO-CROCKPOT COOKING TIME CONVERSIONS:

15–30 minutes in the oven = $1\frac{1}{2}$–$2\frac{1}{2}$ hours on HIGH or 4–6 hours on LOW

35–45 minutes in the oven equals 2–3 hours on HIGH or 6–8 hours on LOW

50 minutes–3 hours in the oven equals 4–5 hours on HIGH or 8–18 hours on LOW

HIGH ALTITUDE HINTS:

Foods that require **boiling** take longer to cook.

Microwaving requires a little more water and a longer cooking time.

Meats cooked in the oven require more time.

Baking requires increased temperature (add 25 degrees), increased liquid, decreased leavening and decreased sugar.

Yeast dough rises more rapidly, so shorten your "rising" time.

PAN SIZES FOR BAKING:

4 cups will fit into
8-inch round cake pan
9-inch round pie pan
9-inch pie pan
4 x 8 x 2¾ loaf pan (small)

5 cups will fit into
7 x 11 x 1¾ -inch pan
10-inch pie pan

6 cups will fit into
8 x 8 x 2-inch square pan
10 x 10 x 2-inch casserole
5 x 9 x 3¼-inch loaf pan (large)

8 cups will fit into
9 x 9 x 2¼-inch casserole
7½ x 11¾ x 2-inch pan

12 cups will fit into
8½ x 13½ x 2½-inch glass dish
9 x 13 x 2-inch pan

Index

When in Rome . . . or in Hot Springs, Arkansas . . . .
Leave your intimidation behind you when you enter Bath House Row—
the mineral baths are worth it!

Index

Index

Index

Index

Best of the Best from
ALABAMA

Best of the Best from
IDAHO

Best of the Best from
MISSISSIPPI

Best of the Best from
PENNSYLVANIA

Best of the Best from
ALASKA

Best of the Best from
ILLINOIS

Best of the Best from
MISSOURI

Best of the Best from
SO. CAROLINA

Best of the Best from
ARIZONA

Best of the Best from
INDIANA

Best of the Best from
NEVADA

Best of the Best from
TENNESSEE

Best of the Best from
ARKANSAS

Best of the Best from
IOWA

Best of the Best from
NEW ENGLAND
*Rhode Island, Connecticut,
Massachusetts, Vermont,
New Hampshire, and Maine*

Best of the Best from
TEXAS

Best of the Best from
BIG SKY
Montana and Wyoming

Best of the Best from
KENTUCKY

Best of the Best from
TEXAS II

Best of the Best from
CALIFORNIA

Best of the Best from
LOUISIANA

Best of the Best from
NEW MEXICO

Best of the Best from
UTAH

Best of the Best from
COLORADO

Best of the Best from
LOUISIANA II

Best of the Best from
NEW YORK

Best of the Best from
VIRGINIA

Best of the Best from
FLORIDA

Best of the Best from
MICHIGAN

Best of the Best from
NO. CAROLINA

Best of the Best from
VIRGINIA II

Best of the Best from
GEORGIA

Best of the Best from the
MID-ATLANTIC
*Maryland, Delaware, New
Jersey, and Washington, D.C.*

Best of the Best from
OHIO

Best of the Best from
WASHINGTON

Best of the Best from the
GREAT PLAINS
*North and South Dakota,
Nebraska, and Kansas*

Best of the Best from
MINNESOTA

Best of the Best from
OKLAHOMA

Best of the Best from
OREGON

Best of the Best from
WEST VIRGINIA

Best of the Best from
WISCONSIN

Best of the Best from
HAWAI'I

*All BEST OF THE BEST STATE COOKBOOKS are 6x9 inches and comb-bound with
illustrations, photographs, and an index. They range in size from 288 to
352 pages and each contains over 300 recipes.*

Recipe Hall of Fame Collection

Lay-flat paper-bound • 7x10 inches • Illustrations • Photographs